Explore Canada

THE ADVENTURER'S GUIDE

Icon Legend

 Birding

Winter sports (including cross-country
skiing, snow-shoeing and dog sledding)

Hiking and camping

Biking

Fishing

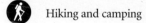 Water sports (including sea kayaking,
whitewater rafting and canoeing)

Trail riding

Explore Canada

THE ADVENTURER'S GUIDE

Marion Harrison and Peter Thompson

KEY PORTER BOOKS

Canadian Cataloguing in Publication Data

Harrison, Marion, 1956–
  Explore Canada : an adventurer's guide

Includes bibliographical references and index.
ISBN 1-55263-041-2

1. Outdoor recreation – Canada – Guidebooks. 2. Canada –
Guidebooks.
I. Thompson, Peter, 1943-   . II. Title.

GV191.44.H37 1998   796.5'0971
C98-932820-1

The publisher gratefully acknowledges the
support of the Canada Council for the Arts and the
Ontario Arts Council for its publishing program.

THE CANADA COUNCIL | LE CONSEIL DES ARTS
FOR THE ARTS | DU CANADA
SINCE 1957 | DEPUIS 1957

Canada

We acknowledge the financial support of the Government of Canada
through the Book Publishing Industry Development Program
(BPIDP) for our publishing activities.

Key Porter Books Limited
70 The Esplanade
Toronto, Ontario
Canada M5E 1R2
www.keyporter.com

Design: Peter Maher
Cover design: Peter Maher

Distributed in the United States by Firefly Books.
Printed and bound in Italy
99 00 01 02   6 5 4 3 2 1

Contents

Introduction 10

Choosing Your Destination 12

Preparing for Your Trip 15

Equipment and Clothing 16

On the Trip 18

British Columbia

Gold River 20

Hot Springs Cove 22

Clayoquot Sound 24

Barkley Sound 28

West Coast Trail 30

Juan de Fuca Marine Trail 32

Johnstone Strait 34

Whistler 38

Garibaldi Provincial Park 42

Tatshenshini–Alsek Wilderness Park 44

The Chilkoot Trail 46

Spatsizi Plateau Wilderness Provincial Park 48

Bowron Lake Provincial Park 50

Wells Gray Provincial Park 52

Mount Robson Provincial Park 54

Cathedral Provincial Park 56

Kettle Valley Railway 58

The Silver Triangle, Kootenay Region 60

Kokanee Glacier Provincial Park 64

Purcell Lodge 66

Glacier National Park 68

Yoho Valley, Yoho National Park 72

The Burgess Shale, Yoho National Park 74

Lake O'Hara, Yoho National Park 76

Kicking Horse River 78

Rockwall Highline Trail, Kootenay National Park 80

Mount Assiniboine Provincial Park 82

Alberta

Maligne Valley, Jasper National Park 84

Rocky Mountain House 88

Icefields Parkway 90

Num-Ti-Jah Lodge, Banff National Park 92

Skoki Lodge, Banff National Park 94

Shadow Lake, Banff National Park 96

The Bow Valley 98

Rats Nest Cave 100

Kananaskis Country 102

Crowsnest Pass 106

Waterton Lakes National Park 110

Dinosaur Provincial Park 112

Milk River and Writing-on-Stone Provincial Park 116

Elk Island National Park 118

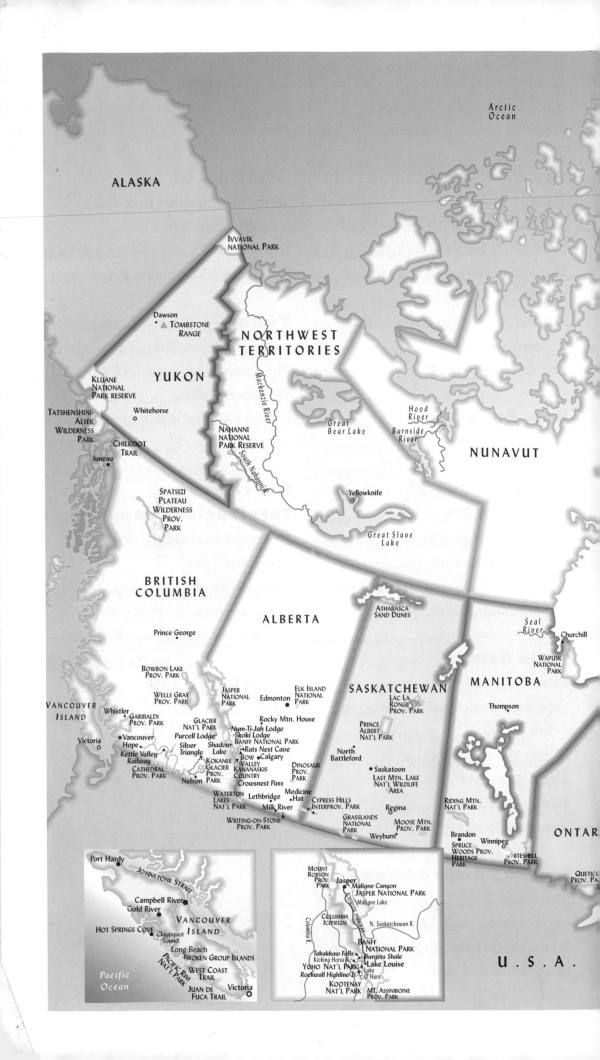

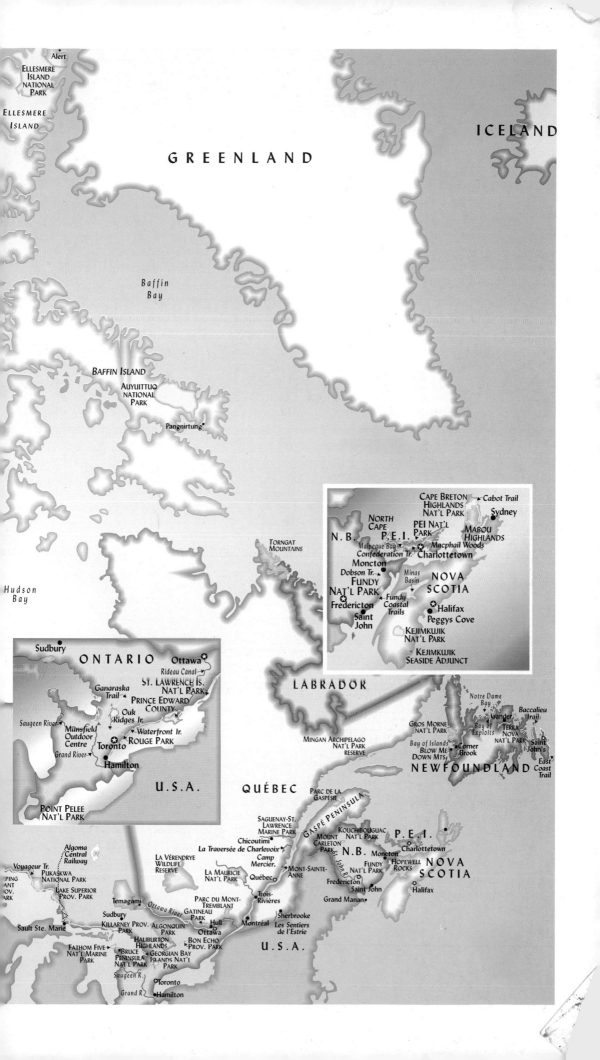

Introduction

Canada is arguably the best country in the world for outdoor enthusiasts and nature lovers. The rugged mountains, countless rivers and lakes, and long, crenelated coastlines offer unlimited opportunities for adventure trips and wildlife viewing. Thanks to over a century of government initiatives, more than 154,440 square miles (400,000 square kilometers) of the most beautiful parts of the country have been preserved as national and provincial parks. From the rainforests of British Columbia to the rocky headlands of Newfoundland, the most scenic of Canada's wild lands have been preserved as national treasures.

Explore Canada shares some of these treasures with you. Our familiarity with the best recreational destinations in Canada stems from our long-term involvement with *Explore,* Canada's premier magazine on outdoor adventure. Together we have endeavored to convey our love for the outdoor world through the magazine, and this book is an extension of that endeavor.

Explore Canada is a vehicle of ideas. It is not a guidebook, but will guide you to what we think are some of the greatest destinations in Canada, from short nature hikes near urban centers to multi-day wilderness trips in the North. We have attempted to include something for everyone: if you enjoy day tripping, there are fascinating areas, such as the Oak Ridges Moraine near Toronto or Elk Island National Park near Edmonton – destinations that are very rewarding and justify repeat visits.

If you prefer family outings with children, destinations such as Kejimkujik National Park in Nova Scotia offer drive-to campgrounds, short trails and activities of interest to all the family. If you are taking your first backpacking steps, areas such as Killarney Provincial Park in Ontario or Garibaldi Provincial Park in British Columbia offer easy-to-reach backcountry campsites. And if you really want to get away from it all, there are remote northern destinations such as Yukon's Ivvavik National Park where you're guaranteed to see more wildlife than people.

Since most of the destinations are in national or provincial parks where native habitats are protected and preserved, the opportunities for bird watching and wildlife viewing are excellent. Special places such as Point Pelee in Ontario, Grand Manan in New Brunswick, or Last Mountain Lake in Saskatchewan offer you the chance to add new bird species to your life list. If you have your heart set on watching polar bears – from a safe distance! – there's Wapusk National Park in Manitoba. If whale watching is more your thing, visit Johnstone Strait on the west coast or the Bay of Exploits on the east coast. Many of the destinations will allow you the chance to see rare or endangered species such as peregrine falcons in Ontario's Bon Echo Provincial Park, beluga whales in Saguenay–St. Lawrence Marine Park, or the elusive cougar in Kananaskis Country, Alberta.

If you're a wildflower aficionado, *Explore Canada* will not only point you toward the best alpine meadows and woodland glades, it will also tell you which are the best months for wildflower viewing. Trees also hold a fascination for nature lovers. You'll find grandeur in the old-growth forests of Vancouver Island's Clayoquot Sound; subtlety in the delicate shades of Rocky Mountain larches in fall; or a riot of color in the maples and birch of Southern Ontario, Québec and the Maritimes.

While hiking is the most common activity in this book, we have not ignored other modes of "self-propelled" travel. Considering the thousands of lakes and rivers in Canada, it seemed appropriate to include plenty of canoeing destinations. The canoe is a vital part of Canada's heritage and is still a cherished, if not revered, object of affection. Enjoy a two-hour paddle in Whiteshell Provincial Park in Manitoba, or a ten-day expedition to the Nahanni River in the Northwest Territories.

Alternative modes of travel are by raft, kayak or bicycle. Whitewater rafting on B.C.'s Kicking Horse River or Ontario's Ottawa River offers the thrill of a lifetime, whereas ocean kayaking offers a slower-paced and serene way of exploring special places such as Newfoundland's Bay of Islands. Cycling is an efficient way to travel long distances and still experience the sights, sounds and smells of such places as Ontario's Prince Edward County or Nova Scotia's Cabot Trail. And travel on skis or snowshoes opens up an entire new world, from the quiet trackset trails of Québec's Gatineau Park to the backcountry grandeur of B.C.'s Glacier National Park.

Planning an adventure vacation is more complicated than simply paying a visit to your local

travel agent. You'll probably be met with a blank stare if you tell your agent you want to go sea kayaking or backcountry skiing. *Explore Canada* will guide you to the correct sources for information, be it a guidebook, tourism office, park headquarters or outfitter. Each destination offers you enough information to begin planning your own trip or have someone plan it for you.

There is a lifetime of adventure in the following pages. You can start with less challenging trips and as you gain experience and confidence, work your way toward the more remote destinations that require commitment in the planning and in executing the plan. We hope you enjoy discovering these special places as much as we've enjoyed writing about them. Happy exploring!

Marion Harrison
Peter Thompson

Choosing Your Destination

Where does your imagination take you? Do you see yourself backpacking in high alpine meadows amid a crazy carpet of wildflowers in bloom? Or skillfully drawing and backpaddling on a frothing river, with wild spray drenching your face and arms? Perhaps you'd like to pack your panniers and cycle quiet country roads, resting your head on a soft pillow every night? Or, binoculars strung around your neck and checklist in hand, you might be looking for a footpath through a forest where you can spot migrating songbirds. Mountains, rivers, country roads, forests: the possibilities in Canada are endless.

Your destination will depend in part on the type of trip you'd like to take. Many of the destinations presented in this book offer a variety of activities; hiking, backpacking, canoeing, kayaking, fishing, mountain biking, bird watching, skiing and snowshoeing are the primary activities we focused on. The icons shown on the first page of the book tell you which of these activities any destination offers. Do you want to dabble in a little bit of everything, say, hike for a couple of days, spend an afternoon paddling on a quiet lake, and put in a day on the bike paths? Many parks offer equipment rentals, which means you don't have to lug everything from home just for a few hours of enjoyment.

If you've already identified a specific activity you're interested in, the choice of destinations may be more limited. For example, sea kayaking will take you to the east and west coasts, Georgian Bay, the St. Lawrence Islands, Saguenay Fjord, the Mingan Archipelago, and a handful of other locales.

Activities may be dictated by season as well. The best times for bird watching are often during spring and fall migration, with the possibility of seeing seasonal residents that nest in Canada during the summer. Permanent residents are often better seen in winter, when leafless trees won't obstruct your view. Interested in watching icebergs off the east coast? May and June are the best months of the year, with a few stragglers in July. Likewise for whale watching – different species will be seen at different times on both coasts and, in the Far North, a small window of opportunity occurs in July and August after the sea ice has broken up.

Lakes won't be affected by spring runoff, but rivers sure will be! Unless you're a skilled whitewater paddler, avoid a river trip in April and May, even June in some parts of the country. By August, some rivers may be too shallow to reasonably paddle.

Mountain biking is best done after the spring melt and early season rain, when less damage is done to the trails, but can carry on well after freeze-up and before the heavy snows fall. Even then, some avid bikers are taking to the trails throughout the winter. You'll find, though, that most parks permit mountain biking from about June to October.

Fishing is often seasonal, especially in national and provincial parks, where it is also subject to special rules and regulations. In national parks, you'll be required to obtain a national park fishing license. These can often be obtained at visitor centers, gateways and kiosks within the parks,

but contact the park for information prior to travel. Lakes and rivers outside park jurisdiction are subject to provincial and territorial permits and restrictions – contact the appropriate tourism agency for details.

July and August are undoubtedly the most popular times to travel, which means you'll be dealing with crowds in some regions of the country. If you must travel during these peak months, be sure to make reservations at campsites well in advance (where possible) to avoid disappointment. If you're hiking or paddling a route that has a quota imposed on it, have a backup plan just in case the quota's been filled.

If at all possible, travel in the shoulder seasons – spring and fall – when there are fewer people and fewer bugs! Cooler temperatures can make hiking much more pleasant during the day. Spring is a fresh time of year, when the trees are in bud or bursting with blossoms, and the days are long and warm. Fall is always a favorite time, when the trees are splashed with color. The trade-off for travel in spring and fall is fewer interpretive services (or none at all), and information centers may be closed or on reduced hours.

Skiing and snowshoeing are obviously limited to the snow season, usually between December and March in most parts of the country. But if you're into backcountry or telemark skiing, don't hang up your skis yet! One of the best times for this activity is April. In the Rockies, the Coast Mountains, the Gaspé Peninsula and other high-elevation areas, the snowpack lasts well into April, when the days are longer and the temperatures milder. The snow-

pack may not be stable, however, so you'll need superior abilities in evaluating – and avoiding! – avalanche terrain.

While you're choosing a destination, you'll need to keep in mind the requirements and interests of those you'll be traveling with. Are you going as a family with children? Most provincial and national parks have excellent interpretive programs that involve activities for children. Short hikes, evening programs around a campfire, slide shows, live animal demonstrations and many other organized activities will keep your kids occupied, and they probably won't realize they're learning something as well! Look for other diversions too, such as a sandy beach and a good swimming lake, tidal pools to explore, canoe or paddle-boat rentals, bike paths, playgrounds – anything that will make your holiday fun for everyone. When it comes to hiking, choose short trails, stop frequently, bring along extra clothes, and consider letting your children carry a small pack with snacks, drinks and a favorite toy or stuffed animal. Remember that the objective is to make the outdoors a pleasant experience for your children, not something they'll groan about.

Whether you're traveling as a couple or with friends, your outdoor activities must be geared to the least experienced member of the party. That means you'll need to (delicately, perhaps!) find out what skills your friends possess. If you're considering a long-distance backpacking trip with friends you've never hiked with before, take a few day hikes together first, then progress to an overnight or weekend trip. Then ask yourself if you could spend a week or two with these people. You need to know this before you embark on a longer trip. More than just getting along, however, you need to make sure your objectives are the same. If your friends are out to "bag a peak" and you just want to "stop and smell the flowers," everyone will be frustrated.

Knowing the skill level of your trip mates is especially crucial on ski trips, when limited daylight hours and an unexpected snowstorm can turn even a short excursion into an unnecessary epic. Again, take short trips first to find out how your skills relate to those of your friends.

If you're traveling solo, you have no one to worry about but yourself. Just be absolutely sure you know what you're doing, and leave your itinerary with someone who will know what to do if you don't return when expected.

If you don't have a friend or family member who's interested in sharing your activities, try an outdoor club. Be mindful, though, that these are volunteer organizations with perfectly ordinary people leading trips. They're familiar with the terrain you'll be traveling in, which is a big advantage if you're new to the area or to the activity. It's always better to go with someone who knows the region than to strike out on your own. Trip leaders, however, are not necessarily required to have special training such as first aid, and they cannot be held accountable should anything go wrong. Do not expect someone else to bail you out if problems occur.

Taking a guided trip is a very good option for some people. Like most things, there are advantages and disadvantages to commercially guided trips. The first consideration is cost, and here's what you'll be paying for with a reputable company: experienced guides; top-quality equipment; transportation of gear to and from the trip area; great food and lots of it; a small-group experience (usually about 10 to 12 "clients" plus two guides); and a guaranteed beautiful area that's been staked out beforehand.

Not only do your guides know every nook and cranny

you'll be traveling through, they know the safest routes and the problem areas. They have all the training pertinent to the activity you're taking part in and are certified in first aid. They also have the last say, which can be annoying when you've paid a lot of money and can't get to your destination because your guide says the water's unsafe or the snow conditions are unstable. Live with it!

Though you can't choose your trip mates, at least you'll be sharing the experience with like-minded individuals, and you'll often come away with lasting friendships. You can't stray from the company's itinerary either, but that means you can sit back, relax, and let someone else take the reins.

How do you choose a tour company? Ask lots of questions! How long have they been in business? A company that has been around for a number of years has likely developed a smooth-running operation and established a reputation. They won't mind sending you references from previous clients, and they'll bend over backwards to answer your questions in detail. What are the guides' qualifications? Do they have first aid training and is it updated annually? How large are the groups and what is the guide-to-client ratio? How would they handle an emergency? What skill level is expected of clients?

Be aware, also, that you have responsibilities when you sign up for a guided trip. You must be fit enough for the planned activities, and you must let the tour company know of any medical conditions, allergies or phobias that might cause problems once the trip has started. It's your responsibility to read the company's brochures and instructions so there are no surprises. Finally, be prepared to be screened out of a trip if the guide or operator thinks it's in your best interest.

It's worth mentioning here the many backcountry lodge operators. These companies not only offer unique accommodation in a wilderness setting, they often supply guides as well. For example, you can spend a week at a wilderness lodge skiing to your heart's content with a guide who knows the very best bowls for carving turns and the most scenic routes for backcountry touring. They'll know the places to avoid as well – and that's worth plenty in unfamiliar terrain. It's an ideal way to spend a winter outing in comfort. Most of the lodges also operate during the summer and offer special-interest trips on outdoor photography, natural history and wildlife.

Are you physically fit for the activity you want to do? Months before you set off on that week-long canoe or backpacking trip, get walking, hiking, jogging, swim-

ming – anything to increase your aerobic capacity and strengthen your muscles. You'll enjoy your trip much more if you're not suffering with aches and pains.

One final word on choosing your destination. Trips to remote areas where you rely on non-scheduled transportation need careful thought and planning. This type of trip can often be made less expensive by sharing a charter plane or boat, or by coordinating your in-going trip with another party's out-going trip, or vice versa. You must be prepared for delays caused by bad weather. This is particularly difficult at the end of a trip, when food supplies may be low, you're psychologically prepared for the return to family and friends, and you have job commitments. Your pickup could be hours or even days late. Ask yourself if you can cope with this type of stress. Sit tight, not *up*tight.

Preparing for Your Trip

As with any type of travel, the more (accurate) information you have, the better the chances that your trip will be a success. This is particularly important when traveling to remote areas. The information given in this book is up to date at the time of publication, but may change, depending on trail conditions, park regulations and a host of other unforeseeable events. Check before you go.

There are two phases to information gathering: prior to your departure, and when you arrive at, or are close to, your destination. Guide-books, maps, park brochures, magazine articles, Websites and numerous other sources can be used to help you plan your trip. For the most up-to-date information, stop at information centers or tourist offices at your destination. Often a bulletin board with current trail conditions,

closures, wildlife activity and a weather forecast will bring you completely up to date.

Expect to pay a fee at all national parks and many provincial parks and recreation areas. In addition to a park entry fee, you may have to pay additional camping and backcountry fees. Permits are required for backcountry camping in most parks, and many impose quotas on popular areas or trails.

Let someone responsible know your intended route and expected time of return, and what to do if you don't return on time. Take advantage of voluntary backcountry registration, but be sure to sign out when you return.

Hot Springs Cove

Tucked away on a peninsula in the northwestern region of Clayoquot Sound is Hot Springs Cove, where a 120°F (50°C) natural sulfur hot spring tumbles over rocky ledges into steaming pools, then into the ocean. Apart from a small marina about a mile (1.6 kilometers) away, the hot springs are undeveloped. Now, the springs are part of Maquinna Provincial Park and as such are protected from commercial development.

There are three ways to reach Hot Springs Cove: by Zodiac or water taxi, by floatplane or by kayak. The fastest and most expensive way is by plane from Tofino or Gold River to the north. During the summer there are daily flights, but take this option only if you are really short of time.

A water taxi will whisk you to the cove in just over an hour, but whale-watching tours using powerful Zodiac inflatables offer a more thrilling, fun and educational experience. Tour operators are knowledgeable about the gray whales' migration paths, and if there are whales in the area they will find them. Zodiac tours are not for the queasy: the ride can be fast, bumpy and wet despite the waterproof coveralls provided.

By far the most rewarding way to reach the hot springs is the self-propelled way – by kayak. Boats can be rented in Tofino or you can join a guided and fully outfitted tour. A guided trip is advisable if your paddling skills are less than intermediate or if you don't want to deal with the logistics of organizing your own trip.

Starting at Tofino, a relatively sheltered route can be followed along the inside passage around Vargas and Flores islands. Protected channels and inlets allow kayakers to travel safely for most of the 37 miles (60 kilometers) to Hot Springs Cove. The round trip can be completed comfortably in seven to eight days.

Depending on conditions, the most hazardous part of the journey can be leaving Tofino. In summer, there is substantial boat and plane

Waterfall at Hot Springs Cove, Maquinna Provincial Park.

Look for bald eagles when leaving Tofino.

traffic in the harbor. Weave your way out cautiously and soon you'll have left most of the traffic behind. Then there'll be time to relax and start counting the bald eagles (you'll soon lose count) or to enjoy spotting seals.

The sandy shore of Milties Beach on Vargas Island makes a good camping spot for the first night. If you're spared morning fog, make an early start and head for Whitesand Cove on Flores Island. As its name suggests, there's excellent camping on a white sand beach and an opportunity to stretch your legs on the Ahousat Wild Side Trail. The route then follows Millar Channel and Hayden Passage around the east side of Flores Island. Here, the campsites are not as spectacular, but there are pleasant grassy spots beside creeks where you can replenish your water supply.

When you go

Tofino Tourism Information Centre
PO Box 249
346 Campbell Street
Tofino, BC V0R 2Z0
Tel: (250) 725-3414

Most paddlers choose Halfmoon Beach on the northwest shore of Flores Island for their final campsite. It offers easy access to the entrance to Hot Springs Cove on the opposite shore, just 550 yards (500 meters) away. Stash your boats at the government wharf and hike the one-and-a-quarter-mile (1.9-kilometer) boardwalk trail through lush rainforest to the hot springs, stopping occasionally to read some of the more interesting inscriptions on the boards.

During the summer, you'll invariably share the hot springs with others, but there's usually room for everyone. If time permits, plan to stay at the small campsite near the wharf, or stay at the self-catering Hot Springs Lodge, and pay a nighttime visit to the hot springs. It's a special thrill to luxuriate in the warmth of the pools by candlelight!

Weather permitting, the outside passage around Flores and Vargas islands can be taken on the return trip. However, the western side of the islands is more exposed to wind and waves and the rough coast has few safe landing sites. Only experienced paddlers should attempt this route. The rewards, though, are the chance to experience truly wild scenery and long expanses of white sand beaches.

Barkley Sound

If you're ready to venture out on your first real kayak camping trip, Barkley Sound on the west coast of Vancouver Island, and in particular the inner islands of the Broken Group, offers an ideal starting place when the weather is settled. Ease of access, a relatively safe paddling environment, and abundant marine life, sea birds and bald eagles make this destination one that families can readily enjoy.

The dozens of islands that dot the sound form two groups: the Broken Group, part of Pacific Rim National Park Reserve, and the Deer Group. The safest and most convenient way to access them is on the *MV Lady Rose* or *MV Frances Barkley* from Port Alberni. These vessels will drop you just north of the Broken Group at Sechart, where canoes and kayaks can be rented. From there it is

a short paddle to campsites on either Hand or Gibralter islands. The Deer Group can be accessed from Bamfield, which in turn can be accessed by road or by the *MV Lady Rose*. The hazardous Imperial Eagle Channel separates the two island groups. It is not advisable to paddle across the channel.

The Broken Group is an extremely popular destination between July and September, and the eight islands with designated

camping areas are often crowded. Consider visiting the islands in the shoulder seasons – May is often dry and warm and summer weather can extend well into September – or plan a trip to the Deer Group, which is usually less crowded.

When preparing for your trip, it is best to be completely self-sufficient and carry an ample supply of fresh water, especially in late summer, when the few available water sources may have dried up or become inaccessible. The campgrounds are generally small and primitive, but the shoreline sites provide spectacular views of the sound. Although the fishing is good, the harvesting of shellfish is limited; check the Department of Fisheries and Oceans regulations. Because of intermittent red tides, which can result in paralytic shellfish poisoning,

Aerial view of Barkley Sound, Pacific Rim National Park Reserve.

Kayaking, the Broken Group, Pacific Rim National Park Reserve.

it is not a good idea to eat filter-feeding molluscs such as mussels anywhere along the coast.

Morning fog is quite common in Barkley Sound, so expect to be shore-bound for part of your trip. In summer, wind and waves can gather strength during the day. It is best to complete your island crossings early, then spend the remainder of the day relaxing or exploring the sheltered coves, beaches or forest.

Barkley Sound is a naturalist's paradise. The bays and coves are brimming with intertidal life, and bald eagles and sea birds are everywhere. There are seals and sea lions and even the occasional passing gray whale. Hiking trails exist on some of the islands, but in general, because of the impenetrable bush, your explorations will be confined to the seashore.

When you're satiated with the islands' natural beauty, look for signs of their cultural and industrial history – middens and stonewall fish traps left by the Nuu-chah-nulth people, remains of a copper-mining operation on Prideaux Island, and logging paraphernalia on Hand Island. You can even visit the remains of a gun emplacement on Turret Island, constructed during World War II to repel invaders from across the Pacific. Today, the site makes a grand lookout.

In calm and settled weather, you can make an exciting foray around the outer islands of both the Broken and Deer groups to experience the raw power of the Pacific swell. Even on a calm day, it will be a thrilling roller-coaster ride. Be sure to stay well away from breaking waves and submerged rock platforms, and start early to avoid the almost daily buildup of wind and waves.

When you go

Parks Canada
PO Box 280
Ucluelet, BC V0R 3A0
Tel: (250) 726-7721
Fax: (250) 726-4720

For information on ferry schedules and boat rentals at Sechart Lodge, contact:
Alberni Marine Transport
PO Box 188
Port Alberni, BC V9Y 7M7
Tel: 1-800-663-7192

Recommended Reading

Official Guide to Pacific Rim National Park Reserve, available from Parks Canada.

McGee, Peter (editor). *Kayak Routes of the Pacific Northwest Coast.* Vancouver: Douglas & McIntyre, 1998.

Juan de Fuca Marine Trail

Missed your reservation on the West Coast Trail? Not up to committing to a long-distance trek? The Juan de Fuca Marine Trail is a new and welcome addition to Vancouver Island's west coast hiking experience. More than just an alternative hiking destination, though, the Juan de Fuca offers something for people of all ages to enjoy.

The trail begins at Botanical Beach near Port Renfrew on the southwest coast of Vancouver Island and follows the shoreline south to China Beach, just west of the community of Jordan River. Four access points along its 29-mile (47-kilometer) length means you can take on as much or as little as you want.

Botanical Beach is not only the northern terminus of the trail; it's a provincial park day-use area worth a visit for families as well as hikers setting out on the trek. Four short trails suitable for children and older folk lead to tide pools teeming with marine creatures. In May or June, when the tides are at their lowest and the water is clear, the pools are a rainbow of purple sea urchins, green anemones and pink starfish.

The first leg of the Juan de Fuca trail follows the shoreline to Parkinson Creek, another day-use park 6 miles (10 kilometers) and about four hours distant. From the shore, the views across the Juan de Fuca Strait stretch all the way to the Olympic Peninsula in Washington. Closer in, seals and sea lions sun themselves on the rocks, or play hide-and-seek in the seaweed.

From Parkinson Creek, the trail continues through old-growth red and yellow cedar, Sitka spruce and hemlock forest. The terrain is moderate, but even day hikers will need good gripping soles on their boots, especially in wet weather, when the trail gets muddy and slick. Watch for signs of bear and cougar here and in all the forested sections, and don't let children wander out of sight.

Five and a half miles (9 kilometers) from Parkinson Creek, you'll find yourself at Sombrio Beach campsite. Yet another day-use area, the large cobble beach is an easy ten-minute walk from the parking lot. Moms and dads can explore the beach with the kids, stay at the rustic campground, surf, or hike east along the beach. Sea caves, tide pools and gray whales swimming in

Hiking along the Juan de Fuca Marine Trail.

Orange starfish, one of the marine creatures seen at Botanical Beach.

the strait make this a particularly interesting area to spend time in. Backpackers will need to rest up here for the challenging 17-mile (28-kilometer) trek from Sombrio Beach to the trail's southern terminus at China Beach. This section, rated "Very Difficult" by the park, has numerous creek crossings and steeper changes in elevation than the rest of the trail. Only well-prepared, experienced backpackers should attempt this portion.

Exhausted hikers will be relieved to reach China Beach, the trail's southern terminus. Day visitors, too, will be delighted with the spectacular ocean view and the fine sand beach, great for picnics, building sand-castles, or just dabbling your toes in the water. It's a short, 20-minute walk from the parking lot along a wide gravel path and through mature forest to the beach.

For those hiking its full length, the Juan de Fuca Trail is a strenuous but rewarding adventure. For day trippers, the four provincial parks along its route give easy access to a spectacular, unspoiled area of the coast.

When you go

BC Parks
South Vancouver Island District
2930 Trans-Canada Highway
Victoria, BC V9E 1K3
Tel: (250) 391-2300
Fax: (250) 478-9211

Discovering the tide pools on Botanical Beach, Juan de Fuca Marine Trail.

Whistler

When Alex and Myrtle Philip built Rainbow Lodge on Alta Lake back in 1914, it's unlikely they had any inkling of what they had started. The quiet fishing lodge in the Coast Mountains north of Vancouver has spawned two world-class ski resorts, a modern, fast-growing recreational town, and more hiking and biking trails than you can shake a stick at. The Philips and the lodge are now gone, along with most of the wilderness they knew, but their legacy – Whistler Village – lives on.

Harmony Lake, Whistler.

Given that Vancouver and the Lower Mainland, with a combined population of over 2 million, are on Whistler's doorstep, you cannot expect a wilderness experience. But you can expect a great recreational experience, especially as a family. The "village" is a modern recreational town with dozens of hotels and B&Bs, but very little by way of campgrounds. You should head for neighboring Garibaldi Provincial Park for a backcountry camping experience.

The problem with Whistler is knowing where to begin. In winter, there's a choice between alpine skiing or snowboarding on Whistler or Blackcomb mountains, nordic skiing or snowshoeing in the valley, and heli-skiing. In summer, it's even more complicated: hiking, mountain biking, canoeing, climbing, whitewater rafting, windsurfing, trail riding, fishing and bird watching are all available within a few miles of the village. You can rent most of the equipment needed for these activities in Whistler.

A good start on a warm, summer day would be a ride on Whistler Mountain's Village Express gondola. In minutes you're whisked 3,800 feet (1,160 meters) from the bustling village into an alpine world of snowy mountain peaks and glaciers. Here you can enjoy guided or non-guided hikes, long or short. A visit to Harmony Lake and meadows is a must. Alternatively, you can skip the $20 ride and spend three hours hiking to the mountaintop. In midsummer it's worth the cost of the ride to escape the valley heat and bugs for the cool ridgetop breezes.

A highly recommended trip for the more adventurous is the 6-mile (10-kilometer) ridgetop trail that traverses the Musical Bumps – Piccolo, Flute and Oboe – and eventually leads to Singing Pass (named for the wind whistling through the trees – dress

Skiing Tips

- Different styles of skiing use different equipment so be sure to buy the correct skis, poles, boots and bindings. Go to a specialty outdoor store for professional advice.

- Decide before visiting a specialty store whether you plan to ski on groomed trails, in the backcountry or at resort areas.

- Be honest with yourself and decide whether you are a novice, intermediate or advanced skier. Your skill level will dictate the model of ski you buy.

- Dress appropriately, especially when skating or skiing quickly. Use a layering system to stay cool when moving and warm when stationary.

- Ski tourers should invest in good-quality outerwear, either a jacket-and-pant combination or a one-piece suit for those occasions when you might take a tumble!

- Remember the old adage "When your feet are cold, put on a hat." About 20 percent of your body heat can be lost through the head.

- Wear good-quality sunglasses or goggles at all times while skiing. Cloudy and whiteout conditions are often the worst for causing snowblindness.

- Use SPF 30 or greater sunscreen, especially in the spring when the sun is strong and the snow reflects damaging UV radiation.

- Carry plenty of water when ski touring. It is easy to become dehydrated, especially if it's cold. Eat snow only in an emergency and in small quantities. Eating too much snow can lower your core body temperature and lead to hypothermia.

- When ski touring, avoid overexerting yourself and sweating profusely. Move at a steady pace and dress appropriately so that you're neither cold nor sweating. Damp clothes and cold, windy conditions are the main causes of hypothermia in winter.

- Small problems can often escalate into big ones in winter because of cold temperatures, fewer daylight hours and changes in snow conditions. Allow plenty of time for delays when planning an outing.

- Select a large day pack when ski touring. Carry a small (1 pint/500 mL) thermos with soup or hot chocolate, food, a headlamp, repair kit (multi-purpose tool, binding screws, duct tape), first aid kit, insulated water bottle, warm jacket, spare gloves and spare socks.

- For longer day trips, take a lightweight stove and small aluminum pot to refill water bottles or brew up a hot drink.

- An inflatable insulated pad to sit on at lunchtime will keep you dry and warmer.

- Essential items for travel in avalanche terrain: a transceiver, also called an avalanche beacon or "Pieps," a sturdy shovel and sectional avalanche probe. All these items are available at specialty outdoor stores that cater to winter-sports enthusiasts.

- Know how to use your avalanche safety equipment. Take courses, practice with your friends, and update your skills every couple of years.

- Knee-length gaiters will help keep the snow out of your boots and provide extra insulation for your lower legs.

Canoeing the River of Golden Dreams, Whistler.

appropriately for this breezy hike). The well built and well signposted trail offers dazzling views of Blackcomb Mountain and the Spearhead Range, and an eagle's-eye view of Cheakamus Lake over 3,600 feet (1,100 meters) below. This outing needs some planning. If you intend to return on the gondola it's best to hike only partway to Singing Pass, allowing enough time to catch the last ride down. If you want the full-day experience, continue to Singing Pass and then take the Fitzsimmons Creek trail back to Whistler, a distance of 14 miles (23 kilometers). The extra effort is rewarded with dazzling displays of lupine-filled meadows near Singing Pass. Save this hike for late July or August when the wildflowers are in full bloom.

If you have energy to spare, or plan to spend a night in the high country, continue your climb beyond Singing Pass to Russet Lake. The additional mile-and-a-quarter (2 kilometers) is well worth the effort. There is an idyllic campground by the lake and a small shelter that can be used in an emergency. With a little time to sit and stare, you might see mountain goats on the slopes of Fissile Peak or deer browsing on the sparse vegetation.

Blackcomb Mountain offers a similar experience and some rewarding hikes to breathtaking vistas of the Cheakamus and Overlord glaciers. You can even enjoy some summer skiing or snowboarding on the Horstman Glacier until early August. Make sure you remember the sunscreen!

If you prefer more of an adrenaline rush, join one of the guided mountain-bike descents of Whistler or Blackcomb mountains. Bikes are provided for the high-speed, bone-jarring descents. All you have to do is hang on and stop occasionally to rest your white knuckles, let the brake pads cool, and take in the views. Definitely not for people who like to stop and smell the flowers. If you like to cycle at a more sedate pace, there are dozens of miles of biking trails in the valley.

For a pure hiking experience that doesn't involve mechanical lifts, consider the 8.5-mile (13.6-kilometer) hike to Brandywine Meadows, about 9 miles (15 kilometers) south of Whistler. A steep 1,150-foot (350-meter) climb through lush forest leads to the flower- and heather-strewn meadows crisscrossed by a pretty meandering stream. You can continue up-valley for as long as your ambition and energy hold out – all the way to the top of 7,316-foot (2,230-meter) Brandywine Mountain, a climb of about 4,300 feet (1,300 meters).

If the weather is not suitable for a mountaintop adventure, take to the 9-mile (15-kilometer) Valley Trail that circumnavigates Whistler, passes by seven lakes and five parks and crosses numerous creeks. The mostly paved pathway is shared among pedestrians, cyclists and in-line skaters in summer, and becomes a cross-country ski circuit in winter. Sections of the Valley Trail are part of the much longer Sea to Sky Trail, an as-yet-unfinished 186-mile (300-kilometer) mountain-biking and hiking trail that runs from Squamish to D'Arcy, north of Pemberton.

The Valley Trail is ideal for families and can be fun even on those dreary rain-filled days for which the coastal mountains are notorious. The whole family can rent bikes or in-line skates, or simply stroll along the pathways, stop at the park for a picnic lunch, or duck into a café for a break. Relax and watch the sailing races on Alta Lake or the windsurfers skimming along with the help of afternoon breezes.

When you go

Whistler Resort Association
4010 Whistler Way
Whistler, BC V0N 1B4
Tel: 1-800-944-7853
Website: www.whistler-resort.com

Recommended Reading

Christie, Jack. *Whistler Outdoors Guide.* Vancouver/Toronto: Greystone Books, Douglas & McIntyre, 1996.

Looking for a leisurely outing? Rent a canoe and paddle Alta Lake and the River of Golden Dreams (named for the honeymooning couples who stayed at Rainbow Lodge). Most of the river is a gentle float, allowing you time for bird watching along the reedy banks and to admire the tall Sitka spruce, a reminder of what most of the valley once looked like. The river

flows into Green Lake, the take-out. Most canoe rental companies will pick you up at the lake and take you back to Whistler.

If you'd like to pick up the pace, try a guided river rafting trip on one of the many rivers that flow out of the Coast Mountains.

Whatever the activity you choose, it's likely you'll be sharing the experience with others. Whistler is not a place to leave behind the madding crowd. However, the people who planned the village knew what they were doing. They chose a prime piece of real estate, easily accessible from Vancouver by car or rail, in the midst of mountain scenery that is guaranteed to attract visitors by the thousands. Now, if only they could do something about that rain and the summer bugs!

Skiing at Whistler Resort.

Garibaldi Provincial Park

A land formed by fire and ice is an apt description of Garibaldi Provincial Park. Volcanic activity and glaciers have each played a role in shaping the awe-inspiring landscape of this 750-square-mile (1,950-square-kilometer) park in B.C.'s Coast Mountains. The Black Tusk, a towering monolith of volcanic rock, is the most impressive legacy of this titan clash, but throughout the park there are lava flows, lakes and glacially scoured valleys that provide spectacular eye candy for jaded urbanites.

The roadless park is bounded on the west by Highway 99, linking Vancouver and Whistler, and on the east by Lillooet Lake and River, which effectively cut off easy access to the rugged eastern side of the park. Most of the park's trails and campgrounds are in the western half and are readily accessed from Highway 99, a.k.a. the Sea to Sky Highway. You can be shouldering your backpack within an hour and a half of leaving Vancouver.

Five distinct recreational areas are worth visiting: Elfin Lakes/Diamond Head, Garibaldi Lake/Black Tusk, Cheakamus Lake, Singing Pass and Wedgemount Lake. In all of these areas, backpacks can be exchanged for skis when the prodigious amounts of coastal rain turn to prodigious amounts of snow.

The 7-mile (11-kilometer) Elfin Lakes trail in the southwestern portion of the park is a very pleasant introduction to the area. Both hikers and cyclists can use the forestry

When you go

Garibaldi Provincial Park
PO Box 220
Brackendale, BC V0N 1H0
Tel: (604) 898-3678
Fax: (604) 898-4171
Website: www.elp.gov.bc.ca/bcparks

Recommended Reading

Copeland, Kathy, and Craig Copeland. *Don't Waste Your Time in the BC Coast Mountains.* Riondel: Voice in the Wilderness Press, 1997.

Ice cave in Helm Glacier, Garibaldi Provincial Park/Black Tusk.

The Black Tusk from Taylor Meadows, Garibaldi Provincial Park.

road that climbs gently through a forest of Douglas fir, red cedar, western hemlock and deciduous trees such as birch and cottonwood. This mixed forest gives rise to spectacular fall colors. Elfin Lakes are the end of the trail for cyclists but hikers can continue toward Diamond Head, the multi-hued volcanic peak that dominates the sprawling scene, or Opal Cone, a remnant of a volcanic rim. A campground and a 34-bed cabin adjacent to the lakes make it possible to stay in the area to explore further.

Arguably the most popular destination in the park is Garibaldi Lake and the surrounding area – Black Tusk, Taylor Meadows and Panorama Ridge. The 5.5-mile (9-kilometer) trail to the lake climbs just over 2,600 feet (800 meters), making it a reasonably challenging hike. The trail starts at the base of the Barrier, a wall of red volcanic rock that formed when a lava flow ran into a glacier. The ice has now melted, leaving the impressive rock wall that dams the waters of Barrier, Lesser Garibaldi and Garibaldi lakes.

The lake and nearby Taylor Meadows can be visited in a day trip, but to do justice to the area, plan to use the designated campgrounds at either the lake or the meadows for at least an overnight stay. From here you can climb through subalpine forest to the heather-strewn Panorama Ridge and views of the

Sphinx and Sentinel glaciers, Garibaldi Lake and Table Mountain. If you're up for a steep scramble, tackle the 2,755-foot (840-meter) ascent of Black Tusk. The final climb up a steep gully to the summit is best left to mountaineers, but even if you don't reach the top, the hike through flower-strewn alpine meadows and the unfolding panorama of Garibaldi Lake, Squamish and the waters of Howe Sound is still a treat.

If you prefer more of a backpacking experience, consider taking the 10-mile (16-kilometer) trail from Black Tusk Meadows via Helm Creek to the Cheakamus River. This would be a three-day, one-way trip if you stayed at the Helm Creek camp ground, conveniently situated about 5 miles (8 kilometers) from Garibaldi Lake. The trail descends steadily to a bridge across the Cheakamus River, a sure sign that your trip is almost over. After you cross the river, the final mile (1.5 kilometers) to the parking lot at the end of the Cheakamus Lake Road is a pleasant stroll through a forest of towering fir, cedar and western hemlock.

A favorite among locals and visitors alike, Cheakamus Lake is a turquoise jewel nestled between mountains that soar up to 5,200 feet (1,600 meters) above the lake. The almost level, 1.8-mile (3-kilometer) forested trail to the lake is ideal for a family outing, either on foot or by bike. For 2 miles

(3.5 kilometers), the trail undulates along the flower-strewn hillside to a small campground at Singing Creek.

Singing Pass, the headwaters for Singing Creek, is well worth a visit, but it must be approached from Whistler, either as a hike up Fitzsimmons Creek or along the Musical Bumps from near the top of Whistler ski resort.

The trail to Wedgemount Lake, the northernmost area in the park accessed from Highway 99, is for fit and determined hikers only. The 4-mile (7-kilometer) trail climbs about 3,900 feet (1,200 meters). En route, you're treated to a breathtaking view of Wedgemount Creek as it tumbles down from the cirque that cradles the lake. As you haul yourself up the last steep section to the rim of the cirque, the mountain vista will take away what little breath you have left. A small, rustic shelter near the lake accommodates six, but it is probably more pleasant to camp and feel closer to nature in this incredible area.

It's difficult to predict the best time to visit Garibaldi Park. The fickle coastal weather will always be ready with surprises, but mid-July through September seems to be the best period to plan an alpine hike. Alpine and glacier touring on skis is best in April and May. If you plan to stay on the valley bottom trails, any time of the year is okay; just be prepared for wet conditions.

Garibaldi Lake/Black Tusk.

Tatshenshini–Alsek Wilderness Park

Edward Glave, the first European to paddle down the Tatshenshini River, in 1890 noted that the river environs yielded "such an incessant display of scenic wild grandeur that ... we can no longer appreciate it." Each year, more than 1,000 people now paddle the "Tat," as it is affectionately called, on a journey back in time to the last Ice Age when snowfields and glaciers dominated the land.

The Tatshenshini – Tlingit for "river of ice" – was catapulted into the spotlight in recent years because of a scheme to operate an open-pit copper and gold mine in the heart of the region. Thanks to the concerted efforts of 50 conservation and environmental groups, the project was quashed and the B.C. government declared the area a Class A provincial park. The Tatshenshini–Alsek Provincial Park that was created as a result of this legislation is a massive 3,700 square miles (9,580 square kilometers), almost twice the size of Prince Edward Island.

Both private and commercial groups run the river between mid-June and August. Competent canoeists, kayakers or rafters may arrange their own trips, but most people choose an outfitter to guide them down the river and supply the specialized equipment. The number of paddlers on the river at any one time is strictly controlled to maintain the quality of the wilderness experience and to avoid logistical problems at the take-out. All groups require a permit costing $100.

The 140-mile (225-kilometer) journey starts at Dalton Post in Yukon, a two-and-a-half- to three-hour drive from Whitehorse. The river flows through the northwestern corner of British Columbia and enters the Gulf of Alaska at Dry Bay. Most groups take 10 to 12 days to complete the trip, which allows time for hikes into the surrounding mountains and to the glaciers.

The trip does require a high

Dall sheep grazing in Tatshenshini–Alsek Wilderness Park.

level of commitment, but not a high level of skill if you join an outfitted group. There are no roads in the park that offer an escape route, so you have to complete the trip in fair weather and foul. If you're not ready to commit to a full-blown wilderness experience, you can take a one-day rafting trip on the upper Tatshenshini, which takes you through some of the best whitewater rapids.

Here you are, though, on the banks of the fast-flowing Tatshenshini, with the equipment stowed and the rafts ready to push off. You're about to embark on a wilderness journey that is acknowledged as one of the best in North America.

For whitewater aficionados the most thrilling part of the journey is near the start, where you bounce through Class III to Class IV rapids in the 6-mile-long (10-kilometer-long) Tatshenshini Gorge. After the confines of the gorge, you're treated to spectacular views of the approaching Alsek and Noisey ranges. This is a slow section of river that meanders through forest and marshland teeming with wildlife. Moose, wolves, bear and beaver all inhabit this corridor, and over 40 bird species have been identified, including rare trumpeter swans and peregrine falcons. If you're extremely lucky, you might catch a glimpse of the "blue" or "glacier" bear.

The size of the river increases enormously during the first few days of your trip, fed by numerous large tributary valleys that

Rafting in Tatshenshini-Alsek Wilderness Park.

have their headwaters in the snowfields and glaciers of the Icefield Range in Kluane. The tributary streams are laden with sediment, giving the river a metallic appearance. The sediments are slowly deposited, creating ever-changing meanders that take considerable skill to navigate.

Most campsites are on riverside sandbars backed by dense willow and shrubs, and fringed with fireweed, Indian paintbrush and wild geraniums. Animal tracks crisscross the sandbars. Great care must be taken to store food properly and give animals all the space they need.

All of the commercial outfitters break up the journey with layover days that allow relaxation in camp or hiking into surrounding hills. Depending on the weather, a variety of hikes can give you an eagle's-eye view of the river – from strolls through flower-strewn alpine meadows to energetic scrambles to high ridges offering panoramic

When you go

For a list of permitted guides, air taxis and expediters contact:
BC Parks
Skeena District
3790 Alfred Avenue, Bag 5000
Smithers, BC V0J 2N0
Tel: (250) 847-7320
Fax: (250) 847-7659

Recommended Reading

Tatshenshini River Wild. Vancouver: Raincoast Books, 1993.

views – your best opportunity to see Dall sheep and mountain goats, wolf and bear.

About halfway through the journey, the confluence with the mighty Alsek River is reached. This is also a rafting river, but part of it – Turnback Canyon – is impassable and must be portaged. The larger commercial outfitters use helicopters. You're now in the heart of the Alsek and Noisey ranges, surrounded by 6,600-foot (2,000-meter-high) peaks and glaciers that flow straight into the river. Welcome to the Ice Age! Here you'll

pass through some of the most spectacular and dynamic scenery on earth.

The Walker Glacier offers an opportunity for a close-up view of the ice, and the glaciers just keep on getting bigger as you travel downstream. At Alsek Lake, the 7-mile-wide (11-kilometer-wide) front of the Alsek and Grand Plateau glaciers continually calves into the lake, creating icebergs up to 65 feet (20 meters) high. It's possible to climb to a rocky promontory and watch the action as the ice groans, cracks and plummets into the water. The backdrop to this surreal scene is Mount Fairweather; its 15,200-foot (4,633-meter) peak is the highest in B.C.

Shortly after leaving Alsek Lake, the final mountain ridge is passed and the next stop is Dry Bay at journey's end. From here, weather permitting, a small plane transports you back to Whitehorse and the return to civilization.

The Chilkoot Trail

Imagine, after two to three days of strenuous effort you've finally reached the top of Chilkoot Pass, tired but with a sense of accomplishment and relief. Now imagine how short-lived that relief would be if you had to retrace your steps and repeat the climb 20 or more times! This was the reality for the stampeders heading to the Klondike's gold fields between 1897 and 1899.

Today, up to 3,000 hikers a year follow in the footsteps of the stampeders, but strictly for recreation. The gold is long gone; only the crumbling shacks, rusting machinery and countless artifacts remain as a reminder of a brief, frantic, greed-filled era.

The 33-mile (53-kilometer) trail starts at Dyea, near Skagway, Alaska, and ends at Bennett, B.C. Skagway, a tourist town that capitalizes on the Gold Rush era, can be reached by road from Whitehorse or by boat via the Inside Passage. The latter option is an excellent way to round out your vacation and see some spectacular coastline. You're allowed to pitch your tent on the upper deck of the ferry, but campfires are frowned upon!

The first obvious evidence of the Gold Rush is at the site of Canyon City, once a thriving community of 1,500. Here was a powerhouse for an aerial tramway that carried goods to the summit of Chilkoot Pass. Shortly after the tramway closed, bought out by its competitor, the White Pass and Yukon Railroad, the town was abandoned. The rusting boiler that provided steam power for the tramway is still there, as are rotting timbers and countless reminders of everyday life – pots, utensils, lanterns – that are now being swallowed by undergrowth and slowly returned to the earth.

Five miles (eight kilometers) beyond Canyon City is Sheep Camp, a good objective for the first day if you plan to reach the pass the following day. There is a shelter here for escaping rain, if necessary, and for swapping stories with other campers.

An early start is advisable for the hike to the pass because it can take up to 12 hours to reach the next campground. As well, depending on the time of year, there is always a threat of avalanches in the afternoon – an early start reduces the risk. The trail climbs 3,100 feet (950 meters) over about 4 miles (7 kilometers) and gradually passes from lush coastal rainforest to barren alpine tundra. On your way to the pass you'll see the ruins of the Scales, where the Northwest Mounted Police supervised the weighing of the stampeders' supplies.

Beyond the Scales, the terrain becomes steeper and more rugged. The final 600 feet (200 meters) are a scramble through rocks with poles in place to show the way in rain or

Hiking up "The Steps" on the Chilkoot Trail.

mist. Depending on the time of year and the previous year's snowfall, you could be kicking steps in snow. As you cross Chilkoot Pass, you leave Alaska and enter British Columbia. The toughest part of the hike is now behind you. Fortunately, there's no border crossing, just a small building and a Canada Parks official who makes sure everyone arrives safely at the top of the pass.

If time permits, you should explore the surrounding area, which is strewn with artifacts. Try to locate the remains of a dozen or more canvas and wood canoes that some bygone entrepreneur hauled to the top of the pass to sell to the stampeders. These particular canoes did not become part of the 7,000-boat flotilla that floated down Lake Bennett en route to the gold fields in the spring of 1898. They were deemed unsafe by the authorities and were not allowed into Canada.

The landscape changes significantly after you enter Canada. The 4-mile (6.4-kilometer) hike to Happy Camp passes through rolling hills dotted with small lakes and few trees. The hiking is pleasant and easy, but the campsite and shelter at Happy Camp will be a welcome sight after a long day on the trail.

On the final 12.5-mile (20-kilometer) leg to Lake Bennett, you descend into a subalpine boreal forest of fir, lodgepole pine, willow and alder. The contrast with the stately spruce and hemlock forest on the "wet" side of the mountain range is striking. At Lake Bennett your journey is over. Catch the afternoon "speeder" that runs on narrow-gauge tracks (and is anything but speedy) to Log Cabin on the Klondike Highway between Skagway and Whitehorse. There is regular bus service to Skagway or you can take the train, which winds through the scenic White Pass.

The slower train gives you a chance to wind down and reflect on your experience and to marvel

When you go

Klondike Gold Rush National Historic Park
PO Box 517
Skagway, AK 99840
Tel: (907) 983-2921

Chilkoot Trail National Historic Site
205-300 Main Street
Whitehorse, YT Y1A 2B5
Tel: 1-800-661-0486 for reservations and hiking permits.

Recommended Reading

Neufeld, David, and Frank Norris. *Chilkoot Trail: Heritage Route to the Klondike.* Whitehorse: Lost Moose Publishing, 1996.

at the fortitude of the 25,000 stampeders who struggled over the pass full of hope. Some returned from Yukon rich, but most returned empty-handed.

The best time to hike the trail is July and August, when most of the snow has gone from the higher ground. You will be sharing the trail with many other hikers, though a quota system now guarantees you a campsite at day's end. Fit hikers can complete the trail in three days; four or five days are more comfortable if you prefer to go slower and explore all the historic sites. Be prepared for rain and cool temperatures. There are five campsites along the trail, some with shelters for cooking and drying gear, but no opportunity to sleep indoors. This is a backpacking trip. Like the stampeders, you must be self-sufficient.

The historic Red Onion Brothel at the start of the Chilkoot Trail.

Spatsizi Plateau Wilderness Provincial Park

British Columbia is a place of superlatives. It has the biggest trees, the wildest whitewater, arguably the most scenic mountains, and one of the largest and most remote wilderness parks in Canada: Spatsizi Plateau Wilderness Provincial Park in north-central B.C. The combined area of Spatsizi and the adjoining Tatlatui and Mount Edziza provincial parks is a stunning 4,050 square miles (10,500 square kilometers) – all of it roadless and all of it wild.

Because of its remoteness and the logistics involved in planning a trip, only a few hundred people visit the 2,500-square-mile

(6,500-square-kilometer) Spatsizi park each year. If you want to experience true wilderness with the opportunity to view lots of wildlife, this is the park for you. The opposite side of the coin is that you have to be extremely well prepared and self-sufficient. If you have any doubts

about your coping skills, join one of the many outfitters that organize hiking, trail riding and paddling trips into the park. All visitors are required to practice no-trace camping/wilderness ethics while in the park.

Most of the park is made up of rolling upland plateau, dissected by broad river valleys. The rugged Skeena Mountains form the western boundary of the park, and the mighty Stikine River defines its northern and eastern boundary. To the south is Tatlatui Park, even more remote and wild than Spatsizi. The relatively mild climate and abundant vegetation support a large variety of wildlife, including moose, mountain goats, stone sheep, woodland caribou, wolves, grizzly and black bear, and arctic ground squirrels. Over 140 species of birds have been identified within the park.

Most people visit Spatsizi in the fall when the hills are ablaze with yellow, orange and red dwarf birch, trails are in better condition, and the cool days are ideal for hiking. The jumping-off spot for the park is at Iskut, about 300 miles (500 kilometers) north of Smithers along the Stewart–Cassiar Highway. Depending on the amount of time available to you and your taste for long days on the trail, you can either fly into Cold Fish Lake in the heart of the park, or follow either of two routes to the same destination. The recommended backpacking route is the 30-mile (50-kilometer) trail up Eaglenest Creek and over Danihue Pass. On your hike you might see the mountain goats after which the park is named. (*Spatsizi* is the Tahltan Indian word for "red goat," a name

Canoeing on the Stikine River, Spatsizi Plateau Wilderness Provincial Park.

A view of the Spatsizi Plateau.

given to the mountain goats in the area that have a habit of rolling in red iron oxide dust.) The other trail up the McEwan River is recommended only for horse travel because of large areas of bog and muskeg.

At the northwest end of Cold Fish Lake there are eight rustic cabins, a sauna and a cookhouse that are available to the public on a first-come, first-served basis. These cabins are the legacy of Tommy Walker and his wife, who established the fishing and hunting camp in 1948. The cabins are in a magnificent setting, overlooking the lake and the Eaglenest Range to the west.

Cold Fish Lake is on the doorstep of the Gladys Lake Ecological Reserve, the domain of stone sheep, mountain goats and grizzly bears, as well as a variety of smaller mammals. Hiking in the reserve is encouraged but camping, hunting and fishing are prohibited. The Plateau, Black Fox, Bug Lake and Danihue Pass trails all offer superb day hikes from the cabins.

The lake is the hub from which a network of routes, ranging from day trips to two- or three-day outings, lead into Spatsizi's alpine tundra. The rolling terrain is covered with moss, heather and splashes of color: red Indian paintbrush, yellow and pink columbines, purple gentian and blue forget-me-nots. Woodland caribou roam these open areas.

Spatsizi is also a great destination for wilderness canoe, kayak or

When you go

BC Parks
Skeena District Office
3790 Alfred Avenue, Bag 5000
Smithers, BC V0J 2N0
Tel: (250) 847-7320
Fax: (250) 847-7659

raft trips, though because of unpredictable obstacles, fluctuating water levels and the remoteness of the rivers, inexperienced paddlers should not attempt them. Less skilled paddlers can take guided trips that are safer and more enjoyable.

There are two major canoe routes in the park: the Spatsizi and the upper Stikine rivers. Of the two, the 43-mile (70-kilometer) Spatsizi River, which involves one 3-mile (5-kilometer) portage, is easier and does not require floatplane access. Most paddlers start their trip down the Stikine in the southwestern corner of the park at either Tuaton or Laslui lakes, both of which can be accessed only by floatplane. The Stikine is a faster and more technical river and involves one mandatory 1.8-mile (3-kilometer) portage, and perhaps two others for inexperienced paddlers. The two rivers join on the eastern boundary of the park and flow through the Stikine River Conservation Area for 110 miles (180 kilometers) to the take-out just north of Iskut at the Highway 37 bridge. Allow eight to ten days for either river trip.

Whether you hike, ride a horse, or paddle in Spatsizi Park, you'll be guaranteed an unforgettable wilderness experience.

Bowron Lake Provincial Park

Mountains are what usually come to mind when you think of British Columbia's interior. Mountains and valleys and forests – and inevitably lakes. In Bowron Lake Provincial Park, amid the Cariboo Mountains, all these features combine to form one of North America's premier canoeing destinations.

Bowron Lake park is a wilderness wildlife reserve with a history closely tied to mining and trapping. The earliest inhabitants, the Takulli people, were nearly wiped out by smallpox with the arrival of prospectors during the 1859 to 1862 Cariboo gold rush. Over the next century, while prospecting and trapping continued, the Cariboo became well known to big-game hunters and fishermen. Hunting ended with the establishment of the park in 1961, but licensed fishing is still allowed.

Canoeing at Bowron Lake Provincial Park.

Today, recreation is the main draw to Bowron Lake park; the seven- to ten-day, 72-mile (116-kilometer) canoe circuit has become a classic. The Bowron chain connects a series of waterways roughly rectangular in shape, starting at the Registration Centre in the northwest corner of the park and heading clockwise with the direction of the flow. Oddly enough, the trip begins with a portage, the first of six totaling 6 miles (9.6 kilometers). Almost all parties use canoe carts, which make for fairly easy going along the wide, smooth paths, but there are canoe rests along each portage for those who prefer to carry their boats.

From the Registration Centre, it's a 1.5-mile (2.4-kilometer) portage to the put-in at Kibbee Lake. In mid-July, you'll be treated to the sight of tall white bog orchids in the marsh just as you reach the lake (named for pioneer trapper and guide Frank Kibbee). A short paddle takes you across the lake to a one-and-a-quarter-mile (2-kilometer) portage leading to Indianpoint Lake. Two other early settlers, the McCabes, built a beautiful cabin on these shores; unfortunately, only the stone chimney remains.

At the far end, Indianpoint Lake narrows to a marsh, with a marked channel leading through a grassy slough. After another short portage, you enter Isaac Lake and paddle the West Arm 4.2 miles (6.8 kilometers) to Wolverine Bay, famous for its lake trout. Isaac Lake turns south here and continues for another 19.4 miles (31.2 kilometers). The distance seems long, but the scenery is unsurpassed, with waterfalls threading their way down the cliffs on one

Cave Wonders

At the headwaters of Huckey Creek, a major tributary of the Bowron River, is a large limestone cave system. When it was first explored in 1971, one excited caver reported wonders of gold-bearing black sand, white frogs and Sasquatch footprints. Later parties found only an overactive imagination to be at work.

side, and the high mountains of the Cariboos on the other. Isaac Lake is subject to high winds and rough water; follow the east shore, where it's easiest to land if a squall comes up. When you reach the end of the lake, you'll have completed a major portion of the circuit.

The next portage takes you into small McLeary Lake, past chutes and whitewater, and 36-foot (11-meter) Isaac Falls. Experienced canoeists can run the whitewater, shortening the 1.7-mile (2.8-kilometer) portage by about a mile (1.6 kilometers). Perhaps this is a warm-up to the

Canoeing on Swan Lake, part of the Bowron Lakes circuit.

next section on the swift Cariboo River, where spills and swampings most often occur. All paddlers must be adept at scouting the river and self-rescue skills.

The Cariboo dumps you into Lanezi Lake, which stretches over 9 miles (15 kilometers) across the southern portion of the park. Follow the north shore to Sandy Lake, a warm, shallow lake with beautiful sand beaches. Now, another section of the Cariboo River links Sandy Lake and Babcock Lake, with a short detour to pretty Unna Lake. Crystal clear, and with fine sandy shores, Unna Lake is the perfect place to stop and take a day off from paddling. Spend some time fishing or just relaxing, and be sure to see the 80-foot-high (24-meter-high) Cariboo Falls.

The Cariboo River is unnavigable beyond Unna Lake, so retrace your strokes to Babcock Creek and line your canoe down the shallow stream to Babcock Lake. The terrain begins to change here – the land of giant mountains, deep lakes and swift rivers gives way to

more rounded hills; the lakes are warmer, and moose graze in the marshy shallows. The last leg of the trip leads you to your final campsite, across Skoi Lake, Spectacle Lakes and Swan Lake, connected by a couple of easy portages, and through a magnificent marsh at the mouth of the Bowron River.

If you have time to spare, paddle a mile or two up the Bowron River and enjoy the variety of birds: coots, mergansers, mallards, widgeons, geese and many others feed

When you go

Canoe circuit reservations:
D.J. Contractors Limited–Hager
Business Services
358 Vaughan Street
Quesnel, BC V2J 2T2
Tel: (250) 992-3111
Fax: (250) 992-6624

Information:
BC Parks District Manager
281–1st Avenue North
Williams Lake, BC V2G 1Y7
Tel: (250) 398-4414
Fax: (250) 398-4686

and nest in the estuary. In the morning, you'll paddle the last stretch of water on the circuit – Bowron Lake. Cottages and motorboats are tell-tale signs that you're heading back to civilization. Travel in the morning when the water is calm and the winds are behind you, and stay to the east side of the lake.

The canoe season begins in June and continues to the end of October. September is likely the best time to go as the summer months are very busy, with up to 50 people starting the circuit each day. There are plenty of campsites, but the choice spots are soon filled during peak season. Novice or inexperienced paddlers should consider going with a guided group, and even experienced paddlers should brush up on their strokes and be fit for portaging, flatwater and river running. Two private lodges on the northwest shore of Bowron Lake rent canoes, paddles, canoe carts and other equipment, and provide accommodation, meals and guided trips. Come prepared for wet weather as well as sunshine – you never know what you'll get in the mountains!

Wells Gray Provincial Park

Located in east-central British Columbia, little-known Wells Gray Provincial Park encompasses over 19,300 square miles (50,000 square kilometers) of untamed wilderness in the heart of the Cariboo and Columbia mountain ranges. It's a feast for the senses: waterfalls thundering into deep plunge pools, wildflowers ablaze during the summer months, and magnificent views from high alpine meadows.

It's also a geological wonder, for the land has been transposed by glaciation, water erosion and volcanic eruptions. The volcanoes were silenced nearly 8,000 years ago, leaving craters, cinder cones, lava flows and basaltic columns scattered throughout the southern region of the park – an awesome exploration ground for hikers and naturalists.

The major access route, Clearwater Valley Road, leads into the park's central corridor. The 43-mile (70-kilometer) road winds through the area most heavily used by day trippers and car campers, and ends at the major jumping-off point for boating and extended canoe tripping. From the road, a network of trails leads to some fascinating formations.

One such network, open to hikers and horseback riders, begins at the Flat Iron trailhead. Several trails follow Hemp Creek and its tributaries to immense lava cliffs, a volcanic mesa and towering hoodoos. Most are easy day trips that can be done in a few hours – or combined to make longer circuits that take in several sights.

Of special interest is White Horse Bluffs. An easy 3.7-mile (6-kilometer) hike through dense cedar and fir forest leads to the top of the bluffs. It's a spectacular 1,070-foot (325-meter) drop to the Clearwater River Valley, with views south over Green Mountain and the Trophy Mountains in the distance. A short, difficult scramble leads to the Rock Roses, an intriguing formation of lava dikes and horizontal columns that looks like a contemporary cubist sculpture.

Farther along the Clearwater Valley Road is the centerpiece of Wells Gray park, Helmcken Falls. The park's existence can be attributed to this stunning cataract that drops 450 feet (137 meters) into a roiling cauldron on the Murtle River. Most visitors see the falls from the lookout, but it's well worth the 5-mile (8-kilometer) (return) hike along the canyon edge to the drop-off. Be careful! The edge can be muddy and slippery at times, and the mesmerizing effect of the falls can make you feel dangerously dizzy. Volcanic forces formed the vertical columns of basaltic lava over which the falls tumble and roar. In winter, the spray rising above the plunge pools gradually forms a gigantic ice pillar as high as 250 feet (75 meters).

Continuing along the road brings you to the trails leading to Pyramid Mountain's volcanic tuya, the historic Ray Farm, and Ray Mineral Springs, one of more than a hundred springs in the park. An easy one-and-a-quarter-mile (2-kilometer) trail will take you to the ancient Dragon's Tongue, a low ridge of jagged lava rubble that cooled and formed over 7,000 years ago. The new campground at Pyramid Mountain now gives easy access to hiking along the Murtle River, past several spectacular waterfalls and gorges. There's good creek

The spectacular Helmcken Falls in Wells Gray Provincial Park.

Photographing wildflowers in Wells Gray Provincial Park.

fishing in the Murtle, and you may see moose, bear and other forest animals along the way.

Trailheads on the east side of Clearwater Valley Road lead to some fantastic alpine hiking through prime grizzly bear country! Here, in the extreme southeast corner of the park, you can hike into supreme alpine meadows covered in wildflowers anytime from late June to the end of August. As the snow recedes, "first bloom" flowers paint the meadows in pastels, with white mountain avens, glacier lilies, spring beauties, wind anemones, marsh marigolds and heather. And when the summer sun has warmed the earth, the "second bloom" bursts upon the scene in a riot of blues, reds and purples – Indian paintbrush, lupine, arnica and valerian.

There are many possibilities for day hikes, but a multi-day traverse of the Trophy Mountains is a fine way to experience the immensity and grandeur of the park. Wells Gray Chalets and Wilderness Adventures, a guiding and outfitting company, has constructed three rustic alpine chalets. They are strategically placed along

the route and make the hike a luxury for backpackers accustomed to tent life.

Just a two-hour hike from the park boundary is the Trophy Mountain Chalet, perched at 7,050 feet (2,150 meters). From a nearby ridge overlooking the Valley

When you go

Wells Gray Provincial Park
RR 2, Box 4516
Clearwater, BC V0E 1N0
Tel: (250) 587-6150

Wells Gray Chalets and Wilderness Adventures
PO Box 188
Clearwater, BC V0E 1N0
Tel: 1-888-754-8735
Tel: (250) 587-6444

Recommended Reading

Goward, Trevor, and Cathie Hickson. *Nature Wells Gray*. Kamloops: The Friends of Wells Gray Park, 1989.

Neave, Roland. *Exploring Wells Gray Park*. Kamloops: The Friends of Wells Gray Park, 1995.

of the Lakes, you can see the 8,400-feet (2,560-meter) peak for which the Trophy Mountain range was named. The 7.5-mile (12-kilometer) hike to the second cabin leads you through the Valley

of the Lakes, over Eagle Pass, then down to lush meadows and the Table Mountain cabin. The hike to the third cabin is an easy but very long 11-mile (18-kilometer) day. This cabin sits on the edge of Fight Meadows, with "52 Ridge" as a backdrop and a vast rolling meadow spread before it. Caribou are easily spotted from the front window of the cabin.

Wells Gray Chalets and Wilderness Adventures also guide ski tours through the Trophy Mountains and canoe trips on the lakes. One of their canoe trips involves a six-day, 40-mile (65-kilometer) circuit of Clearwater and Azure lakes, two of British Columbia's premier paddling lakes. During the day you paddle past cascades of water pouring off the rugged mountains, and at night, set up camp on sandy beaches in the midst of old-growth cedar forest. There is plenty of great fishing for rainbow trout, and good possibilities of spotting deer, moose, grizzly bears and wolf. In spring, you may see these animals swimming across the lake to gain their summer grounds in the higher alpine areas.

Mount Robson Provincial Park

There are dozens of majestic and visually appealing mountains in the Canadian Rockies, but the uncontested monarch of them all is Mount Robson. It is not only the highest in the Rockies at 12,969 feet (3,954 meters), but it also has the most vertical relief, about 9,840 feet (3,000 meters). Its glacier- and snow-clad faces soar to a permanently snow-covered summit, a prize sought but not

often won even by experienced mountaineers.

Fortunately, you don't have to be a mountaineer to enjoy views of Mount Robson; you just need to be lucky! Its usually cloud-capped summit can be seen from the Yellowhead Highway, 52 miles (84 kilometers) west of Jasper, at the Mount Robson Viewpoint Centre. This is also close to the starting point for the 13.5-mile (22-kilometer) Berg Lake trail, one of the most scenic and popular hiking trails in the Rockies, which gives unsurpassed views of the mountain.

Mount Robson and the Berg Lake trail are both within the 838-square-mile (2,170-square-kilometer) Mount Robson Provincial Park, created in 1913. Despite its large area, there are few maintained trails and backcountry campgrounds. Most of the park's resources are spent on maintaining the trail and the seven backcountry campgrounds en route to, or just beyond, Berg Lake. Both hikers and trail riders share parts of the trail,

Berg Lake and Mount Robson.

Who First Climbed Mount Robson?

The Reverend George Kinney, accompanied by Curly Phillips, an outfitter, claimed the first ascent of Mount Robson in 1909. However, Phillips later recanted, saying they didn't quite reach the top. Kinney never admitted their failure. The first undisputed ascent was by Conrad Kain and two others in 1913 via the steep north face, now called the Kain Face.

Hiking the Glacier–Mumm Basin loop in Mount Robson Provincial Park.

and mountain biking is allowed on the first 5.5 miles (9 kilometers).

There can be no guarantee of fine weather anywhere in the vicinity of Mount Robson. Because of its height and bulk, the mountain is capable of creating its own weather. The summit is often obscured by cloud even on a clear day, and rain should be expected at any time. Be prepared for the worst and if the weather gods smile on you, be thankful.

There are four campgrounds spaced at regular intervals on the way to Berg Lake. Strong hikers can reach Marmot campground at the south end of the lake in one day, but if you are not pressed for time, take two and linger at the sensational viewpoints.

The trail starts amid a lush forest of Douglas fir, western hemlock, western red cedar and white pine, a reminder of the moist climate in these parts. The noisy Robson River, the outflow from Berg Lake, tumbles along beside the trail. The first 3 miles (5 kilometers) to Kinney Lake, a blue-green glacier-fed lake, and the next three are relatively gentle. Beyond the delta that feeds the lake, the trail becomes steeper as it enters the Valley of a Thousand Falls. There is no respite now until the campground at Berg Lake is reached.

Numerous waterfalls cascade down the mountain slopes on both sides of the trail, but by far the most impressive are those on the Robson River: White Falls, Falls of the Pool and the much-photographed Emperor Falls, which is well worth the short side trip from the main trail.

Your appetite should now be whetted for the main event, the first view of Berg Lake and the mile-and-a-quarter-high (2-kilometer-high) Emperor Face of Mount Robson. The jaw-dropping view improves as you follow the western shore of the lake, bringing into sight the north face of Robson and Berg Glacier. Icebergs or growlers regularly calve off the glacier into the lake, bobbing around like giant ice cubes.

Berg Lake campground is the most popular on the trail and is often full. Allow a little extra time to hike to the less crowded Rearguard or Robson Pass campgrounds, 875 yards (800 meters) and 1.2 miles (2 kilometers) respectively from Berg Lake. Stay a while. Spend a day exploring the 6.5-mile (10.8-kilometer) Snowbird Pass trail that climbs alongside the Robson Glacier for much of its length. Or for even better views of Mount Robson, take the 9-mile (14.8-kilometer) Hargreaves Glacier–Mumm Basin loop. The trail climbs high above Berg Lake, giving uninterrupted views of the Berg and Mist glaciers and the incredible north face of Robson.

If you have been blessed with good weather and clear views, the memory of your trip to Berg Lake will remain vivid for many years to come.

When you go

BC Parks
Prince George District
4051 18th Ave, PO Box 2045
Prince George, BC V2N 2J6
Tel: (250) 565-6759/6340
Fax: (250) 565-6940

Cathedral Provincial Park

In a province full of recreational gems, Cathedral Provincial Park stands out like a crown jewel. The park is a 127-square-mile (330-square-kilometer) mountain wilderness that straddles the transition zone between the wet Cascade Mountains and the dry Okanagan Valley, providing the best of both worlds. Packed into the relatively small park are forests of Douglas fir, lodgepole pine and Engelmann spruce, alpine lakes and meadows, and geological formations that intrigue and delight visitors.

The park is about 15 miles (25 kilometers) south of Keremeos on Highway 3, a five-hour drive from Vancouver. The southern

boundary of the park is the 49th parallel. Mountain bikes and dogs are not allowed in the park.

Near the center of the park is Cathedral Lakes Lodge on Quiniscoe Lake, a recreational complex that can accommodate up to 53 guests in the main lodge and has eight outlying cabins. Both guests and non-guests (by prior arrangement) can

be driven from the park boundary to the lodge by four-wheel drive on the park's only road. Purists can eschew a ride and spend a day hiking into the park via any of three access trails, the shortest being the 10-mile (16-kilometer) Lakeview Trail. There are two campgrounds in the core area that are open from June 1 to mid-October.

All trails eventually lead to Quiniscoe Lake, the largest of seven lakes that are collectively called the Cathedral Lakes. Each has its own charm: Lake of the Woods is enclosed by subalpine forest and has an idyllic campground; Ladyslipper Lake contains trophy-sized rainbow trout; and Glacier Lake is fringed with grassy meadows and larches. Quiniscoe Lake offers both good fishing and the opportunity to enjoy some paddling (rowboats and canoes are available for rent at the lodge). Pyramid Lake also offers great fishing for pan-sized cutthroats. The tiny but scenic Scout Lake and Goat Lakes, about 1 mile (2 kilometers) and 5 miles (8 kilometers) respectively from Quiniscoe Lake, are also well worth visiting.

Over 37 miles (60 kilometers) of well-maintained trails radiate from the vicinity of the lodge and lead to alpine lakes, alpine meadows and high ridges. The park's showpiece is the Cathedral Rim Trail, a 7-mile (11-kilometer) mountaintop traverse, most of it above the treeline. Not only are the views magnificent, but there are fascinating geological formations as well. Add to this the possibility of wildlife sightings – mountain goats, California bighorn sheep, marmots and mule deer – and you have a truly memorable day-long outing.

The Rim Trail starts at Quiniscoe Lake, then follows the east ridge of Red Mountain to its

Glacier Lake, Cathedral Provincial Park.

"Smokey the Bear" rock formation at Cathedral Provincial Park.

summit at 8,098 feet (2,469 meters). From here the trail stays high and offers uninterrupted views of the North Cascades and the Coast Mountains over 60 miles (100 kilometers) away. A succession of geologic features will then make your ridgetop ramble even more interesting. The Devil's Wood Pile is a formation of columnar-jointed basaltic rocks, said to look like the ingredients for Satan's furnace. Stone City is a bizarre jumble of quartz monzonite (granitic) rocks that have been rounded by incessant wind and water action. Perhaps the most impressive formation is the Giant Cleft, a vertically sided chasm that was formed when a layer of softer basalt rock was eroded from between the surrounding harder granite.

When you go

BC Parks
Okanagan District
PO Box 399
Summerland, BC V0H 1Z0
Tel: (250) 494-6500

Cathedral Lakes Resort
RR 1 Cawston, BC V0X 1C0
Tel: 1-888-255-4453 for reservations
Website: www.cathedral-lakes-lodge.com

If the weather doesn't justify a trip to the ridgetops, numerous trails connect with the lakes and offer exquisite forest hiking. It's an opportunity to try to identify some of the 36 or more species of birds and well over 500 varieties of plant life that have been documented in the park.

A special time of year is late September, when the Lyall's larches are ready to shed their leaves. The contrast between the blue lakes and the yellow larches is stunning, making this an ideal time to visit.

Kettle Valley Railway

For 80 years a major transportation route, the Kettle Valley Railway has seen the last of the railcars chugging through the mountains and valleys of B.C.'s southern interior. These days, it's an important route that carries a cargo of outdoor enthusiasts on a journey steeped in history.

The KVR, as it's commonly called, is an abandoned railway corridor that winds through nearly 370 miles (600 kilometers) of diverse B.C. landscapes. In a region known as the Okanagan–Similkameen, the multi-use trail cuts through arid desert, lush orchard country, high mountains and deep valleys linking the town of Midway to the city of Hope.

The history of the railway is brief, but exciting. In 1910 the Canadian Pacific Railway began construction of the KVR and its off-shoots. This was dubbed an engineering miracle. The CPR was

Little Tunnel on Okanagan Mountain, Kettle Valley Railway.

competing with its U.S. rival, the Great Northern Railway, for access routes to the seaports in Vancouver. The freight was gold, silver, copper, lead and coal from the rich mineral fields of the West Kootenays, as well as fruit, forest products and even ice!

The railway's progress was hampered by lack of manpower, equipment and supplies, as well as by economic depression and war. Add the rugged terrain, extreme weather, forest fires, washouts and other natural hazards, and the complexity of the project becomes clear. Steep mountainsides and deep river valleys were connected by dozens of trestles, bridges and tunnels, and many men were injured or killed in the process of building and maintaining the KVR.

As mineral resources dwindled and other modes of transport became more accepted, the expensive upkeep of the Kettle Valley Railway could not be justified. Parts of the railway were closed in 1961, and the final section abandoned in 1990. Meanwhile, numerous groups and individuals have coordinated their efforts with the provincial government to convert the KVR to a multi-use recreational trail. While much of it is open to hiking, cross-country skiing, horseback riding and cycling, the latter is the most common way of exploring the trail.

You might think following a

mostly flat rail bed with occasional 2.2-percent grades would make for boring cycling. Not so! Apart from the fabulous views around every bend, the KVR offers diverse challenges not encountered on a typical bike trip. Every year, washouts, landslides, fallen trees and flooding add new obstacles to overcome.

But the easy grade does make the KVR suitable for short family outings and day trips, or, with

TCT Partner

The Kettle Valley Railway will be the backbone of the Trans Canada Trail in British Columbia. The entire route will be designated as part of the TCT when all property issues are settled.

advanced planning, extended touring. There are historic hotels, cabins, B&Bs, campgrounds and resorts along the way – and access is easy. The KVR is split into five subdivisions, and each leg can be connected by bus or car.

The Carmi Subdivision is the longest leg and perhaps the most traveled, given its incredible scenery. It begins at the Midway Station (now a museum) and ends 133 miles (215 kilometers) later in Penticton. The three- to four-day cycle trip follows the Kettle River Valley, gradually climbs to the Okanagan Highlands, then gently descends to Penticton. There are several campgrounds, cabins and resorts for overnight stays.

A very good weekend trip from McCulloch Lake Resort to Chute Lake Resort and ending in Penticton takes in the highlight of this section,

One of 18 trestle bridges in the Myra Canyon section of the Kettle Valley Railway.

Myra Canyon. No fewer than 18 trestles and bridges, totaling 4,860 feet (1,482 meters), cross the magnificent canyon. The trestles and bridges have decks and handrails, installed by the Myra Canyon Restoration Society, but it's still wise to dismount and walk your bike across. The heights are dizzying, so don't risk slipping and plummeting to the rocks below.

Several historic sites and ruins along the way add even more variety: water towers, old railway sheds, station foundations, rock ovens, mines, and the oldest operating hotel in British Columbia, the Beaverdell Hotel. You pass through several tunnels en route to Penticton and detour around a particularly unique spiral tunnel. The walls and ceiling of Adra Tunnel, the longest on the KVR, have given way in sections, making it too dangerous to enter.

On the final descent into Penticton, the KVR skirts Okanagan Lake, with beautiful views down the valley. This is orchard country,

land of roadside fruit stands, wineries and pick-your-own fruit farms. From Penticton, it's an easy day trip in the 36-mile (58-kilometer) Osoyoos Subdivision. Riding through Canada's only true desert makes this the hottest section on the KVR; carry lots of water, and

When you go

The best source for information is *Cycling the Kettle Valley Railway* by Dan and Sandra Langford. (Calgary: Rocky Mountain Books, 1997.) This kilometer-by-kilometer guide is essential to exploring the KVR. Includes maps, equipment lists, safety tips, historic notes, tour operators and accommodations. Current conditions and notes are provided on their Website: www.planet.eon.net/~danl/kvr.html.

head for the beach when you reach Osoyoos.

Princeton Subdivision is 109 miles (175 kilometers) long, starting in Penticton and heading west. The 38.5-mile (62-kilometer) section from Princeton to the pretty village of Brookmere is particularly enjoyable. It follows the

clear green Tulameen River to Coalmont, where the old hotel recalls the pre-1930s boom at the Blakeburn coal mine.

The Merritt Subdivision, 29 miles (47 kilometers) long, runs from Brookmere to Merritt. This branch line was frequently used in the winter when the Coquihalla Subdivision was closed because of heavy snow or other obstructions. Don't miss the scenic stretch along the Coldwater River Valley.

The Coquihalla Subdivision is one of the most challenging, taking you 56.5 miles (91 kilometers) from Brookmere to the end of the line in Hope. Completed in 1916 and abandoned in 1959, this rugged section now follows much of the Coquihalla Highway, and only half the cycling trip follows the old rail bed. There are always surprises here, not the least of which are problems with property ownership and legal liability. Future access for the public is uncertain.

The Silver Triangle, Kootenay Region

If you've ever heard anything about the Kootenays, it probably conjured up images of the 1960s hippie culture – peace, love and groovin' to the music. While an ambience of peaceful, simple living still pervades, the Kootenays offer much more to the visitor: a colorful history, unparalleled scenic beauty and friendly communities.

On this tour, we follow a shortened version of the driving route called the Silvery Slocan Heritage Tour – dubbed the Silver Triangle by cyclists. The 135-mile (217-kilometer) route roughly forms a triangle, with the towns of Nelson, Kaslo and New Denver at its points. The trip can be divided into three days of 43, 30 and 62 miles (70, 47 and 100 kilometers), or any variation of this, depending on the time you have. Following Kootenay and Slocan lakes, with the Selkirk and Valhalla mountains competing for your attention, the route travels through an area filled with the ruins of old mining towns and abandoned mines left over from the silver boom of the late 1800s.

The tour starts in Nelson, but don't be in too much of a rush to leave this pretty town. Although mining and logging played a lesser

Artifacts decorate a shed in the old mining town of Sandon.

View of Slocan Lake from Idaho Lookout, Kootenay Region.

role in the development of Nelson than elsewhere, it became the governmental and service center of the Kootenays. There are 350 heritage buildings, museums, art galleries, craft shops, bakeries and restaurants, all worth more than just a cursory glance. If you have the time, spend a day exploring the town, and set off to Kaslo the next morning.

From Nelson, head north on Highway 3A. On your right is long, narrow Kootenay Lake, almost always in sight through the trees and cottages that line its shore. Just outside of Nelson, you'll see the top deck of the *SS Nasookin*, the largest of the sternwheel ships to run on Kootenay Lake in the first half of the century, now refurbished as a private residence.

About 12.5 miles (20 kilometers) out of Nelson is the access road to Kokanee Glacier Provincial Park, a beautiful alpine wilderness where hiking and fishing are popular in the summer, backcountry skiing in the winter. Directly opposite is the turn-off to Kokanee Creek Provincial Park. If you're there from mid-August through September, it's well worth a stop at the artificial spawning channel to watch the kokanee salmon.

Ainsworth Hot Springs, 28 miles (45 kilometers) from Nelson, is your next stop. Its unusual horseshoe-shaped cave supplied by hot mineral springs is actually an abandoned mine shaft. Before the arrival of European settlers, it was a meeting place for the Kutenai and Lakes people, who believed there were healing properties in the mineral water. You'll want to test this theory with a long soak in its steamy pool!

Across the lake is the hamlet of Riondel, the site of the Bluebell Mine. The discovery of its lode brought the first serious wave of prospectors to the area in 1882. The claim was disputed, leading to murder and a hanging – just one of many legendary stories arising from the silver boom.

You'll likely want to stop for the night at Kaslo, a picturesque village known for its local art and craft shops. There are a number of good restaurants, two campgrounds and a variety of hotels, cabins and B&Bs. Unlike other settlements in the region, Kaslo was a logging center before mining fever struck. It was also world famous for its apple and cherry orchards, which were unfortunately wiped out by disease in the early 1900s. Take time to visit the *SS Moyie* steamship museum. Now a national historic site, the *Moyie* is the oldest surviving passenger sternwheeler in the world and was in use from 1898 to 1957.

The steep ascent out of Kaslo is a bit of a cruel awakening in the morning, but you're eventually rewarded with a long ride down into New Denver. Following Highway 31A,

Cycling Tips

What's the single most important thing if you're cycle touring? Comfort! Here are some tips to keep your body happy.

- Add bar-end extensions, wear padded cycling gloves, fit your handlebars with cushioned grips and shift hand position frequently to avoid numbness.

- Wear cycling shorts with special padding in the crotch. Now you can buy padded shorts that look like regular shorts, so you don't have to feel self-conscious when you stop for a snack!

- Buy a certified helmet and wear it! If you don't, your head will resemble a smashed pumpkin if it ever meets the pavement. For off-road cyclists, a helmet will save your noggin from head-level branches and from those rocks, ruts and stumps you're flying over.

- Always wear sunglasses to protect your eyes from exposure to UV, wind, bugs (keep your mouth closed!), and stones (you know what stones can do to your windshield …). Proper fit is important, too; you don't want your glasses constantly sliding down your nose or rattling up and down as you negotiate a rough downhill.

- A note to women: Most bike frames are made to fit the average male, who tends to have shorter legs and a longer torso than a woman of the same height. When buying a bike, make sure you're not stretched out too much or you'll end up with back and shoulder pain. Get properly fitted in a specialized bike shop.

- Be kind to your behind: replace that hard saddle with a gel-padded seat.

- For long-distance road touring, use a mountain bike. Today's versions are almost as fast and lightweight as road bikes, but give you greater freedom to go "off-road"— even if it's just a gravel road or an unpaved shoulder. And if you break down, there's a better chance of obtaining parts for a mountain bike.

- Make sure you have a wide range of gears on your bike. On hilly stretches, you'll be grateful for the "granny" gears, and those at the other end of the spectrum will allow you to take full advantage of descents.

- Purchase racks that are light but strong enough to bear heavy loads. Buy water-resistant panniers and ensure there's enough heel clearance when they're mounted.

- When packing your bike for a multi-day tour, load the heavier items in the rear panniers, evenly distributed to balance the load. If you must use front panniers, load them with light, bulky items. Use a seat bag for your tool kit, and a small handlebar bag for your maps, camera, sunscreen, snacks and other things you might want to keep handy.

- Invest in a steel U-lock. It's heavy, but essential.

- Be visible: wear bright clothing.

---

the total distance is only 30 miles (47 kilometers), but several detours on the way will add time and distance. This leg of the Silver Triangle is the heart of the Slocan mining area, the "Valley of the Ghosts." Silver, lead and zinc were discovered here in the 1890s, and for a time it was the richest silver mining region in Canada. The route is lined with the relics of towns and mines that once thrived. Eventually, the mines shut down and the communities disappeared.

Take the turnoff to Sandon, about 24 miles (39 kilometers) west of Kaslo, and cycle the 5-mile (8-kilometer) dirt road to the remains of a boom town once known as the "Monte Carlo of Canada." In the 1890s, there were 29 hotels, 28 saloons and 50 buildings in the Red Light District; it was a wild town with a wild reputation, and there are plenty of stories about the characters who lived here. In the space of just 30 years, Sandon went from boom to bust and continued to decline through to the 1960s. The Sandon Historical Society is currently restoring many of the derelict buildings; the general store, city hall, powerhouse and laundry are open to the public during the summer.

Back on the highway, continue cycling west to New Denver on the

Slocan Lake. There's a campground right on the lake, a hostel and a handful of B&Bs and hotels. Near the campground, the Nikkei Internment Memorial Centre commemorates the internment of over 6,000 Japanese-Canadians in the Kootenay region during World War II. During the silver boom, New Denver – or Eldorado as it was called then – served as the center for recording mine claims for the Slocan region, and artifacts from the late 1800s are preserved in the Silvery Slocan Museum. As is true in the rest of the Kootenays, logging has replaced mining as the main industry.

South from New Denver, the highway follows the shoreline of Slocan Lake with the rugged mountains of Valhalla Provincial Park rising abruptly on the opposite side. A steep climb out of Silverton leads to a spectacular viewpoint high above the water. The route to Slocan was once a frightening, one-lane road in parts, clinging to the mountain on one side, with knuckle-whitening drops on the other. Now, though still hilly and winding, it's a wide highway, with plenty of shoulder room for cyclists.

Beyond the town of Slocan, the terrain rolls gently through farmland and small orchards, and the road is lined with fruit stands and health food stores. The valley was settled by Russian Doukhobors, then draft dodgers and hippies, who continue to give the valley its unique character.

After turning onto Highway 3A east to Nelson, it's a leisurely ride following the Kootenay River back to your starting point. There are a number of hydroelectric dams on this section, some of which are open to the public.

The Silver Triangle can be cycled anytime from May to the end of September. You may run into rainy, dismal weather – the price you pay for mountain scenery – so be prepared to stop and wait it out, or keep your rain gear handy. On the other hand, don't forget to pack the sunscreen, as summer temperatures can reach the low 80s (high 20s), and there's not much escape from the sun when you're riding a bike. As a final note, do some conditioning before you set out on this hilly ride – your legs will thank you!

When you go

Nelson Chamber of Commerce and Visitor Information Centre
225 Hall Street
Nelson, BC V1L 5X4
Tel: (250) 352-3433
Fax: (250) 352-6355
E-mail: chamber@netidea.com

Silver Triangle region.

Kokanee Glacier Provincial Park

Hiking in the mountains is one of those immensely pleasurable pastimes, and nothing could be more rewarding than a day in the high alpine. But what if it were every day, and what if you were hauling heavy equipment and supplies up and down steep slopes all day?

That's exactly the history that lies behind Kokanee Glacier Provincial Park in the West Kootenay region of British Columbia. Set in the rugged Kokanee Range just north of Nelson,

with the Kootenay and Slocan lakes on either side, the park was once worked by miners seeking silver, lead and zinc. One of the oldest parks in

the province, Kokanee Glacier was established in 1922. Trails built and used by miners at the turn of the century now make up the system of about 55 miles (85 kilometers) of trails used by hikers today.

The park is accessed by road and trail via five deep valleys that radiate from the center of the park. The most common access is 12 miles (19 kilometers) north of Nelson on Highway 3, then 10 miles (16 kilometers) up the Kokanee Creek gravel road to Gibson Lake. This is a very popular fishing spot with an easy (level!) 1.5-mile (2.5-kilometer) trail around the lake, picnic tables and a day-use shelter. It's also the starting point of the 5.5-mile (9-kilometer) hike to the historic Slocan Chief Cabin and nearby campground.

The trail immediately begins to climb steeply through lush subalpine forest, with views through the trees becoming ever more impressive as you gain elevation. After about a

Slocan Chief Cabin in Kokanee Glacier Provincial Park.

Yum, brake lines

At some trailhead parking areas, you may notice that the lower parts of vehicles have been wrapped in chicken wire or stucco wire. This prevents porcupines from climbing up into the engine, where they love to snack on rubber hoses and cables. Pick up some wire at your local building supplies store before your trip to Kokanee Glacier Park.

Hiking up to the Kokanee Glacier for some spring skiing.

mile (1.5 kilometers), the trail begins to level out, and hiking becomes less demanding. At about the halfway mark, you reach Kokanee Lake, the largest lake in the park and a great fishing spot for cutthroat trout. Skirt the western shore, then climb gradually to Kokanee Pass through open, rolling, rocky terrain. Just past Kaslo Lake is your first view of Kokanee Glacier, flanked by Kokanee Peak and the Battleship.

It's not long now until you reach the cabin, a beautiful log building that was once a miners' bunkhouse. The cabin sleeps 12 in the second-story loft (first come, first served), and the main floor has tables, a propane cook stove and cupboards for storing food. Most people prefer to camp during the summer, especially if the weather is fine, as the cabin is fairly dark inside.

There are a number of very scenic, moderate day hikes from

the cabin. The short, one-hour Smuggler Ridge Trail leads to the ruins of the Smuggler Mine, high up on the mountainslope above. In the opposite direction, Helen Deane Lake is just a short jaunt away, and an excellent spot for fishing and swimming. The trail beyond the lake is closed from mid-August to early October to allow grizzly bears to feast on ripe berries. The hike to the toe of

When you go

BC Parks
Site 8, Comp 5, RR 3
Nelson, BC V1L 5P6
Tel: (250) 825-3500
Fax: (250) 825-9509

Kokanee Glacier allows spectacular views of the park; hiking on the glacier itself is not recommended without the aid of ropes, crampons and ice axes. The longer hike to

Sapphire Lakes heads past Kaslo Lake, over Lemon Pass, and into a large alpine basin. The lakes are nestled in pockets of exposed bedrock, surrounded by dwarf subalpine fir and wildflower meadows. A scramble to the top of the ridge behind the lakes gives a long view over Lemon Creek Valley.

Two other cabins in the park, Woodbury and Silver Spray, are accessible, but more remote.

Wherever you hike in the park, you'll encounter mine workings and well-preserved high-elevation mine sites dating from the turn of the century.

From December to May, a small number of backcountry skiers take advantage of Kokanee's deep snowpack. The Slocan Chief and Silver Spray cabins are booked in October through a lottery system; contact the BC Parks district office for information.

Purcell Lodge

After all those years of roughing it at primitive campsites in all kinds of weather, do you feel the occasional need to be pampered? Is the promise of a hot shower and comfortable bed the only way you can coax your spouse or friends into the backcountry? If you're nodding assent to either of these propositions, Purcell Lodge could be the place for you.

Situated near the eastern boundary of Glacier National Park, Purcell Lodge offers luxurious accommodation in a wilderness setting. The lodge is open summer and winter, though in winter the only means of access is by helicopter from nearby Golden. In summer, there is the option of hiking or flying in. The 7-mile (11-kilometer) hiking trail starts in the Spilimacheen Valley and climbs 1,970 feet (600 meters) to Bald Mountain, the largest alpine meadow in southern British Columbia. The lodge is situated atop the meadows and offers a magnificent view of the mountains of Glacier park to the west, in particular Mount Sir Donald.

When it was first built in 1989, the lodge was a state-of-the-art facility. It generates its own electricity with a mini hydro plant and has flush toilets and a waste management system that ultimately releases pure water back into the ground. Only grease and non-combustibles are flown out. The cost of this environmental stewardship is high, so expect to pay between $150 and $200 a day, depending on the season.

The food also is superb. Most guests cannot wait to return to the lodge after a day's hiking or skiing to see what culinary delights the resident chef has prepared. Comfortable rooms with snug duvets and spectacular mountain views, a sauna, and a friendly ambiance combine to make a vacation at the lodge a unique experience.

In summer, lodge-based naturalist guides offer daily trips, long or short depending on your preference, to explore the fauna and flora of the meadows. A hike to the top

Purcell Lodge: luxurious accommodation in a wilderness setting.

The normal access to Purcell Lodge is by helicopter.

of Copperstain Mountain will reward you with breathtaking views of Glacier park to the west, and to the east the snowy peaks of the Rockies stretching from horizon to horizon.

In late July and August the meadows are a cornucopia of color: red paintbrush, yellow asters, blue gentian and white spring beauties. Above, prairie falcons, red-tail hawks, bald and golden eagles patrol the skies looking for an easy meal. Larger mammals such as elk and black bear can often be seen, especially in the area of the Copperstain Burn, north of the lodge.

In winter, Bald Mountain is coated with up to 10 feet (3 meters) of snow. The rolling hills make perfect terrain for beginner ski touring. More ambitious skiers can tackle the slopes of Copperstain Mountain or the Copperstain Burn, where the gray skeleton trees make a great slalom course. All ski tours are guided, and guests are offered an easy or more demanding ski tour, depending on their preference and ability. At the end of the day, a sauna and a gourmet meal await.

When you go

For reservations contact:
Places Less Travelled
PO Box 1829
Golden, BC V0A 1H0
Tel: (250) 344-2639
Website: www.purcell.com

Glacier National Park

In the heart of the Selkirk Mountains, the Trans-Canada Highway follows a pass through a wild, mountainous area that has been a playground for outdoor enthusiasts for over a hundred years. The mountain pass is named after Major A. B. Rogers, a Canadian Pacific Railways surveyor, and the surrounding mountains are part of Glacier National Park.

Rogers Pass was the key to the completion of the CPR rail link between Montreal and Vancouver. In 1887, shortly after the rail link was completed, Glacier House was built by the CPR to cater to mountaineers, naturalists, artists and sightseers. The hotel is long gone, but mountaineers as well as hikers and skiers still flock to this mountain Mecca.

The remains of the stone railway trestles in Rogers Pass, Glacier National Park.

Because areas of the park adjacent to the highway are easily accessible, it makes an ideal stopover for cross-country travelers in both summer and winter. Plan to spend at least two or three days exploring some of the 30 trails in the park. The park's weather is influenced mostly by moist Pacific air, so expect cool rainy days in summers and mild (23° to 14°F/-5° to -10°C) snowy days in winter. However, infrequent arctic fronts can send temperatures plunging to -20° to -25°F (-25° to -30°C).

A variety of accommodations are available in the pass, from the comfortable Glacier Park Lodge to roadside campgrounds by the Illecillewaet River and Loop Brook. The Alpine Club of Canada operates the Wheeler Hut, a rustic log building near the Illecillewaet campground. Non-club members can reserve the hut. Much of the park's backcountry is seldom visited, and random camping is permitted here. In popular backpacking areas, such as the Bald Hills/

Copperstain Loop, designated campsites are provided. In all cases, hikers must carry a Wilderness Pass, obtainable at the Rogers Pass Centre.

Your trip to the park should start with a visit to the center, adjacent to the lodge. Park staff will update you on trail conditions and closures, if any. (Because of the large grizzly bear population, some areas of the park are closed during the summer to avoid problem encounters and give the bears undisturbed use of important habitats.) The center also contains wildlife exhibits, historic photos, a theater, a bookstore and a wide selection of videos that can keep you occupied for hours, an attractive prospect during periods of bad weather.

When the weather is fine, though, you should head for one of the many trails that will take you through forests of towering Douglas fir, western hemlock and western red cedar. The girth of many of the

The Nakimu Caves

A special attraction of the park is the Nakimu Caves, a multi-entrance labyrinth of passages developed in a narrow band of limestone. The caverns were first explored in the early 1900s and were a popular destination for visitors to Glacier House. These hardy individuals negotiated steep, slippery wooden staircases by the light of flickering lanterns but were rewarded with a unique adventure experience. With the demise of Glacier House, the cave tours stopped and the stairs and walkways fell into disrepair. To avoid accidents and preserve the delicate formations found in the caves, they have been gated and locked. Access to the 3.5-mile-long (5.9-kilometer-long) system is made available to caving groups, both commercial and non-commercial, by a lottery system for a limited number of dates each spring.

trees attests to the fact that this is a rainforest fed by an average of 56 inches (1,450 millimeters) of precipitation annually. If you don't have a lot of time, the 440-yard-long (400-meter-long) Hemlock Grove Boardwalk is a fascinating introduction to the rainforest. Or check out the one-mile (1.6-kilometer) Loop

Brook Interpretive Trail, where you can still see stone pillars that once supported the elevated rail bed, remnants of a bygone age. Keep to the trails. The underbrush can be thick and full of prickly devil's club, the bane of early explorers.

The 3-mile (5-kilometer) trail to Balu Pass, which starts behind the

View of Rogers Pass from Abbott Ridge, Glacier National Park.

Cougar Creek flowing through the labyrinthine Nakimu Caves.

lodge, is an excellent introductory hike. The trail climbs 2,520 feet (788 meters) along a steep-sided valley to spectacular alpine meadows in the vicinity of the pass. In the lower valley, keep a lookout for the American dipper, often seen bobbing and flitting around in the creek in search of insects and larvae.

If you are planning a full-day hike, head up into the high country to get a first-hand view of the glaciers and snowfields. Glacier park is aptly named because permanent snow and ice cover about 12 percent of its 520 square miles (1,350 square kilometers). At the turn of the century, even more of the area was ice-covered, but the glaciers have been receding at a rapid rate ever since. Hiking trails now take you into rock-strewn areas that have only recently emerged from the Ice Age. These trails are often snow-covered well into July, so the best time to hike into the high country is August and September.

The Illecillewaet Glacier and névé, one of the largest in the park, can be viewed from two vantage points – from Perley Rock, a 3.5-mile

(5.6-kilometer) trek, and from Glacier Crest, about a third of a mile (half a kilometer) shorter. Both trails will have you panting for breath on the steep upper sections. But the effort is worth it: on a clear day you will be rewarded with eye-popping views of the glacier and of 10,486-feet-high (3,277-meter-high) Mount Sir Donald. Its classic pyramidal shape has lured mountaineers for over a century, but it is a long and demanding climb as many benighted climbers have found to their cost.

The challenging 4-mile (6.5-kilometer) hike to the Asulkan Glacier climbs almost 3,300 feet (1,000 meters) but is one of the must-do hikes if you'd like a panoramic view of the park. There is the option of staying overnight at the Asulkan cabin, which must be reserved through the Alpine Club of Canada. At the start, the trail passes the old Glacier House site, then climbs gently at first alongside Asulkan Brook and through majestic cedar, fir and spruce forest before breaking out into the alpine. You'll cross many alder-covered avalanche

paths, testimony to the frequent slides that scour the slopes in winter. The steep upper part of the trail brings you to the edge of the Asulkan Glacier. Do not venture onto the snow and ice without proper equipment and training.

Near the eastern edge of the park are two backpacking trails that offer an alternative to rock and ice. The Beaver Valley and the Copperstain Valley trails are tree-lined for most of their distance, but do eventually climb into lush alpine meadows. The 14-mile (23-kilometer) circuit from the Beaver Valley to the Copperstain Valley via Bald Mountain and Copperstain Pass is one of the most scenic yet challenging in the park. The trail climbs over 4,160 feet (1,300 meters) to the flower-strewn alpine meadows atop Bald Mountain.

The railway line over Rogers Pass was abandoned in 1916 because of the extreme avalanche danger and is now routed through the 8.5-mile-long (14-kilometer-long) Macdonald Tunnel. The highway is protected by avalanche sheds but is still closed occasionally in the winter when travel is deemed unsafe. The immense snowfall at the pass, up to 60 feet (18 meters) between November and March, is both a boon and a bane to skiers. Good ski conditions are almost guaranteed, but the avalanche danger can be extreme. If you plan to ski in the park, it's essential that you check the current avalanche conditions at the Information Centre near the summit of Rogers Pass.

Winter accommodation is available at Glacier Park Lodge, which has special rates for skiers, and at the ACC hut and the

When you go

Mount Revelstoke and Glacier National Parks
PO Box 350
Revelstoke, BC V0E 2S0
Tel: (250) 837-7500
Rogers Pass Centre: (250) 814-5232

Recommended Reading

Woods, John. *Glacier Country: Mount Revelstoke and Glacier National Parks.* Vancouver: Douglas & McIntyre, 1987.

Asulkan cabin. Rogers Pass is famed for its powder snow, which can accumulate at the rate of three feet (a meter) a day during a Pacific storm. There is terrain for every

level of ability, but because the valleys are relatively short and steep-sided, there is far more skiable terrain for advanced skiers or snowboarders. If you do not have the necessary skills to travel safely in avalanche terrain, you can employ a guide at the lodge or contact the Alpine Club of Canada, which occasionally organizes courses and tours.

Beware! If you ever experience a day of skiing in knee-deep "champagne" powder beneath an azure sky, you could be hooked for life. Addicts count the days until the next ski season starts!

Mount Sir Donald, Glacier National Park.

Yoho Valley,
Yoho National Park

I n his efforts to publicize the Canadian Rockies, CPR president William Cornelius Van Horne borrowed two Cree words – *takakkaw* (magnificent) and *yoho* (a Cree exclamation of astonishment) – to describe the wonders of a remote glacier-encircled valley. The publicity campaign worked and countless visitors have now gasped at the sight of thundering Takakkaw Falls in the Yoho Valley.

While the falls is the centerpiece of the park, numerous other waterfalls and a network of trails make this valley a hiker's delight. On a single day hike you can pass through forests of towering Engelmann spruce and see crashing waterfalls, glaciers and alpine meadows strewn with wildflowers.

Because it is so accessible and has trails of varying lengths, the Yoho Valley is ideal for day trips. Accommodation is available at Cathedral Mountain Chalets, the closest to the valley, or in nearby Lake Louise, or at the secluded Emerald Lake Lodge.

The 8-mile (13-kilometer) Yoho Valley Road leads from the Trans-Canada Highway into the heart of the Yoho Valley. On stepping out of your vehicle, you're greeted by the sound and fury of 830-foot-high (254-meter-high) Takakkaw Falls. The water strikes a ledge near the top of the falls, leaps outward then crashes to the valley floor, creating a plume of flying spray. It's an impressive sight at any time of the year, but especially during periods of hot weather when the volume of glacial meltwater increases substantially.

All the hiking trails are located on the west side of the valley and start from either the Whiskey Jack hostel, which offers overnight accommodation, or the parking area at the end of the road. The 5-mile (8-kilometer) valley bottom trail to Twin Falls climbs gradually alongside the lively Yoho River and offers gentle hiking along a forested trail. This is a perfect trail for an introductory or an early-season hike. Numerous diversions such as hidden lakes, waterfalls and a side trip to the Twin Falls chalet for afternoon tea can easily turn this hike into a day-long excursion. Overnight accommoda-

Takakkaw Falls in the Yoho Valley, Yoho National Park.

tion is available at the chalet between mid-June and September.

The more scenic but challenging hikes follow broad terraces that are reached by steep uphill climbs. The classic 7-mile (11.3-kilometer) Highline Trail follows a terrace above a 660-foot (200-meter) cliff band for much of its length. Numerous lookouts offer panoramic views of the valley and the surrounding peaks and icefields. Mountain goats can sometimes be seen at trailside, but more often on the slopes above.

The Iceline Trail, the park's showpiece, follows an even higher terrace and contours into the Little Yoho Valley, a classic "hanging" valley that is above and perpendicular to the Yoho Valley. The steep ascent from the valley bottom is through an area of ancient trees, lush ferns and rich, wet wildflower meadows. The trail climbs 1,150 feet (360 meters) to the rock-strewn terrace with spectacular views of Takakkaw Falls, the Yoho Glacier and the icefields beyond.

Close inspection of the bedrock will reveal striations or grooves in its surface, caused by rocks embedded in the ice being scraped over the bedrock. The orientation of the striations tells us the direction of the ice

When you go

Yoho National Park
PO Box 99
Field, BC V0A 1G0
Tel: (250) 343-6783
Fax: (250) 343-6330

Recommended Reading

Beers, Don. *The Wonder of Yoho.* Calgary: Rocky Mountain Books, 1989.

Fall larches in Yoho National Park.

movement. The Emerald Glacier now clings to the mountainside above the trail, a fraction of its former size, though in places seemingly close enough to touch. This is a stark, beautiful but moody environment: friendly and inviting in sun-

shine, but ugly when rain and mist descend from the peaks. Be prepared for all types of weather on this trail.

Various connectors link the valley bottom trail, the Highline and the Iceline trails. A day trip ranging in length from 7 to 14 miles (11 to 22 kilometers) can be planned, depending on time available and your ambition.

The Little Yoho Valley is an ideal place to overnight, either at the campground or at the nearby Stanley Mitchell hut, managed by the Alpine Club of Canada. The meadows in the upper part of the valley will be awash with alpine flowers in late July. At the head of the valley is Kiwetinok Lake, a spectacular glacier-fed lake that is well worth the short hike from the campground. Being one of the highest lakes in the Rockies, however, it is often frozen over until August.

In winter, peace and quiet return to the valley. The road is closed at the Trans-Canada Highway so only the most determined skiers tackle the long slog into the Stanley Mitchell hut. Those that do are rewarded with exceptional backcountry skiing and, in spring, the option of long glacier tours.

View of the Rockies, Yoho National Park.

The Burgess Shale, Yoho National Park

Imagine, if you can, a creature with five eyes and teeth at the end of a long stalk, or one with seven snapping tentacles on its back. Stars of yet another Hollywood horror movie? No, these are fossil remains of arthropods, small marine animals that lived over 500 million years ago. They were preserved in soft black mud that is known today as the Burgess Shale, the discovery of which turned the scientific world on its ear. Located in Yoho National

Park, the Burgess Shale was declared a World Heritage Site on the basis of the fossil discoveries.

Mount Stephen, Yoho National Park.

Curious, and fit, hikers can visit the Burgess Shale in the company of licensed private guides. For a small fee, groups of up to 15 are taken to two sites, both of which involve steep climbs of over 3,300 feet (1,000 meters). One site, on the north flank of Mount Stephen near Field, is rich in well-preserved trilobite fossils. The other site, near the top of Mount Field, involves a 6-mile (10-kilometer) hike and occupies a full day. This is the site of the Walcott quarry from where, beginning in 1909, over 65,000 fossils were removed for scientific study.

Because the sites are at relatively high elevations, the guided tours operate only between July 1 and September 30 when the snow has melted and the trails are drier. Registration is by phone or e-mail, and groups meet in Field for the seven- to ten-hour trips. There is a display of fossils at the Field Visitor Centre and at the Lake Louise Visitor Centre for those who are unable to visit the fossil beds in person.

The fossil beds on Mount Stephen are reached via a well-defined one-and-a-quarter-mile (2-kilometer) trail that zigzags up the face of the mountain, affording panoramic views of the Kicking Horse Pass and Yoho Valley to the north. The trail goes to the edge of the fossil beds, where you will be exposed to the wonderful world of trilobites.

The hike to the Walcott quarry starts at the trailhead to Yoho Pass near Takakkaw Falls. Beyond Yoho Pass the trail climbs along the flanks of Mount Field toward Burgess Pass and the quarry site. Along the way,

Mount Stephen, site of the main beds of the Burgess Shale, Yoho National Park.

wonderful vistas open up as the trail gains height. There are, in fact, two small quarries and a rich stash of fossils where the Royal Ontario Museum occasionally pitches a cataloguing tent. Here, the guides come into their own and help with fossil identification.

Access to both fossil sites is allowed only with a licensed guide, who will take pains to point out that it is illegal to collect and remove the fossils. Stiff fines back up the law for those who don't comply.

Why are the fossils of the Burgess Shale so important? The brief answer is that the exquisitely preserved remains give paleontologists a detailed snapshot of the wide variety of marine life that existed over 500 million years ago. When the fossils were studied closely, it became apparent that many were new phyla that

When you go

To make reservations contact:
The Yoho–Burgess Shale Foundation
PO Box 148
Field, BC V0A 1G0
Tel: 1-800-343-3006
E-mail: burgshal@rockies.net

Detail of a fossil in the Burgess Shale.

could not be classified within any known group, and that the range of biodiversity was much greater than anyone had imagined. This led Stephen Jay Gould to suggest in his book *Wonderful Life: The Burgess Shale and the Nature of History* that evolution moves not linearly, but as a branching network of adaptations advanced or cut off by catastrophic events. According to Gould, there is no such thing as an evolutionary "dead end." All organisms adapt to fit their environment and survive or disappear based only on chance.

The jury is still out on this view of evolution, and new discoveries constantly add grist to the mill of scientific debate. One thing is certain: the diversity and complexity of the fossils you will see on your trip to the Burgess Shale will leave you full of wonder.

Lake O'Hara, Yoho National Park

Since before the turn of the century, the Lake O'Hara region has been one of the most popular hiking and mountaineering destinations – if not *the* most popular – in the Canadian Rockies. Its popularity stems from the magnificent alpine scenery, ease of access to over 50 miles (80 kilometers) of hiking trails, numerous lakes and ample accommodation, from tenting to a comfortable historic lodge. There is a trail to suit every level of ability.

The jewel is Lake O'Hara itself, which has attracted artists, photographers, hikers and fishermen since its discovery in 1887. Viewed from up high on a calm, sunny day, the turquoise lake and surrounding grandeur leave a lasting impression on every visitor. The other two large lakes in the region – Lake Oesa and McArthur Lake – are arguably even more impressive than Lake O'Hara but are more difficult to reach.

Like many scenic and easily accessible areas, Lake O'Hara was in danger of being "loved to death" by throngs of outdoor enthusiasts, so in 1976 Parks Canada imposed a quota system for summer visitors. The quota is enforced by busing most visitors from the trailhead, 7 miles (11 kilometers) west of Lake Louise on the Trans-Canada Highway, to Le Relais, a small concession and day-use area near Lake O'Hara itself. Bus reservations must be made in advance and permits obtained for overnight camping. Because of the popularity of the region, you may be disappointed to

find all the permits allotted when you apply. Have a backup plan just in case. Parks Canada staff will help with suggestions if necessary.

Lake O'Hara, Yoho National Park.

Choose from three levels of accommodation, according to your style and budget. Near the lakeshore is Lake O'Hara Lodge, a relatively luxurious log building with additional lakeshore cabins. Make reservations, especially for summer,

well in advance. The bus service delivers guests right to the door. A 30-site campground is available for the more budget-conscious or people who prefer tenting. A camping permit must be obtained before boarding the bus or hiking in. If you like a roof over your head but balk at the lodge rates, try the Alpine Club of Canada's Elizabeth Parker hut, which is self-catering and can be reserved by non-club members. All accommodation is located within 600 yards (a kilometer) of the lake.

All of the trails and lakes are in a compact area surrounded by soaring rock walls and snow-covered peaks. Because of the well-designed trails, it's relatively easy, though strenuous, to gain altitude quickly and gaze down on the deep blue waters of the lakes and across to the rock walls encircling the valley. If you're sharp-eyed, you may spot mountain goats on ledges high above the valley floor.

If you are able to spend only a day in the region, the 5.5-mile (9-kilometer) Lake Oesa–Yukness Ledge–East Opabin circuit is highly recommended. The trail climbs steeply to Lake Oesa, which although ice-bound much of the year, makes a glorious picnic spot on a summer's day. En route you may see hoary marmots sunning themselves on rock piles, or now-tame ground squirrels waiting at trailside for a handout (resist the temptation to feed them, though). The trail along Yukness Ledge is thrilling and in parts quite airy; you need a head for heights and the ability to scramble up and down rock ledges. The final section is along the sparsely treed Opabin Plateau, followed by a steep descent to the lake. This circuit should be attempted only on a fine day when the views will be awesome and the trails dry.

In inclement weather, or if you are short of time, numerous trails offer easy hiking. The 1.8-mile (2.9-kilometer) Shoreline Trail that circumnavigates the lake is a must. Keep a lookout for dippers bobbing by the shoreline. Other trails lead to Schäffer Lake, a small but pretty alpine lake below McArthur Pass. Just one mile (1.6 kilometers) beyond Schäffer Lake and 660 feet (200 meters) higher is McArthur Lake, a spectacular lake that is worth the steep climb. Surrounded by imposing rock walls and a hanging glacier, its waters are free of ice only during late summer and fall. The area around McArthur Pass is often closed by the Parks Service to avoid encounters between humans and grizzly bears. Heed the warning notices.

When you go

Yoho National Park
PO Box 99
Field, BC V0A 1G0
Tel: (250) 343-6783

Lodge reservations:
Tel: (250) 343-6418 (summer)
Tel: (250) 678-4110 (winter)
ACC hut reservations:
Tel: (403) 678-3200
Bus reservations and O'Hara campground reservations:
Tel: (250) 343-6433
(mid-March to September 30)

Recommended Reading

Beers, Don. *The Wonder of Yoho*. Calgary: Rocky Mountain Books, 1989.

Much of the Lake O'Hara region is close to the treeline, which makes it prime larch territory. As September draws to a close the higher ground, especially the Opabin Plateau, is ablaze with golden larch – summer's last hurrah before winter sets in for six months or more.

Visiting doesn't stop with the onset of winter, though. After the summer visitors leave, enthusiasts arrive with their skis and snowshoes. Both the lodge and the Alpine Club hut are open in winter. Hardy types can still use the campground with its heated picnic shelter for cooking and for drying gear. Access is by ski or snowshoe only via the 7-mile-long (11-kilometer-long) access road. (Lodge guests can choose to have their luggage taken in by snowmobile.)

Since the Lake O'Hara region is located on the western side of the Continental Divide, it receives more snowfall than, say, Banff or Lake Louise. This ensures good ski conditions through most of the winter, but the down side is an increased avalanche risk, especially since steep mountains enclose the lake and its environs. It is best to stay on established trails on the south and west side of Lake O'Hara if you are not practiced in route-finding in avalanche terrain.

Cabins at Lake O'Hara Lodge in winter, Yoho National Park.

Rockwall Highline Trail, Kootenay National Park

It may seem odd that a park owes its existence to a highway, but that's exactly the case for Kootenay National Park. In exchange for a highway linking Alberta's Bow Valley with the Columbia Valley west of the Rocky Mountains, the province of B.C. handed over 5 miles (8 kilometers) of land on either side of the proposed road. The federal government completed the highway and in the process established a national park in 1920 that covered 560 square miles (1,450 square kilometers).

Highway 93, a.k.a. the Banff–Radium Highway, a.k.a. the Kootenay Parkway, has produced winners all around, not the least of which are visitors to the national park. The highway serves a useful purpose to hikers and backpackers looking for a wilderness experience, and the Rockwall Highline Trail does not disappoint.

The Rockwall Highline offers classic Rocky Mountain hiking at its best: steep-walled valleys, rushing streams, plunging waterfalls, alpine

meadows, high passes, glaciers and – of course – the rugged mountains themselves. The Rockwall Highline is named for the 33-mile-long (53-kilometer-long) rock rampart that extends northeast from Floe Lake to the Ottertail Valley in Yoho National Park. Towering limestone cliffs rise up to 2,950 feet (900 meters) in an almost unbroken wall, and paralleling its length is the excellent Rockwall Highline Trail.

For strong hikers, the 43-mile (70-kilometer) trail provides a number of options. The entire route can be hiked over a four- or five-day period, with a choice of five well-spaced campgrounds. Or it can be broken down into two- or three-day

hikes, using any of three side trails leading back to the highway.

The trail begins at the Floe Lake parking lot, just off the Kootenay Parkway about 37 miles (60 kilometers) west of Banff. It descends first to the Vermilion River, then gently ascends toward Floe Lake, following Floe Creek. It's a pleasant hike through lush forests of Douglas fir, spruce and lodgepole pine and across wide avalanche slopes. This is grizzly country, so be sure to sing or talk loudly to avoid any surprise encounters. In the upper valley, the forest turns to massive Engelmann spruce, some towering 130 feet (40 meters) above your head. The last 1.5 miles (2.5 kilometers) to the campground is a long, steep grunt, gaining 1,300 feet (400 meters) in elevation. But what a delight to reach the lake! Nestled

Ceremonial Colors

The Paint Pots are formed by three active cold mineral springs that percolate up through the clay soil. Rich in iron oxides, the springs stain the clay yellow, orange and red, forming the Ochre Beds on a wide floodplain downhill from the pots. The clay was a valuable commodity for the Kutenai natives, who traded it with other native tribes. During the 1700s, they shaped the clay into cakes, baked it in a fire, then mixed it with fish grease or animal fat to make a body paint used in rituals and ceremonies.

Larch trees and the Rockwall on the Rockwall Highline Trail, Kootenay National Park.

Wolverine Plateau on the Rockwall Highline Trail, Kootenay National Park.

below the imposing Rockwall, Floe Lake mirrors the headwall and the glacier that clings to its lower slopes. From Floe Lake, the trail winds through subalpine larch forest to the highest point on the Rockwall Trail, Numa Pass, at 7,780 feet (2,370 meters). As you approach the pass, you'll be constantly glancing over your shoulder at the spectacular view of Floe Lake and the Rockwall glowering over it.

After crossing Numa Pass, it's downhill all the way to Numa Campground, a knee-jarring descent of 2,760 feet (840 meters) over 4 miles (6.8 kilometers). The day's total distance is 6 miles (9.5 kilometers). Numa Campground is the only scenic disappointment on the trail. The campsites are surrounded by dense forest that hides any view of the surrounding peaks. If your time is limited, you can leave the Rockwall Trail here by following Numa Creek Trail to the Kootenay Parkway for a circuit of 16.8 miles (27 kilometers).

Otherwise, continue on to Tumbling Creek Campground, 5 miles (8 kilometers) from Numa Creek. The trail crosses numerous avalanche slopes grown over with various berry bushes (grizzly warning!), climbing steadily to a lovely boulder-strewn meadow. Soon you come to the spectacular view of Tumbling Glacier, and the rubble-covered slopes pouring off it. Given the views, the campground at the head of the valley has to be one of the most scenic locations in the Rockies.

Once again, you can exit the Rockwall Trail here, following the

When you go

Kootenay National Park
PO Box 220
Radium Hot Springs, BC V0A 2K0
Tel: (250) 347-9615

turbulent Tumbling Creek to the Paint Pots parking lot on the Kootenay Parkway. From Floe Lake parking lot, you will have completed a 23.5-mile (37.7-kilometer) circuit.

From Tumbling Creek Campground, ascend yet another short but grinding uphill section that leads eventually to the broad subalpine meadows of Wolverine Plateau. A giant cleft in the cliffs, Wolverine Pass is the only break in the Rockwall. If the weather cooperates, you can see beyond the Beaverfoot Valley below to the lofty Bugaboo Spires in the Purcell Range, some 40 miles (70 kilometers) to the west.

The Rockwall Trail continues to the alluvial flats of Helmet Creek and a pretty little campground in the valley. From here, you get a distant view of the impressive Helmet Falls, which plummet 1,200 feet (365 meters) from the Rockwall.

There are two options from here. If you have an extra day, you can hike up to Goodsir Pass and cross the boundary into Yoho National Park. The steep ascent to the pass is rewarded with a hike through wonderful high alpine meadows and awe-inspiring views. Then it's a steady descent to the campground on a ridge overlooking the Ottertail Valley. The final 9-mile (15-kilometer) leg follows an old fire road through the forested valley to the trail's terminus at the Trans-Canada Highway.

The other option is to hike out Ochre Creek from Helmet Falls Campground, a distance of about 5 miles (8 kilometers). A pleasant trail meanders down through lush forest to the Paint Pots to emerge at the Kootenay Parkway and the end of a truly classic Canadian Rockies hike.

Mount Assiniboine Provincial Park

When William Van Horne, president of the Canadian Pacific Railway, uttered his now famous remark, "If we can't export the scenery, we'll import the tourists," one of the places he had in mind was the Mount Assiniboine region in southeastern B.C. Thanks to a huge publicity campaign, the CPR did attract tourists by the thousands to the Canadian Rockies by using Mount Assiniboine, referred to as the Matterhorn of the Rockies, in their poster campaign.

Mount Assiniboine, named after the prairie natives who hunted in the region, is the picture-perfect mountain. The soaring ridges of this pyramidal peak, the Rockies' sixth highest at 11,870 feet (3,618 meters), never fails to impress first-time visitors. Yet the mountain is only the centerpiece of a remarkable area that offers superb hiking, mountaineering, skiing, fishing and trail riding.

The scenic value of the region, and the need to protect it, was recognized in 1922 when the 150-square-mile (390-square-kilometer) Mount Assiniboine Provincial Park was created. Though small, the park has everything a visitor to the Rockies looks for: Mount Assiniboine itself, large expanses of alpine meadows awash with wildflowers in summer, and numerous lakes that nestle among towering peaks and ridges. In 1991 the park was designated a UNESCO World Heritage Site in recognition of its unique scenic and historic value.

Though modest in size, the park now boasts four campgrounds and over 37 miles

(60 kilometers) of hiking trails. The Naiset cabins, four log shelters, are available for people who prefer not to camp, as is the rustic but comfortable Assiniboine Lodge. The privately operated lodge and outlying cabins accommodate up to 30 guests and can be reached on foot or by helicopter. Most of these amenities are centrally located near Magog Lake in the shadow of Mount Assiniboine.

Western anemone in its seed phase (locally known as "hippy on a stick"), Mount Assiniboine Provincial Park.

Unfortunately, the popularity of the park has resulted in damage to the alpine meadows by indiscriminate hikers and trail riders. However, BC Parks is reversing this trend by closing and re-vegetating braided trails and by asking users to stay on properly maintained trails. Random camping is prohibited, and trail riding is permitted only on certain trails.

There are various ways to reach the park. A helicopter can whisk you from the Shark Mountain helipad to the heart of the park in a matter of minutes, though flights are allowed only on Sunday, Wednesday and Friday. If time permits, choose one of the five backpacking routes into the park. Trails converge on Magog Lake from north, east and west. The most direct is the 16.5-mile (27-kilometer) trail from the Shark Mountain trailhead via Bryant Creek and Assiniboine Pass.

Many of the scenic attractions are concentrated in the core area around Magog Lake. The 3-mile (5-kilometer) circuit to Elizabeth Lake via Sunburst and Cerulean lakes is one of the most rewarding in the park; the sweet song of the hermit thrush can often be heard in the surrounding forest of spruce, lodgepole pine and subalpine fir. (There are over 60 species for birders to identify in the Assiniboine region.) The view of the lakes is even better from Nub Ridge, a 650-foot (200-meter) climb from Elizabeth Lake. The reward for the extra effort is an unsurpassed view of Mount Assiniboine.

With a permit (available at the lodge), anglers can try their

Mount Assiniboine Provincial Park.

luck at catching lake trout in the lakes that are open for fishing. The fishing season is July 1 through September.

Farther afield, try the 4-mile (7-kilometer) return trip to Wonder Pass. The trail skirts Gog Lake (Gog, along with Og and Magog, are names plucked from the Old Testament) then passes through alpine meadows carpeted with Indian paintbrush, western anemone ("hippy on a stick" during its seeding phase), arnica, vetches and fleabane. It is well worth the effort to go a little beyond Wonder Pass to the lookout, where there is an excellent view of Marvel Lake far below.

Another panoramic view is from Windy Ridge, a 1,300-foot (400-meter) ascent from Magog Lake. The 5-mile (8-kilometer) trail winds through grassy, flower-strewn meadows before climbing toward Og Pass. As you climb the ridge above the pass, through a band of larch and a high alpine meadow, the vista unfolds to reveal a sea of snowy peaks. You can turn this excursion into an energetic full-day trip by crossing Og Pass, descending to Bryant Creek and then climbing back over Assiniboine Pass to complete the circle.

The prime time to visit the park is between mid-July and October. By July the snow has mostly melted, the trails have dried out and the wildflowers are at their best. In mid-to late September the larch trees put on their annual show, their needles turning from green to gold before being shed for the winter.

By December, the lakes, meadows and peaks lie beneath a blanket of snow that can attain a depth of up to 10 feet (3 meters) by spring. The park is just as magical, if not more so, in winter as in summer. The network of hiking trails is transformed into ski trails of every level of difficulty from beginner to advanced. When you stay at the lodge, which is open for only part of the winter, guides will take you on a ski trip tailored to your skills. The Naiset cabins can be reserved in the winter through the lodge. Self-guided parties are advised to have some training in avalanche awareness because there are notoriously unstable slopes in parts of the park. The best time for skiing is March and April, when the days are longer and warmer, and the snow is more settled.

When you go

BC Parks
Area Supervisor
PO Box 118
Wasa, BC V0B 2K0
Tel: (250) 422-4200
Fax: (250) 422-3326
E-mail: agreen@galaxy.gov.bc.ca

Mount Assiniboine Lodge
PO Box 8128
Canmore, AB T1W 2T8
Tel: (403) 678-2883
Fax: (403) 678-4877
E-mail: assinilo@telusplanet.net

Recommended Reading

Beers, Don. *Banff–Assiniboine: A Beautiful World.* Calgary: Highline Publishing, 1993.

Maligne Valley, Jasper National Park

The French fur traders called the river wicked (*maligne*) because its fast and dangerous waters were difficult to cross. Kids today use "wicked" to mean *awesome* or *impressive*, which seems far more appropriate for the Maligne River and the valley of the same name.

Scenic valleys with mountains, lakes, rivers and canyons are commonplace in the Rockies, but none surpasses the Maligne Valley in Jasper National Park. Surrounded by snow-capped mountains and subalpine forest, Maligne Lake gives birth to the Maligne River, part of which flows through Maligne Canyon, a deep narrow gorge at the lower end of the valley. Midway between the lake and the canyon is Medicine Lake at

the base of a half-mile-long (a kilometer-long) section of smooth, high-angled limestone slabs. Add to this scenic mix some of the most spectacular hikes in the park, and you have a truly "wicked" place.

The valley is an outdoor adventurer's paradise. There's canoeing and fishing on Maligne Lake, hiking and trail riding in the surrounding mountains, whitewater rafting,

cycling and, in winter, skiing and ice climbing. No roadside camping is allowed in the Maligne Valley, but daily forays from nearby Jasper are easy and convenient. Backcountry campgrounds operate on a quota system, and sites must be reserved in advance.

Start your exploration of the valley at Maligne Lake, 30 miles (49 kilometers) from Jasper. The Maligne Lake Road begins just 2.5 miles (4 kilometers) from Jasper and extends to the day-use area at the north end of the lake and the outlet where the Maligne River begins. This 13.5-mile (22-kilometer) lake, the longest in the Canadian Rockies, pokes its way into the mountains like a long, bony finger. The lake is glacier-fed, giving

Canoeing on Maligne Lake, Jasper National Park.

it a milky jade or turquoise color, depending on the time of year.

In May of each year, harlequin ducks visit Maligne Lake to nest. They're the only North American ducks to migrate inland from their seaside homes on the Pacific. The small drakes with their striking plumage of dark blue, rust and bold white streaks can sometimes be seen bobbing on the lake's waters. Unfortunately, their numbers are declining because of loss of habitat, overhunting and environmental pollution.

The recreational choices are varied: take a boat cruise to the end of the lake; rent a canoe, rowboat or kayak; or launch your own canoe. Try to reach the Narrows, about halfway along the lake and close to the much-photographed Spirit Island. In season, you're very likely to land a rainbow trout or two from the once stocked lake. If an adrenaline rush is more your style, take one of the guided whitewater rafting trips down the Maligne River.

If you prefer to stay on dry land, try one of the numerous hiking trails that either follow the shoreline or climb to viewpoints high above the lake. An exquisite view is from the Bald Hills lookout, a 2,000-foot (610-meter) climb into a sparsely treed area that is awash with alpine flowers in late June and July. The nearby Opal Hills, named for the alpine bluebells that grow at the timberline, is also well worth the strenuous climb. Your efforts might be rewarded with a sighting of mountain caribou, goat, sheep or a distant grizzly.

The ever-popular Skyline Trail also starts at Maligne Lake. As its name implies, the 28-mile (45-kilometer) trail climbs to a high ridge separating the Athabasca River valley and the Maligne Valley. Much of the route stays high and crosses three passes, the highest at 8,240 feet (2,510 meters). The views from here are unsurpassed. On a clear day you can see peaks such as Mount Robson, over 56 miles (90 kilometers) away. The trail descends to the Maligne Lake Road via the 5.2-mile (8.4-kilometer) Signal Mountain fire road, a rather anticli-

mactic finish to a great hike.

Because of the Skyline Trail's high elevation, it is best to tackle the hike later in the season when the trail has dried out and the alpine flowers are in full bloom. Mid-July to mid-August usually provides the best window of opportunity. The two- to three-day hike is a deserved favorite among backpackers, necessitating a strict quota system. If you're unable to reserve a campsite, consider a day hike from either end of the trail, or

from an intermediate trailhead such as the Watchtower Basin. An alternative is to travel light, stay at the privately owned Shovel Pass Lodge, which is conveniently located at about the midway point, and complete the walk in two days.

The upper valley around Maligne Lake is undoubtedly the most scenic, but the lower valley has its attractions, including a mystery. At numerous points along the Maligne Lake Road, the large and turbulent

Maligne Canyon in winter, Jasper National Park.

Maligne River can be seen flowing toward Medicine Lake. The river enters the lake at its southern end, but at its northern end, the presumed outlet, the riverbed is dry. Where did the water go?

To obtain the answer, you have to continue down-valley to Maligne Canyon. This popular roadside tourist spot is equipped with a teahouse, walkways, bridges and railings to prevent overly curious people from falling into the canyon. Some still manage to anyway and don't live to tell the tale! Six bridges cross the 1.8-mile-long (3-kilometer-long) canyon, allowing dizzying glimpses of crashing waterfalls and roiling cauldrons far below. Up to 180 feet (55 meters) deep and so narrow that boulders and trees become jammed between its walls, the canyon is a dramatic example of the erosional power of water. Ferns and mosses grow along the spray-dampened canyon walls that are also home to rare black swifts.

Between the fourth bridge and the sixth, the farthest downstream, the mystery is solved. The Maligne River resurfaces as a series of large springs, increasing the flow of the river eightfold or more. Linking Medicine Lake and the lower canyon is an as-yet-unexplored cave system with no obvious access.

In winter, parts of the canyon can be explored on foot. The floor and walls become draped with ice and the larger waterfalls become an ice climber's playground. Seeing the deep canyon from the inside is a special treat, made safe by professionals who offer guided tours.

The Maligne Road is kept open for most of the winter so the entire valley is accessible to skiers and snowshoers. There are no facilities open during the winter. Over 12.5 miles (20 kilometers) of summer-use trails are trackset in winter.

Spirit Island on Maligne Lake, Jasper National Park.

The more challenging open terrain of the Bald Hills and Opal Hills is ideal for ski touring. However, steep open slopes are also potential avalanche slopes. Use caution, or join a guided group if your avalanche awareness skills are not up to snuff.

The upper valley is caribou wintering ground. Avoid approaching or disturbing the animals – they need all their energy to survive the winter and the wolves that stalk them.

Though the better skiing is in the upper valley near the lake, there are more accessible ski trails in the lower val-

When you go

Jasper National Park
PO Box 10
Jasper, AB T0E 1E0
Tel: (780) 852-6161

Recommended Reading

Beers, Don. *Jasper–Robson: A Taste of Heaven.* Calgary: Highline Publishing, 1996.

Maligne, Valley of the Wicked River. Ottawa: Dept. of Supply & Services Canada, 1979.

ley, closer to Jasper. The 5.6-mile (9-kilometer) Signal Mountain fire road near Maligne Canyon climbs gradually to a fire lookout that offers fine views in clear

weather. Stay in the shelter of the trees if the wind is blowing or the visibility poor. The steep climb to the Watchtower Basin a little farther up-valley is worth the effort for the spectacular views from this huge, open basin.

Thanks to advance planning and effective management by Parks Canada, the Maligne Valley is relatively free of commercial development. An extensive network of trails gives rapid access to backcountry areas and an opportunity to view the abundant wildlife in the valley. Truly a "wicked" place!

Rocky Mountain House

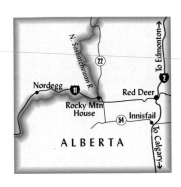

To an outsider it may look like mayhem, but to Steve Taylor the sight of twenty or so rambunctious dogs jumping up and down, yelping or rolling in the snow, is a perfectly normal start to one of his dog-sledding trips. The excited huskies just cannot wait to get on the trail. Finally, Steve gives the word, you pull the snow hook and you're off like a shot out of a cannon, hanging on for dear life.

Welcome to Ice Haven Expeditions, a dog-sledding company owned and operated by Steve and Carol Taylor in Rocky Mountain House, about two and a half hours by car from either Calgary or Edmonton. Their trips start from Nordegg near the eastern boundary of Banff National Park and follow the Wapiabi River north into the forested foothills of the Rockies.

The Taylors believe in a "hands-on" experience. After an introductory spiel on toboggan control, you get to help harness the dogs – somewhat like trying to dress a squirming two-year-old – then you handle your own five-dog team for the duration of the trip. Fortunately, after the frantic start the excited dogs quickly settle down into a steady trot, and everything seems more manageable.

There are two things you quickly learn about dog sledding. First is the importance of the brake, a metal bar that you push into the snow with your foot. On your first downhill slope, you'll notice a tendency for the toboggan to try to overtake the dogs. This is a concern to the wheeler dogs, those directly in front of the toboggan, they will cast anxious looks over their shoulders as it gains on them. Second is the importance of the snow hook, a wicked-looking two-pronged metal hook you thrust into the snow every time you step off the toboggan. Forget, and your team could take off on a cross-country trip without you.

There are other subtleties to learn, such as being relaxed around the dogs. Nervous people make dogs nervous. Successful drivers are relaxed and quiet of soul. Then there are the dog relationships: who's in heat, who's feuding with whom, who's feeling out of sorts. It all makes for an exciting and unique experience.

A moderate level of fitness is required for a trip of this type. On the steeper uphill sections you have to dismount and try to keep up with the dogs. This can leave you wheezing at the top of the hill, but there's usually lots of time to recover your breath before the next uphill.

Dog sledding the Wapiabi River valley, Alberta.

By the time you reach the Taylors' bush camp, 20 miles (32 kilometers) from the trailhead, you'll be feeling like an expert, having maneuvered the toboggan up and down hills, around sharp corners, and across icy creeks. After the dogs are fed – it's quite a sight to see them wolf down a couple of pounds (about a kilogram) of food in less than a minute – you can make yourself comfortable or help with camp chores. The camp consists of three wooden-floored canvas tents with wood-burning stoves, cozy yet having that pioneer feel. The meal tent has some distinctly non-pioneer

When you go

Ice Haven Expeditions
RR 2
Rocky Mountain House, AB T0M 1T0
Tel: (403) 845-5206

touches: elegant candles, tablecloths, and bottles of good wine to accompany a gourmet three-course dinner.

Your night's rest might be interrupted by the dogs and the resident coyotes having a songfest, but the fresh air, exercise and a relaxing sauna will usually guarantee a good night's sleep.

Most novices head back to Nordegg the following day, having enjoyed a challenging, exciting and novel experience. More ambitious guests have a choice of trips lasting up to ten days. These trips use larger dog teams, cover greater distances each day over more challenging terrain, and use mobile camps. It's a chance to become a truly competent dog handler and to shed much of the stress of modern life.

The cost of this unique experience ranges from $195 a day for the two-day trip to $325 a day for a ten-day trip. All equipment, food and snowmobile support is provided.

Dog sledding near Rocky Mountain House, Alberta.

Icefields Parkway

"Twenty Switzerlands in one," enthused Banff's *Crag and Canyon* when the Icefields Parkway was opened in 1940. Though the praise is a slight exaggeration, the 140-mile (230-kilometer) ribbon of highway that connects Jasper to Lake Louise through the heart of the Canadian Rockies is one of the most scenic and awe-inspiring in the world.

Millions of people have seen the Icefields Parkway from the cocoon of a bus or car, but few have *experienced* it. On a bicycle you experience the sights, sounds and smells at a pace you set. The ride can be completed in three days with few side trips. If time permits, take four or five days and make frequent stops at the many roadside attractions. Your rear end will appreciate the sorely needed rest!

If possible, plan your trip for June or September. July and August see thousands of buses, motor homes and cars on the highway, necessitating frequent maneuvering around parked vehicles and an increased risk of accident. In general, though, the wide shoulder on most of the highway makes for safe cycling. Fortunately, transport trucks are not allowed on the parkway.

There are several ways to tackle the logistics of the ride: be self-sufficient and camp; stay at hostels or cabins to reduce the weight you carry; or take a guided tour and have all your meals and accommodation provided. Eleven campgrounds and six hostels are spaced at convenient intervals along the route. However, unless you are a strong cyclist you'll find the first option rather punishing. The easiest, though most inflexible, option is to join a guided group. You carry only the necessities, roadside snacks are provided, and a "sag wagon" will scoop you up if you need a break or some bicycle repairs.

Like the bird that gets the worm, the early riser has a decided advantage when cycling the Icefields Parkway. Early mornings are usually cool, windless and relatively free of traffic, ideal conditions for cycling. Sightings of browsing elk, deer and moose are more likely in the early morning, too. It's heart-lifting to see the rising sun painting the snowy peaks with a beautiful alpenglow. Later in the day, when the heat and wind have both risen to uncomfortable levels, you can be enjoying a siesta or a cool walk in the woods.

Most cyclists prefer to ride north to south, from Jasper to Lake Louise.

Athabasca Glacier, Columbia Icefields.

The Columbia Icefields

The 125-square-mile (325-square-kilometer) Columbia Icefields is at the hydrographic apex of North America. Rivers originating from the icefields flow into three oceans: the Columbia River flows west into the Pacific; the Athabasca River joins the Mackenzie River, which flows north into the Arctic Ocean; and the North Saskatchewan River flows east to Hudson Bay. The Athabasca Glacier, though large, is just a small part of the massive icefields, which are large enough to create their own weather system.

Athabasca Glacier and the Icefields Parkway, Alberta.

It's a gentler start and the winds are usually at your back. There are two grueling climbs at Sunwapta Pass and Bow Pass, but take heart – for every uphill grind, there's an exhilarating downhill glide. At the Columbia Icefields, just before Sunwapta Pass, the Athabasca Glacier and the Icefields Centre deserve a stop. The center has a very impressive (free) interpretive gallery. If time permits, plan a brief hiking trip to the alpine meadows at Parker's Ridge. Here, you can celebrate: you're halfway to Lake Louise!

Beyond Saskatchewan River Crossing, where you can stock up on junk food, the road climbs steadily

When you go

Jasper National Park
PO Box 10
Jasper, AB T0E 1E0
Tel: (780) 852-6161

Recommended Reading

Helgason, Gail, and John Dodd. *Bicycle Alberta.* Edmonton: Lone Pine Publishing, 1984.

to Waterfowl Lakes and views of Mount Chephren, one of the most impressive peaks along the route. The only remaining hurdle is the steep climb to Bow Pass, at 6,790 feet (2,069 meters) the route's highest point. Take a well-deserved

rest at the summit and visit the alpine meadows and Peyto Lake viewpoint. Refreshments can be bought at the historic Num-Ti-Jah Lodge on Bow Lake. The remaining 25 miles (40 kilometers) to Lake Louise are, relatively speaking, a piece of cake.

If you still have energy and enthusiasm, the ride can be extended 37 miles (60 kilometers) to Banff along the Bow Valley Parkway, a quiet tree-lined route that parallels the much busier Trans-Canada Highway. There is a voluntary closure on this road from 6 p.m. to 9 a.m. in recognition of its importance as a wildlife corridor.

Num-Ti-Jah Lodge, Banff National Park

The late 1800s and early 1900s were busy times in Rocky Mountain history. The Canadian Pacific Railway had opened up the vast wilderness to prospecting, trapping, exploration and, inevitably, tourism. Scientists, big-game hunters, alpinists, even artists, flocked to the mountains, and every one of them needed a guide.

Jimmy Simpson was one of that rare breed of mountain men who came to the Rockies at an early age, became skilled in the ways of the wilderness, and eventually made his living guiding in the mountains he loved. He dreamed of building a lodge on the edge of Bow Lake, but commercial development in Banff National Park was restricted even then, and it wasn't until 1940, four decades after he first arrived in the area, that he was able to erect a six-room guest house. By 1950, though, it had expanded to a beautiful log and stone lodge, with 25 guest rooms, dining room and library. He called it "Num-Ti-Jah," a Stoney Indian word meaning "pine marten."

In 1972, Jimmy died, leaving his dream lodge to his son, Jimmy Simpson Jr., and in 1996, the property left the family. But Num-Ti-Jah hasn't lost any of the charm and warmth that the Simpsons brought to it. Today, the lodge is much as it's always been – spacious, simple and welcoming.

During the summer, the lodge is packed to the rafters with tourists from all over the world who come to enjoy the fresh mountain air. Horseback riding is a favorite activity, and guests of every age can saddle up for as little as an hour or as much as a full day, following some of the trails Jimmy Simpson once guided on. Beautiful Bow Lake, just outside the lodge's front door, invites visitors to cast a line or simply enjoy a quiet morning paddle on its glacier-blue waters.

Hikers have an unlimited choice of trails in the immediate vicinity. A half-day trip could take you around the Bow Lake shoreline, or 2.8 miles (4.5 kilometers) up to the Bow Glacier Falls, through a deep canyon and scrambling across glacial moraine. In winter, the falls are frozen in motion, and ice climbers cling to its solid surface.

More ambitious hikers can head to the high alpine, where the meadows are brimming with wildflowers

Hiking in the summer.

in July and early August. Crowfoot Mountain, Bow Summit, Observation Peak and Helen Lake are all superb day hikes that offer spectacular, unobstructed views of the mountains and icefields.

Winter is a special time at Num-Ti-Jah. Outside, the snow-covered lake sparkles, and the harsh, slate-gray mountains now look soft and innocent in white. Snowshoers and cross-country skiers can set out across the frozen lake or take to the forests surrounding the lodge, blazing their own trails or following the zigzag of hare tracks in the snow. Experienced backcountry skiers can ski up to Crowfoot Mountain or Bow Glacier for long runs back down to the valley. A short distance from the lodge are a number of telemark slopes that offer particularly good spring skiing that lasts well into May.

At the end of the day, it's wonderful to come back to a hot shower and an elegant meal at Num-Ti-Jah. Evenings can be spent sipping wine in front of a blazing fire, playing a game of pool in the lounge, or reading a good book in the library. The lodge is open in the summer from mid-May until mid-October, and in the winter from Christmas to mid-March. Room rates start at $100 in the summer, $65 in the winter.

When you go

Num-Ti-Jah Lodge
PO Box 39
Lake Louise, AB T0L 1E0
Tel: (403) 522-2167
Fax: (403) 522-2425
E-mail: reserve@num-ti-jah.com
Website: www.num-ti-jah.com

Recommended Reading

Hart, E.J. *Jimmy Simpson, Legend of the Rockies.* Canmore: Altitude Publishing, 1991.

Num-Ti-Jah Lodge, Banff National Park.

Skoki Lodge, Banff National Park

You're curled up in front of the stone fireplace, sipping a mug of steaming Cougar's Milk and toasting your toes in the warmth of the fire. Still full from a gourmet dinner and sleepy after a long, satisfying day in the mountains, you relax with the other lodge guests and swap stories about your adventures. On the log walls surrounding you, black and white photos tell similar stories of people just like you, who came to Skoki Lodge half a century ago.

And their experience was not so different from yours, despite the passage of time and technological inventions. The lodge and three cabins are kept cozy with wood stove or propane heaters and are lit by kerosene lantern; only the kitchen has advanced with the addition of modern appliances. There are no showers or indoor plumbing, but there is a wood-fired sauna, and the walk to the outhouse is magical on a moonlit night.

When you go

Skoki Lodge
PO Box 5
Lake Louise, AB T0L 1E0
Tel: (403) 522-3555
Fax: (403) 522-2095
E-mail: thelake@telusplanet.net
Website: www.banff.net/skoki/

Even the trip into the lodge has changed little over the years. Guests once started hiking or skiing from the train station in the village of Lake Louise. Nowadays, the usual access starts at the Fish Creek parking lot at Skiing Louise, owners of Skoki Lodge. Guests are bussed to the end of the road near the ski resort's Temple Lodge, where the trail begins. Winter or summer, it's 7 miles (11 kilometers) on foot to Skoki, across the treed slopes of the ski resort, past the Halfway Hut – reputed to be visited by the ghosts of mountaineers – and over the jumbled slopes of Boulder Pass. You'll likely be bending into the wind here and as you cross (or, in summer, hike around) Ptarmigan Lake. The climb up Deception Pass is rewarded with a long downhill past the Skoki Lakes to the lodge.

Skoki Lodge, Banff National Park.

Skoki. The word means "marsh" in Stoney Indian. And though it's set in a low-lying alpine meadow, the lodge is situated at 7,100 feet (2,164 meters) elevation, the highest guesthouse in any of the national parks. Built in 1930, with an addition in 1936, the lodge was one of the first of its kind in the Canadian Rockies, and a precursor to today's downhill ski resorts.

Manager Blake O'Brian and staff are always on hand to recommend a hike or ski route suited to your abilities and desires. If you're hiking or cross-country skiing, Blake might suggest the circle tour around the base of Skoki Mountain to the Red Deer Lakes or to Merlin Meadows. On a clear day, he might direct you to the summit of Skoki Mountain. Even from this low peak, you gain a superb view of your surroundings: the Skoki Lakes near Deception Pass to the south, the Red Deer Lakes to the north, and to the southwest, Merlin Lake, flanked on three sides by the Wall of Jericho, snowy Mount Richardson (10,125 feet/3,086 meters) and Merlin Castle.

For a full day out, you might be interested in the hike to Natural Bridge to see the waterfalls that gush through a slit in the limestone cliff. Strong hikers could tackle the difficult Castilleja and Merlin lakes route, hiking along the boulder slope on the Wall of Jericho. If fishing is your forte, Blake will suggest heading to the Red Deer Lakes, Baker Lake or the upper waters of Baker Creek – all well known spots for rainbow trout.

For telemark skiers, he'll point you to Merlin Ridge below Mount Richardson. From high up on the ridge, the panorama is breathtaking, and in good conditions, the ski back down is heaven. In fact, if his chores are done, Blake may even be tempted to carve a few turns with you.

Pick your pleasure! In the morning, after an energizing breakfast, build yourself a lunch from the mounds of food set out on the sideboard and be on your way. At Skoki, there's terrain suitable for beginner and intermediate cross-country skiers and telemarkers, and plenty of hikes to choose from. Just beware of the wet spots in summer, and avalanche danger in the winter.

Sometime during your stay at Skoki, you might run into mountain legend Ken Jones, hauling water or chopping wood. Now in his 80s, Ken – or Greybeard, as he's affectionately known – helped build the main lodge at Skoki in 1936 and has been working there on and off ever since. In the early years, Ken skied in from Lake Louise with supplies every day, carrying packs that weighed up to 90 pounds (40 kilograms). His recipe for Cougar's Milk is a favorite with backcountry enthusiasts in the Rockies.

Some visitors do the trip to and from Skoki in a day, stopping at the lodge for tea and baked goodies (open from 11 a.m. to 4:30 p.m.). Only very determined skiers and hikers should attempt this, even though the trail is rated beginner/intermediate. Those staying overnight at the

> ### Recipe for Cougar's Milk
>
> Place two teaspoons (10 milliliters) of sweetened condensed milk into a mug. Add boiling water and stir, then add overproof rum to taste. Top with a dash of nutmeg, pull up a chair by the fire and enjoy.

lodge must be able to carry a pack with extra clothing, equipment, a lunch, and perhaps a bottle of wine to sip with dinner. In the winter, telemark or backcountry ski gear is best, although some guests do use light touring equipment.

The lodge is open from Christmas to April, and late June to September. Rates (including transportation to the trailhead and all meals) begin at $120/person/night and drop with longer stays.

Skoki Lodge, Banff National Park.

Shadow Lake, Banff National Park

Fall is the perfect time of year for hiking in the Rocky Mountains. The days are cool, the air is crisp, the bugs have disappeared and a light brush of snow in the high country adds a special sparkle to the changing colors. The Rockies don't get the brilliant reds and oranges that Eastern Canada enjoys, but they do get a poor-man's version – the soft golds and yellows of alpine larch.

Larch trees, found only at high altitudes, are deciduous conifers that shed their needles every fall. Their soft, pale green needles turn golden yellow, then drop to the ground, revealing twisted, gnarled trunks with thin, brittle branches.

The third weekend of September is "larch weekend" in Alberta, when hikers flock to the mountains to catch the peak change of these delicate trees. So lace up your boots and head to the high country around Shadow Lake Lodge in Banff National Park. Once a CPR rest house, and now owned and operated by the Brewster family, the lodge re-opened in 1990 and caters to hikers, horseback riders, mountain bikers and, in winter, the cross-country ski crowd.

In summer and fall, mountain biking is a reasonable alternative to hiking up the 7.5-mile (12-kilometer) fire road to the lodge. Starting from the Redearth Creek parking lot on the Trans-Canada Highway, 12 miles (19 kilometers) west of Banff, the steep, wide trail leads to the turnoff to Shadow Lake. From here on, the trail is off-limits to cyclists, so lock your bikes at the bike racks and hike the remaining mile and a quarter (2 kilometers) to the lodge.

Plan to arrive at the lodge in time for tea, served from 11 a.m. to 5 p.m. every day. For a mere $6.50, hikers can sample homemade cakes and cookies, served buffet-style in the main lodge. Have a quick snack, drop your packs in your cabin, and hike toward Ball Pass to work up an appetite for dinner. You'll be glad you did! Huge hiker's portions and a few glasses of wine will have you feeling sleepy and content after dinner, and before long you'll be snuggled under a toasty down duvet.

In the morning, after a hearty breakfast, head up to Gibbon Pass, a

Shadow Lake and Mount Ball, Banff National Park.

Shadow Lake Lodge, Banff National Park.

short (2.5 miles/4 kilometers) but steep hike to expansive subalpine meadows and larch forests. The pass is flanked on the east and west by mountains – if you have a keen eye, you may spot the mountain goats that are often seen here, scrambling along the cliff bands. The views north and south are superb. On a clear day you can see the pyramidal outline of Mount Assiniboine, the "Matterhorn of the Canadian Rockies," to the south, and Mount Hector to the north, near Lake Louise.

After lunch, if you're feeling adventurous, take the 7.5-mile (12-kilometer) round-trip hike to the toe of Ball Glacier. A rough but well defined trail follows the north shore of Shadow Lake to the west end of the lake. From there, follow the obvious trail toward the amphitheater on Mount Ball's eastern flank, past two lovely waterfalls and through subalpine meadows to the moraine at the base of the glacier. Looking east, the views of the lake are unsurpassed from any other vantage point. A little farther up, you'll come to an ice cave carved out of the toe from glacial meltwater.

A long day trip would take you 6.8 miles (11 kilometers) from the lodge to Whistling Pass via Haiduk Lake, tiptoeing through boggy meadows crazy with wildflowers in the summer. At the top of the pass, listen for the shrill whistle of the resident hoary marmots (thus the name of the pass), and survey the views. The Pharaoh Peaks have been your companions as you gained the pass, and

When you go

Banff National Park
PO Box 900
Banff, AB T0L 0C0
Tel: (403) 762-1550

Shadow Lake Lodge
PO Box 2606
Banff, AB T0L 0C0
Tel: (403) 762-0116
Fax: (403) 760-2866
E-mail: shadow@telusplanet.net

now, looking south, you'll see Egypt and Scarab lakes. This is a beautiful area and an excellent hike (from Sunshine Village via Healy Pass) at any time of year. It's sometimes used as an alternative route to Shadow Lake by hardy backpackers. Unfortunately, its beauty and accessibility make Egypt Lake a too-busy spot; you'll seldom find solitude there if that is what you're after.

Another alternative route to the Shadow Lake area begins in Kootenay National Park, over the provincial border in British Columbia. Take the 7.5-mile (12-kilometer) Hawk Creek Trail from Highway 93 to the Ball Pass Junction Campground. The trail, though obvious and well marked, is not well maintained. Be prepared to clamber over uncleared deadfall.

The trail climbs steadily to Ball Pass, and the views from here are well worth the effort. To the north is glacier-capped Mount Ball – normally admired from the east end of Shadow Lake – its 10,860-foot (3,311-meter) bulk dominating the valley. You are now sitting on the crest of the Continental Divide: on the west side of the pass, all water drains to the Pacific Ocean; on the east, to Hudson's Bay and the Atlantic Ocean. Below you, the 1-mile (1.6-kilometer) length of Shadow Lake stretches east from the base of Mount Ball. You can just make out the shiny yellow log walls of Shadow Lake Lodge and cabins glinting through the trees at the far end of the lake. Once you reach the Ball Pass Junction Campground, it's a further 3 miles (5 kilometers) to the lodge, through wet, low-lying meadows. On the way, you'll catch glimpses of golden larch stands on the surrounding mountains. Hurry along – you don't want to miss afternoon tea at the lodge!

The Bow Valley

For many years, the lower Bow Valley was viewed simply as the gateway to Banff and the national park. Traffic from Calgary sped by the small town of Canmore on the eastern edge of the park, hardly giving it a second glance.

All of that started to change in 1988, when Canmore was selected as the site for the nordic events at the Winter Olympic Games. In more recent years, Canmore has benefited from the development slowdown in Banff, so that now the two towns are similar in size and Canmore has become a destination in its own right. Located 66 miles (106 kilometers) west of Calgary on the Trans-Canada Highway, Canmore straddles the Bow River and is surrounded by soaring peaks, including the famous Three Sisters.

The recreational opportunities in the Bow Valley are immense, from hiking, biking, fishing, canoeing, rafting and kayaking in the Bow Valley and nearby parks, to caving or sport climbing.

When you go

Travel Alberta/Canmore Visitor Information Centre
2801 Bow Valley Trail
Canmore, AB T1W 3A2
Tel: 1-800-661-8888

Recommended Reading

Daffern, Gillean. *Canmore and Kananaskis Country.* Calgary: Rocky Mountain Books, 1994.

In winter, nordic, backcountry and alpine skiing are all accessible within a few miles of the town. Equipment for most of these activities can be rented in Canmore, and guides and instructors are readily available. There are also three sizable campgrounds in the valley.

A legacy of the 1988 Winter Olympic Games is the Canmore Nordic Centre, which features a 43-mile (70-kilometer) network of trails open to recreational skiers in winter and mountain bikers and hikers in summer. World-class bike and ski races, and dogsled races during the annual week-long Winter Festival, are also held at the center. There are 1.5 miles (2.5 kilometers) of lighted trails for night-time skiing.

Just up the hill from the Nordic Centre is the 1.5-mile (2.5-kilometer) trail to the Grassi Lakes, an ideal

The town of Canmore in the Bow Valley.

hike for families. Built by master trail builder Lawrence Grassi, the footpath winds its way up the mountain in easy stages. Carefully placed stone steps ease you over the steep sections to two small lakes that were special to the Kutenai Indians. Look for the Kutenais' pictographs on a nearby rock; they are thought to be over 1,000 years old. Carry on past the lakes through a boulder-strewn limestone canyon to a small dam and a gravel road leading back to Canmore.

If you're up for a more strenuous outing, the 3,150-foot (960-meter) ascent of Pigeon Mountain, 6 miles (10 kilometers) east of the Grassi Lakes, is very rewarding. The 4.8-mile (7.7-kilometer) trail offers carpets of alpine forget-me-nots in spring, and an easy summit ridge with views of the valley and the flat prairie beyond.

Numerous tributary canyons to the Bow Valley make interesting hiking. One of the most popular and scenic is Grotto Canyon. Keep a lookout for the faint Indian pictographs that decorate the sheer canyon walls.

Bow Valley Provincial Park is located near the entrance to the valley, about 9 miles (15 kilometers) from Canmore. The park is a naturalist's paradise and an ideal family destination. The eco-zone is classed as montane forest, and the resulting mosaic of fauna and flora is unique to this part of Alberta. Prairie western meadowlarks can be spotted in the same area as mountain chickadees; yellow mountain avens grow close to three-flowered avens. Add to this mix interesting glacial features such as eskers, kames and moraines, a series of springs that harbor meat-eating butterworts and orchids, and you have a truly fascinating park.

An equally interesting area is the Jewell Pass/Quaite Creek Valley, due south of Bow Valley Provincial Park. A 12.5-mile (20-kilometer) section of the Trans-Canada Trail crosses this area, starting at Barrier Lake on Highway 40 and ending at Dead Man's Flats on the Trans-Canada Highway. The first 8-mile (13-kilometer) leg to Heart Creek offers easy hiking or biking through pockets of moss-covered old-growth fir. Considering the proximity of a

major highway and areas of urban and industrial development, the trail has a remarkable backcountry "feel." To break the trip into two short days, you can stay at the quiet Quaite Valley campground. Much of the trail between Quaite Creek and Dead Man's Flats clings to the mountainside high above the Trans-Canada Highway. The final 4-mile (7-kilometer) section to Dead Man's Flats is quite technical for mountain bikers.

Visitors to the valley cannot help but notice the massive cliffs of Yamnuska Mountain north of the highway. While the cliffs are the domain of rock climbers, hikers can take a 2-mile (3.5-kilometer) trail to the east ridge of the mountain. The trail angles up through aspen forest onto open slopes with sensational views of the broad valley dotted with small lakes and crisscrossed by the meandering Bow River. In early season, crocuses and western wood lilies are abundant.

Ambitious hikers can complete a 9-mile (15-kilometer) circumnavigation of Yamnuska. Descend from the east ridge (north) into the CMC Valley, then follow the valley upslope (west) to a prominent col between the west end of Yamnuska and Goat

The Bow Valley from Yamnuska.

Pictograph at Grassi Lakes in the Bow Valley.

Peak. Complete the loop by traversing under the imposing cliffs back to the east ridge, or take one of many climbers' trails down to the valley bottom.

In general, hiking and biking trails in the lower Bow Valley are accessible much earlier and later in the season than those in Banff National Park's higher mountains. The Bow Valley enjoys warm, dry summers and relatively mild winters, though the occasional arctic front can bring bone-chilling cold. May and September usually offer the most stable weather. However, there are sufficient recreational opportunities around Canmore and the Bow Valley to make any time of the year enjoyable.

Rats Nest Cave

Imagine a world with no breeze, no rain or snow or sleet. No stars, sun or moon – no sky! Now imagine yourself in it, the world underground.

At least a thousand caves have been discovered in Canada. A handful – like Rats Nest Cave just east of Banff National Park – are open to the public. Rats Nest was designated a Provincial Historic Resource in 1987 to protect it from quarrying by the mining companies in the region. Now, it is gated and locked to discourage illegal entry by careless adventurers who may damage the fragile cave environment. Canadian Rockies Cave Guiding operates trips into the cave for small groups of

physically fit adventure seekers. Led by highly experienced cave scientists, the company provides a safe and educational outing.

The trip starts with a half-hour hike through a canyon to the cave entrance. This is limestone country, the perfect environment for caves. Slightly acidic groundwater seeps

through cracks and fissures in the limestone, chemically reacting with it and dissolving the bedrock over time to form intricate passages, chambers and caverns. At Rats Nest, glacial outflow – rivers gushing off the melting glaciers – was an important force that enlarged the cave system.

Upon reaching the cave, you stop to don climbing harness, coveralls (you will get muddy!), helmet, battery pack, headlamp and gloves. Just inside the gate is the "twilight zone" (you can still see without the aid of a headlamp). While you nervously adjust your helmet and test your headlamp, your guide begins his introduction. "The cave is estimated to be a million years old, and the oldest formations within have been dated at 750,000 years. The temperature remains a constant 41°F (5°C) year round, with 100 percent humidity."

The guide points out the 65-foot (20-meter) drop to the "Bone Beds" and invites you to carefully lean over the edge for a look. The skeletal remains of 36 different mammalian species have been found here, along with prehistoric Indian "points" and a stone tool. Now turn on your headlamp and clamber through the first of many holes on your journey into the unknown.

If you've never been in a "wild" cave – no stairs, no boardwalks, no handrails, no sound and light show – you'll be overwhelmed by the experience. Only the circular beam from your headlamp illuminates a small area of the cave. You must stop and take your eyes from the rocky floor at your feet and focus on the walls, the ceiling, the pockets and passages leading off every which way, the jumble of boulders, and slabs of rock made slippery with mud and the passing of hundreds of people before you.

Rats Nest Cave.

While the gate now keeps out large animals, the cave is still a refuge for others, notably pack rats, bats and spiders. Your guide points out a rat's nest, a small, round pocket set on a rocky ledge strewn with nesting material – sticks, pine needles, the fluff from an abandoned fleece jacket, and other loot. Pack rats are the garbage collectors of the cave.

You haul yourself over a ledge, then squeeze along a diagonal slit to the "pitch." Here, depending on your experience, you'll rappel or be lowered down on a rope 65 feet (20 meters) to the cavern below. The physical experience is perhaps the most exciting aspect of caving. A cave trail is a three-dimensional, multi-level walk, crawl, slip, slide and shimmy using ropes, ladders, legs, arms, stomach, back or whatever is required to get you through the maze. Fitness and a sense of adventure are essential!

Eventually you come to one of the testing grounds for novice cavers – The Chimney. A narrow squeeze through a 33-foot-long (10-meter-long) passageway, The Chimney requires an on-your-back,

feet-first, slithering approach through a downward sloping tube. Then a right-angle bend at the bottom of the tube, switching to a head-first stomach drag through a channel that suddenly spits you out into a stand-up chamber. Whew! Did you feel a bit of panic, with

your guide's headlamp disappearing ahead of you, your helmet banging against the floor and the ceiling above, your battery pack and cable catching on jutting rocks? Don't worry – the adrenaline will keep you going!

You make your way now to the Grand Gallery and the Grotto, two large chambers decorated with "speleothems"– mineral formations caused by dripping, flowing, seeping, pooled and/or condensed water. The sloping walls and ceiling allow water to run down inclined

rock and precipitate calcite as thin, translucent curtains and draperies. Frozen, honey-colored streams and waterfalls, called "flowstone," cascade over the walls and floor. Rimstone dams, terraced like rice paddies, form from water splashing into pools, depositing calcite around the edges. Soda straws and stalactites hang from the ceiling, and stalagmites build up from the floor, occasionally meeting a stalactite to form a column.

At a large pool of water, you see a rope suspended above the "sump": the line scuba divers follow into passages beyond your reach. This is the perfect spot to sit quietly, turn off your headlamp and "see" nothing. Although your eyes strain to become accustomed to the dark, the darkness is absolute. Time to return to the familiar world.

Exploration of Rats Nest Cave continues today. The mapped and surveyed section currently measures over 2.5 miles (4 kilometers) – the ninth-longest cave in Canada. Next time you hike in limestone country, stop and contemplate the hidden world that may lie beneath your feet.

When you go

Canadian Rockies Cave Guiding
2512–19th St. N.W.
Calgary, AB T2M 3V4
Tel: (403) 282-6177
Tel: (403) 678-8819 (Canmore)

Flowstone in Rats Nest Cave.

Kananaskis Country

Most towns and cities have a park or recreation area close by that offers the chance to escape urban life and enjoy some form of outdoor activity. Just so with Calgary, except the local escape is over 1,500 square miles (4,000 square kilometers) in area, encompasses two alpine ski areas, one alpine village, interpretive centers, campgrounds, a custom-made canoe and kayak course, and over 600 miles (1,000 kilometers) of hiking, biking and ski trails. It's called

Indian paintbrush.

Kananaskis Country, or K Country by the locals, created by the government of Peter Lougheed in the late '70s, during the oil-boom years.

Within K Country is Peter Lougheed Provincial Park, a protected area that has well maintained trails and facilities. This is the park you should head for if you're looking for excellent hiking, biking or skiing trails. The park can be broadly divided into two areas: the Kananaskis Lakes region, and the more northerly region adjacent to the Smith–Dorien/Spray Trail. In general, the northerly region offers more rugged trails, whereas the lakes region is more suited for family hiking, biking and fishing.

Start your trip by dropping in at the Visitor Centre, an impressive building with interpretive displays and up-to-date information about the park such as summer bear closures and winter avalanche conditions. The center is the jumping-off spot for a network of over 30 miles (50 kilometers) of hiking and biking trails, including a paved cycle path, catering to all levels of ability. There is ample accommodation at six roadside campgrounds and two group campgrounds. Come winter, cross-country skiers take over the trails, many of which are trackset. The Boulton Creek Trading Post in the heart of the area makes a welcome stop for refreshments in both summer and winter.

The two Kananaskis Lakes are in fact reservoirs, dammed to provide hydroelectric power. The upper lake is more scenic than the lower lake, and has more interesting trails. The 9.2-mile (14.8-kilometer) trail that circumnavigates the upper lake is a rewarding hike that offers views of crashing waterfalls, narrow gorges and flower-strewn meadows. There are numerous picnic spots overlooking the lake or by the lakeshore, where you can watch anglers casting for elusive rainbow or cutthroat trout.

If you prefer a more panoramic view as you eat lunch, take the 1.5-mile (2.5-kilometer) trail from the upper lake to the viewpoint on Mount Indefatigable, named after a World War I battle cruiser that was sunk at the Battle of Jutland in 1916. The steep trail climbs 1,650 feet (503 meters) along a lightly forested ridge to a superb lookout with a view of both lakes. If lunch revives you sufficiently, you can climb a further 1,410 feet (430 meters) along grassy slopes to the rocky south summit of the mountain and even more spectacular views.

For the more adventuresome, there are well maintained, signed trails that take you into incredibly scenic backcountry areas. The 6.3-mile (10.2-kilometer) hike to

Three Isle Lake and South Kananaskis Pass, 1.8 miles (3 kilometers) farther, is a classic overnight trip, but you have to work for the prize. It's a grueling 2,050-foot (626-meter) climb to the pass. Another gem is the 9-mile (14.8-kilometer) trek to the campground at Turbine Canyon and North Kananaskis Pass, 1.3 miles (2.2 kilometers) beyond the campground. With the expenditure of more effort, you can climb to a viewpoint overlooking the Haig Glacier, where cross-country ski racers train during the summer. The reward is a magnificent view of Mts. Sir Douglas, Robertson and French, some of the highest peaks in the park.

The 25-mile (40-kilometer), gravel-surfaced Smith–Dorien/ Spray Trail links Peter Lougheed park

with Canmore. It follows a high, broad valley and is open year round except for occasional winter closures to clear snow. Along the road, which reaches an elevation of 6,230 feet (1,900 meters), is a mountain biking area, a lodge, numerous trailheads that lead into the mountains on both sides of the valley, and Spray Reservoir, a popular fishing spot. Because of the easy access to high country meadows and peaks, it's a popular day-use area for both hiking and skiing.

There are limited opportunities for mountain biking along the Smith–Dorien. In summer, you'd be choked by dust if you attempted to ride on the main road! Instead, drive to the Smith–Dorien Cross-Country Skiing and Mountain Biking Trail System, also known as the Sawmill trails.

Lower Kananaskis Lake in Kananaskis Country.

Kananaskis Country in summer.

A network of about 18 miles (30 kilometers) of old logging roads on the east side of the highway has been cleared, allowing you to bike or ski a series of loops. Some of the trails are quite steep and challenging, but there is something for every level of ability. An alternative is to head for the Mount Shark Cross-Country Ski Trails at the south end of the Spray Reservoir. Summer biking is allowed on selected, well-maintained trails.

The mountains adjacent to the highway are a hiker's Mecca. Because you start at a high elevation, there's no slogging through endless forest to reach scenic lookouts. On a day trip you can easily reach high alpine meadows and ridges with stunning views. The trails are more rugged than those in the lower-lying area near Kananaskis Lakes – expect unbridged stream crossings, deadfall on the trail and steep, sometimes muddy, sections.

The classic hike in this area is the 5-mile (8-kilometer) trail to Burstall Pass. The final mile and a quarter (2 kilometers) to the pass are through meadows strewn with a succession of flowers. In spring you'll see yellow glacier lilies, then columbine, paintbrush, mountain avens and many other species. In fall, larches add a further splash of color to the scene. This can also be the first leg of a backpacking trip into the Spray Valley to the west and Leman Lake, a popular fishing spot.

There are no campgrounds along the Smith–Dorien/Spray Trail, but there is Mount Engadine Lodge, a Swiss-style chalet that can accommodate up to 24 guests. The lodge is popular with the day-hiking crowd who drop by for afternoon tea and homemade strudel and cake.

Spray Lakes Reservoir is the next landmark if you're heading north to Canmore. The road follows the east shore past notable peaks such as Mount Lougheed, Sparrowhawk (once the proposed site of an alpine ski area) and the Windtower. While these are not technically difficult climbs, there are no well marked trails, and any attempt to climb them will be an exercise in route finding.

A road along the west shore accesses the only campgrounds in the valley. They are popular with families and fishermen and are often full on summer weekends. The road is closed to vehicles after 3 miles (5 kilometers), but you can continue by mountain bike another 10.5 miles (17 kilometers) from the closure to the end of the reservoir.

The relatively high elevation of the Smith–Dorien/Spray Trail usually guarantees good early-season skiing. Backcountry tourers can be seen testing the slopes by late November, and by mid-December the ski season is in full swing. The season lasts through April in the high country, by which time hikers are taking their first steps on the valley bottom trails. K Country is truly a year-round playground.

When you go

Kananaskis Country
201, 800 Railway Ave.
Canmore, AB T1W 1P1
Tel: (403) 678-5508
Fax: (403) 678-5505
Website: www.gov.ab.ca/~env/nrs/kananaskis/

Recommended Reading

Daffern, Gillean. *Kananaskis Country Trail Guide.* Calgary: Rocky Mountain Books, 1997 (two volumes).

Daffern, Gillean. *Kananaskis Country Ski Trails.* Calgary: Rocky Mountain Books, 1996.

Lake at Kananaskis Country.

Crowsnest Pass

Straddling the border between Alberta and British Columbia, the Crowsnest Pass, the Rockies' southernmost pass, is an area in transition. It is slowly moving from its industrial roots in mining and forestry to a future in tourism and recreation. The area is rich in recreational opportunities: hiking, mountain biking, caving, canoeing, fly-fishing, windsurfing and skiing.

Because most of the moisture is wrung out of the clouds in B.C., the Crowsnest Pass enjoys long, dry, hot summers, with only occasional rain. The area is known for its strong winds, which frequently gust to more than 60 miles (100 kilometers) per hour. Crowsnest Lake at the summit of the pass is often white-capped and inviting only to expert windsurfers. Winters are relatively mild and frequent chinooks allow shirtsleeve skiing along the low-lying forested trails.

Small communities such as Bellevue, Hillcrest, Blairmore and Coleman dot Highway 3 on the Alberta side of the pass. These

Site of 1903 Turtle Mountain landslide that killed 70 people, Crowsnest Pass.

communities seem frozen in time; development stopped when the last of the coal mines closed down in 1983, after a long period of decline. Only now are the communities being spruced up and tourist facilities introduced. The situation is much the same on the B.C. side of the pass, with the exception of Sparwood, a modern and prospering mining community.

For the tourist, all this translates to plentiful and inexpensive accommodation. There are nine drive-to campgrounds within a few miles of Highway 3, but no official backcountry campgrounds, unlike the situation in most national and provincial parks. If you choose to do a multi-day trip you will have to select your own campsite. Because of the extensive industrial activity in the area, most

of it has never earned provincial or national park status.

When you approach the pass from Highway 3 in Alberta, an unmistakable feature is the Frank Slide, a massive scar on the side of Turtle Mountain and a 90-million-ton pile of rock. It is worth a visit to the Interpretive Centre and the trail that meanders through the house-sized limestone blocks that crushed the town of Frank in 1903, killing more than 70 people.

The second unmistakable feature is Crowsnest Mountain itself, an isolated volcanic-looking peak soaring to 8,950 feet (2,730 meters). Though there are small outcroppings of volcanic rock elsewhere in the pass, Crowsnest Mountain, like all the other mountains in the region, is composed mostly of limestone and

Karst

The term *karst* is applied to limestone terrain that has no, or very little, surface drainage. Rain and snowmelt, made slightly acidic by combining with carbon dioxide in the air, sink into the soluble rock via tiny fissures. Over time, the fissures are enlarged to form caves and sinkholes, some many yards in diameter. Below the surface, streams combine to form large cave systems and subterranean rivers that resurface as springs. In the Rockies, most cave systems are not accessible because the sink points are blocked by either rock debris or snow and ice.

Fly-fishing in Alberta.

Gargantua Cave in Crowsnest Pass.

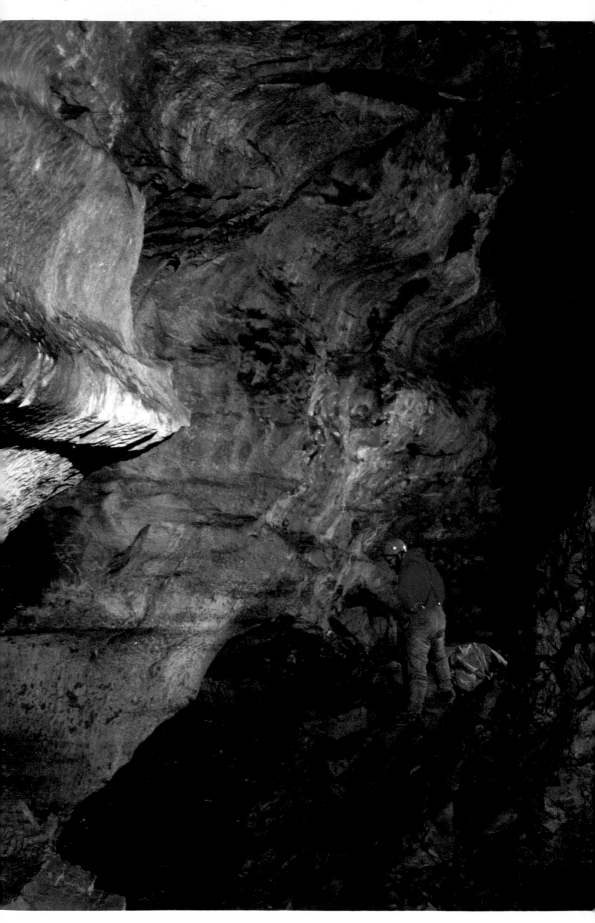

shale. Though it appears to be a technically difficult climb, the north side offers a relatively easy scramble to the summit. In midsummer, start the climb very early in the day to avoid the searing heat and desiccating winds for which the area is famous. Carry lots of water. The 3,600-foot (1,100-meter) climb ascends a series of loose scree slopes and gullies that require considerable care and close attention to the route, which is marked at all of the strategic spots. From the summit and to the west, the Front Ranges of the Rockies extend north and south as far as the eye can see. Turn around and the bald prairie stretches away to the eastern horizon.

If an energetic climb is not to your liking, there are dozens of trails that will lead you more gently onto the high ridges and peaks. The 7.8-mile (12.6-kilometer) hike along Livingstone Ridge is one of the better day trips because of the open terrain and panoramic views.

The Crowsnest Pass region is famous for its caves and karst features, the most obvious of which is the "Source of the Old Man River," a large spring that flows from under a rock arch into Crowsnest Lake, and which is visible from the main highway. Springs such as this are fed by rain and meltwater that originate in the alpine areas north and south of the pass, then course through intricate cave systems to emerge in the valley bottoms.

An impressive karst area is located south of the pass between Sentry Mountain and Mount Ptolemy and is accessed via Ptolemy Creek, a 5-mile (8-kilometer) trek partly along an old seismic line. A steep climb from the end of the line takes you to the first karst area, a small alpine plateau with outcrops of deeply fissured limestone, collapsed cave passages and sinkholes. A further climb of 660 feet (200 meters) takes you over the Continental Divide into B.C. (one of the few locations where B.C. is *east* of Alberta) and the Andy Good Plateau, a much larger karst plateau with no surface drainage and many deep pits. Here, water can be scarce, especially in late summer when most of the snow has melted. Be self-sufficient and carry your own water supply.

If you are interested in venturing underground, guided tours of some of the caves can be arranged locally.

Most of the lakes and rivers, especially the Crowsnest, Oldman and Castle rivers and their tributaries, offer excellent fly-fishing for rainbow, cutthroat and bull trout. Some lakes are stocked annually.

A maze of forestry, mining and gas well access roads, as well as seismic lines, offers ample opportunity for mountain bike trips. Many of the tracks are confined to the mixed spruce, pine and poplar forests, but some climb to high ridges and passes with spectacular views. In many places you'll see evidence of abandoned mines and railway lines and the resultant ghost towns.

The Grassy Mountain–Gold Creek loop offers a gentle introduction to the area. This 15-mile (24-kilometer) ride starts near the Frank Slide Interpretive Centre and passes the abandoned townsite of Lille and the open-pit mines of Grassy Mountain. Much of the route passes through clearings and open forest that offer little shade and no water. In midsummer be prepared for a hot, dry ride.

A more challenging but very scenic ride is the 23.5-mile (38-kilometer) Deadman Pass–Phillipps Pass loop. The trail starts north of Highway 3 at Chinook Lake, one of the more attractive campgrounds in the area, and ascends along cut lines and rutted tracks to Deadman Pass. Here, the open pine and poplar forest allows views of Crowsnest Mountain and the ridges and peaks of the High Rock Range. An exciting descent leads to an easy 5.3-mile (8.5-kilometer) section along the Alexander Creek Road, followed by another steep climb up and over Phillipps Pass, a route used by rumrunners during the Prohibition era in Alberta. A small tarn at the top of the pass makes a great swimming hole on a hot day.

In winter, the network of seismic, mining and logging roads offers countless opportunities for ski touring. Expect to share some of the trails with snowmobilers. Because of the frequent chinooks that ruin the snowpack for skiers, and less snowfall in general compared to areas north and west, the pass is not renowned for its cross-country skiing. One of the better areas is the Allison Creek Recreation Area, an extensive system of ski trails that is closed to snowmobiles. Its sheltered location and higher-than-average snowfall guarantee good skiing all winter.

When you go

Travel Alberta
PO Box 2500
Edmonton, AB T5J 2Z4
Tel: 1-800-661-8888

Recommended Reading

Eastcott, Doug, and Gerhardt Lepp. *Backcountry Biking in the Canadian Rockies.* Calgary: Rocky Mountain Books, 1993.

Ross, Jane, and William Tracy. *Hiking in the Crowsnest Pass.* Calgary: Rocky Mountain Books, 1992.

Dinosaur Provincial Park

When the voyageurs first passed through the dry region bordering the Red Deer River in southern Alberta, they called it *mauvaises terres* – bad lands – and quickly continued on their way. Dry and inhospitable it is, but the region is now recognized for its immeasurable worth as a rich source of fossil dinosaur remains, for its scenic badlands, and for its special riverside ecosystems. Dinosaur Provincial Park, a 28-square-mile (73-square-kilometer) area straddling the Red Deer River, was established to preserve these natural values and to allow excavation of fossils in a protected environment. The park is now a UNESCO World Heritage Site.

The park is 29.5 miles (48 kilometers) northeast of Brooks, about midway between Medicine Hat and Calgary on the Trans-Canada Highway. It can be accessed either by car or by canoe. With some shuttling of vehicles, you can follow in the footsteps of the voyageurs and paddle from near Drumheller to Dinosaur park, a distance of 50 miles (80 kilometers) that takes two to three days. It's advisable to paddle the river in June or early July, when the water level is high and the current strong. There are other put-in points to make the trip longer or shorter. Just consult a detailed road map.

Whether you arrive by car or canoe, plan to spend a couple of days exploring the prairie grasslands, coulees and riverside cottonwood groves. The park's well maintained hiking and interpretive trails are all close to the centrally located camp- ground. A 1.8-mile (3-kilometer) loop road adjacent to the campground allows a stop-and-start driving tour of the main features of the park.

If your knowledge of dinosaurs was sketchy at the beginning of your trip, after a couple of days in the park you'll feel like an expert. There are interpretive displays, dinosaur replicas, and a bookstore with a wealth of information about dinosaurs as well as the fauna and flora of the park. Save some time and enthusiasm for a trip to the Royal Tyrrell Museum near Drumheller, about two hours by car northwest of Brooks. This world-class museum displays the granddaddy of dinosaurs, Tyrannosaurus rex, and many local discoveries, including some from Dinosaur Provincial Park. Allow a full day to visit this fascinating museum.

When dinosaurs roamed this region about 75 million years ago, the climate was subtropical, much like northern Florida today. For reasons still unknown, the dinosaurs became

Mule deer, Dinosaur Provincial Park.

Dinosaur Provincial Park.

extinct over a relatively short period of time, but conditions were right for the preservation of their remains. Over time, mineralization of the bones took place, turning them into fossils.

The process of erosion that uncovered the fossils started only about 13,000 years ago and is continuing today. The combined effects of wind, rain, sun and frost cause the relatively soft sedimentary layers to erode quite fast, exposing new fossils each year. An argument for removing and preserving the fossils now is that eventually they would be washed into the river and lost forever.

Fossil remains of fish, amphibians, reptiles, birds, mammals and a total of 35 species of dinosaurs have been identified in the park. Over 150 complete dinosaur skeletons have been recovered, ranging from 5-foot-long (1.5-meter-long) bird-like Theropod dinosaurs to 33-foot-long

(10-meter-long) Hadrosaurs, or duck-billed dinosaurs. This is a prolific area, but don't expect to collect fossils within the park. Amateur fossil hunting is not allowed and active excavations are in restricted areas of the park, inaccessible to the public. It is possible to visit old sites such as one excavated by Barnum Brown of the American Museum of Natural History. Law prohibits the removal of any fossils.

About one-third of the park is set aside as a natural preserve, and access is restricted to guided groups only. Between mid-May and mid-October, daily hikes and bus tours enter the preserve to visit areas of interest and digs, including the Centrosaurus bone beds, where thousands of individuals are thought to have died en masse. These two- to three-hour tours are a great way to become acquainted with the world of paleontology. If you're really keen,

you can watch scientists at work in the Royal Tyrrell Museum Field Station, a short distance from the campground.

If you prefer to explore the park at your own pace there are three distinct habitats that can be accessed by five trails. Be aware that the park is in a region classed as semi-desert and daytime temperatures can soar to 95°F (35°C) in July and August. All of the hikes are short, however, so you're never too far from water and shelter.

The multi-hued layers of rock that have been exposed by the river's downcutting enhance the desert-like feeling. And the sages, cacti, prairie rattlers, black widow spiders and scorpions seem quite at home in this environment. By staying on the trails, you'll avoid encounters with these less savory desert-dwellers.

The Prairie Trail, right at the park entrance, leads you through often tinder-dry, flat prairie. Grasshoppers

Clouds above Dinosaur Provincial Park.

leap among sagebrush, prairie grasses and prickly pear cactus. In June, the red and yellow flowering cacti provide a special visual treat. If you're fortunate, you may see a coyote loping through the grasses or a pronghorn antelope bounding away to safety.

In contrast to the prairie, the 870-yard (1.4-kilometer) Cottonwood Flats Trail explores the riparian habitat of the valley bottom. The relatively moist environment and shade offered by the rough-barked cottonwoods and willows encourage many birds and animals to call this area home. Early in the morning you're likely to see and hear mourning doves, rock wrens, warblers, goldfinches and brown thrashers, just a few of the more than 160 species that have been identified in the park. Sightings of cottontails, mule and white-tailed deer are almost guaranteed.

The third type of habitat, and by far the most unusual, is between the rim of the river valley and the valley bottom. Here, streams have dissected the layered sediments forming steep-sided coulees and leaving mushroom-like hoodoos. The general lack of vegetation, the deeply grooved slopes and the oddly shaped formations create the impression of a lunar landscape. The half-mile (0.9-kilometer) Coulee Viewpoint Trail offers splendid views of this terrain. Try to view the area in the evening when the rocks are painted a warm red by the setting sun. The Badlands Trail leads you through this eerie world as interpretive signs explain how the badlands were created.

In places, the ground is covered with what appears to be popcorn. These are areas where clay surfaces have cracked, shrunk and curled up under the hot sun to form popcorn-like aggregates. They are delicate and should not be walked upon, especially in wet weather. The clay surface quickly absorbs water and becomes very slick, making it almost impossible to keep your footing on a sloping surface.

Dinosaur Provincial Park is one of the most unusual environments you will encounter on your cross-Canada travels. Allow a day and a half to two days to absorb the numerous interpretive displays. Reservations are recommended.

When you go

Dinosaur Provincial Park
PO Box 60
Patricia, AB T0J 2K0
Tel: (403) 378-4342
Fax: (403) 378-4247
Tel: (403) 378-4344 for bus and hike tour reservations
Tel: (403) 378-3700 for campsite reservations
Website: www.gov.ab.ca/~env/nrs/dinosaur

Hoodoos at Dinosaur Provincial Park.

Milk River and Writing-on-Stone Provincial Park

Following the last Ice Age, the glacial rivers of southeastern Alberta cut through the soft sedimentary layers of the prairies like a knife through butter. In very short periods, geologically speaking, deeply incised river valleys formed. The verdant valleys are like oases, sheltered from the desiccating winds that sweep across the prairies, nurtured by the creeks and rivers that flow along them. Like all oases, they attract birds, animals – and people.

A particularly fine example is the Milk River Valley. Originating in Montana, the Milk flows briefly through Alberta, then turns south to join the Missouri River. From here, a determined paddler could reach the Gulf of Mexico! Most people, however, are content to tackle the two-day stretch from the town of Milk River to Writing-on-Stone Provincial Park. Though only 22 miles (35 kilometers) as the crow flies, the meandering river covers almost twice that distance. If canoeing isn't to your liking, plan to drive to the park anyway. The rock art alone is worth the journey.

Every twist and turn reveals new wonders: stands of stately cottonwoods, soaring sandstone cliffs, and steep-sided coulees that invite exploration. Hardly a minute goes by without sighting wildlife of some kind.

As its name implies, the river has the appearance of milk-laced tea, but it's definitely not drinkable. Rapid erosion of the clay and mud riverbanks, especially after a thunderstorm, results in the movement of thousands of tons of sediment annually. The meandering river constantly changes its course, eating away its banks and leaving abandoned channels or oxbows.

Late spring to early summer is the best time to paddle the river. By mid-July the water level may be too low for safe paddling. The numerous rock gardens along the river are easy to navigate in high water and impassable at low water.

The beauty of the river is that you can drift or paddle gently most of the time while scanning the banks for birds and wildlife. Look for mule or white-tailed deer browsing on riverside vegetation, or skittish antelope bounding along the valley rim. Beavers and badgers will occasionally poke their noses out of their riverbank burrows. Overhead, kestrels and hawks are a constant presence.

Occasionally, you'll catch glimpses of the "real" world: baleful

Writing-on-Stone Provincial Park.

cattle mired in riverside mud, irrigation pumps, fences and cliff-top houses. Though civilization is never far away, it's mostly out of sight, beyond the confines of the river valley. The feel, if not the reality, is of wilderness. There are no official campgrounds between the put-in and Writing-on-Stone. You simply choose your spot roughly midway along the route on one of the flat river terraces. During the night, you'll almost certainly be serenaded by the mournful howls of coyotes.

Early morning is a great time to do some bird spotting. With over 160 species identified, the Milk River is a bird watcher's paradise. The birds range in size from the great blue heron to the ruby-throated hummingbird. Killdeer, sandpipers and curlews are common along the river. Cliff swallows nest by the hundreds beneath overhangs and are a constant presence. If you're sharp-eyed, you might spot the nests of prairie falcons, golden eagles or ferruginous

hawks on the high sandstone ledges.

As the river winds its way toward Writing-on-Stone, the valley sides become steeper and higher. The river makes sharp turns, undercutting the hillsides and causing extensive slumping. Numerous

When you go

Writing-on-Stone Provincial Park
PO Box 297
Milk River, AB T0K 1M0
Tel: (403) 647-2364

coulees branch off from the main river valley and are well worth exploring as a break from paddling. Scramble up the steep-sided coulees to the top for a panoramic view of the river and the distant Sweetgrass Hills in Montana.

Two leisurely days of paddling will bring you to Writing-on-Stone Provincial Park. This area had special significance for the Plains people, mostly Blackfoot and Shoshone,

who left behind over 50 rock art sites depicting thousands of figures. The 7-square-mile (18-square-kilometer) park was created in 1957 to protect the rock art, some of which is thought to be up to 3,000 years old. The more recent petroglyphs depict the arrival of horses and guns in the mid-1700s.

The most famous site is the Battle Scene, an elaborate rock art carving that is thought to depict a battle between the Peigans and Gros Ventre in 1866. It is part of the self-guided Hoodoo Interpretive Trail that parallels the river for one and a quarter miles (2 kilometers) and ends at the Police Post viewpoint. The old NWMP post lies across the river at the entrance to Police Coulee, an old whiskey smuggling route.

The western section of the park is an archaeological preserve that is closed to casual visitors. Park interpreters provide daily guided tours into the preserve from mid-May through Labor Day. Phone ahead for tour times and information.

Milk River in Writing-on-Stone Provincial Park.

Elk Island National Park

" Oh give me a home, where the buffalo roam. " Gone are the days when this lonesome cowboy's yearning could possibly be fulfilled. The millions of buffalo that once roamed freely across the vast prairies have all but disappeared, hunted nearly to extinction. Fortunately, before they were totally wiped out, these massive animals were recognized as a valuable species – apart from simply providing meat and hides.

Originally created to protect what was believed to be one of the last remaining herds of elk on the prairies, Elk Island National Park is better known these days for its herds of buffalo, or "bison" as they're commonly called in the scientific community. Located 28 miles (45 kilometers) east of Edmonton, the 75-square-mile (194-square-kilometer) park is Canada's only entirely fenced national park, creating an "island" sanctuary for the bison and many other wildlife species. The region, about 200 feet (60 meters) higher than the surrounding plains, is characterized by "knob and kettle" features – small hills and depressions typical of a glacier-scarred landscape.

Two distinct herds of bison are protected in the park – wood bison and plains bison – along with an estimated 1,700 elk, about 350 moose and healthy populations of deer and coyote. And while many visitors are drawn to the park to view the wildlife, where its small size and fenced enclosures ensure great opportunities, the park is also well known for its network of over 60 miles (100 kilometers) of trails for hiking and cross-country skiing. Most trails are easy

When you go

Elk Island National Park
RR#1, Site 4
Fort Saskatchewan, AB T8L 2N7
Tel: (780) 992-2950
Fax: (780) 992-2951
E-mail: elk_island@pch.gc.ca

Plains bison, Elk Island National Park.

outings suitable for families. In the summer, wear waterproof hiking boots or rubber boots, as the trails are often wet and muddy.

One major road, the Elk Island Parkway, gives access to the trailheads north of Highway 16, starting with Tawayik Lake. One of over 250 lakes and ponds that cover 20 percent of the park's area, Tawayik is a resting place for birds on migration, and a sanctuary in which to nest and raise their young. A boardwalk extends over the lake's marshy shoreline, and two spotting scopes on raised platforms are well positioned for bird watching.

Three trails start from the picnic area. The Tawayik Lake Trail leads to the "narrows" at Little Tawayik Lake, 3 miles (5 kilometers) away. The narrows are flooded all summer and impassable to hikers, but in the winter, you can ski a full 10.5-mile (16.8-kilometer) circuit around Tawayik Lake, linking up with the Shirley Lake Trail and ending at the parking lot. From here, the short, 2.8-mile (4.6-kilometer) Simmon's Trail is a good challenge on skinny skis, traversing large meadows and open aspen forests over rolling hills.

East of the parkway is the 7.5-mile (12-kilometer) Hayburger Trail, which leads through generally flat terrain where plains bison graze. Plains bison, once numbering in the millions in the 1700s, were depleted to near extinction with the introduction of the horse and rifle. In 1907, the Canadian government shipped nearly 400 bison from Montana to Elk Island park, and later to present-day Wood Buffalo National Park, in an effort to re-establish a herd. About 50 remained in Elk Island, becoming the nucleus of today's herd, which now numbers over 600. Along the Hayburger Trail and throughout the park, you'll notice the "wallows" – depressions in the meadows or on hillsides where bison roll in the dirt, scratching and dusting themselves in the summer heat.

Farther along the parkway is the trailhead for Moss Lake Trail. The knob and kettle terrain makes this 8-mile (13-kilometer) trail the most challenging in the park for cross-country skiers. In the spring and summer, the many ponds, meadows and marshes are great wildlife-viewing grounds.

Eight and a half miles (14 kilometers) north of Highway 16 is the Astotin Lake area, where most of the park's services and facilities are concentrated. During the 1920s and '30s, Sandy Beach, on the east shore of the lake, was a lively meeting place for people from miles around who gathered for family picnics and ball games. No motorboats are allowed on the lake, which means both wildlife and canoeists can enjoy the quiet waters.

In the Astotin Lake area, several short but very interesting trails lead through wetlands on floating boardwalks, past busy beaver ponds and through sedge meadows. Beaver, muskrat, moose and bison are often seen, and interpretive exhibits explain the history and geography of the park. Each fall until freeze-up, Astotin Lake may be closed to allow young trumpeter swans introduced to the park lakes to bond to adult birds that use the lakes for "staging" before their migration south to the United States.

South of Highway 16, a 12-mile (19-kilometer) loop trail around Flyingshot Lake once led through the wood bison enclosure. Due to heavy flooding caused by beaver dams, the trail is now closed, but the wood bison are easily seen from the highway. Like their plains cousins, wood bison suffered drastic reduction in their numbers, from a peak of about 170,000 to a low of 300 in 1891. In 1965, 23 wood bison were shipped to Elk Island to ensure the survival of the species. Today, about 400 roam freely in the fenced portion of the park south of Highway 16, where they are isolated from the plains bison.

When walking or skiing in the park, exercise caution around both wood and plains bison. These huge animals can be dangerous and should be given a wide berth. Especially avoid close encounters during the rut, from late July throughout the fall.

Moose on Elk Island.

Cypress Hills Interprovincial Park

The Cree called them the "beautiful highlands," forested hills that rise nearly 2,000 feet (600 meters) above the surrounding plains, reaching an elevation of 4,566 feet (1,392 meters) across a plateau 80 miles (130 kilometers) long. In places, the elevation is higher than the town of Banff in the Rocky Mountains, and the stands of lodgepole pines are native to the foothills of the Rockies. Yet these are the Cypress Hills, surrounded on all sides by the prairies and cattle ranches of southern Saskatchewan and Alberta.

The lodgepole pines are a welcome oddity on this prairie plateau. First Nations people lived in the Cypress Hills for at least 7,000 years, using the straight shafts of the lodgepole pine for construction of their lodges, teepees and travois. In the mid-1800s, Métis families established wintering grounds in the hills, camping in the protection of the coulees and hunting game in the forests that wasn't found on the open prairie. French-Canadian fur traders mistook the coniferous stands for the jack pines found in Quebec. Called *cyprès* in French, the colorful misnomer has never been replaced.

This is Cypress Hills Interprovincial Park, the highest point of land between the Rockies and Labrador. Straddling the Saskatchewan/Alberta border, it was proclaimed Canada's first interprovincial park in 1989. There are three sections to the park: the Centre Block in Saskatchewan, separated from the West Block by a 12.5-mile (20-kilometer) valley called The Gap, and the Alberta portion. Three secondary roads access the park from the Trans-Canada Highway. An east–west road links Saskatchewan's Centre Block with the West Block, but a couple of long clay and gravel stretches make it impassable in wet weather.

At the core of Saskatchewan's Centre Block is a small resort surrounding the tiny Loch Leven. The park's administration office and nature center are located here, as well as several summer campgrounds and a large hotel. Loch Leven was created in 1931 – the year the park was established – by damming a creek. Loch Leven and Loch Lomond are the only bodies of water in the park large enough to be explored by boat, and canoes are available for rent. The lakes are stocked with rainbow trout, making them popular fishing spots.

Two driving tours are suggested to familiarize yourself with the park's features. You can stand at any of the lookout points en route and watch the hawks soaring overhead, in search of a dinner of rodents in the prairies below.

Three self-guided nature trails allow easy exploration of the woodland, wetland and grassland environments found in the park. Because of their elevation, the Cypress Hills have a wetter and milder climate than the plains, and the variety of ecosystems supports a wealth of wildlife. Elk, moose, deer, lynx, bobcat, coyote and pronghorn antelope are some of the larger mammals at home in the park. And about 200 species of birds have been recorded

Cypress Hills Interprovincial Park.

Fort Walsh National Historic Site, Cypress Hills Interprovincial Park.

here, including wild turkeys, trumpeter swans, sharp-tailed grouse, saw-whet owls and the mountain bluebird. Plant species far removed from their normal range are found in abundance in the hills, among them 18 species and two varieties of the exquisite orchid family.

Cypress Hills is a geological anomaly. The hills were formed from deposits of sand and gravel washed down from large rivers spilling off the newly forming Rocky Mountains about 55 to 65 million years ago. During the last Ice Age, giant glaciers scoured the surrounding plains, but left the top 330 feet (100 meters) of the Cypress Hills unscathed.

The West Block is considered the "wild" section of the park, with thick forest, open grassland and steeply contoured coulees. Hiking is permitted on the newly constructed 12.5-mile (20-kilometer) stretch of the Trans Canada Trail, opened in 1997. Hikers can stay at primitive campgrounds just off Battle Creek Road, and equestrians have the use of a separate campground with cor-

When you go

Cypress Hills Interprovincial Park
PO Box 850
Maple Creek, SK S0N 1N0
Tel: (306) 662-4411

Cypress Hills Provincial Park
PO Box 12
Elkwater, AB T0J 1C0
Tel: (403) 893-3777

rals, a small paddock and parking for trailers. Check with park staff before setting out and take plenty of water, food and extra clothing. Temperatures can reach 104°F (40°C), and snow has been recorded in nearly every month of the year!

Fort Walsh National Historic Site, on the southern edge of the West Block, is the site of a reconstructed North West Mounted Police fort and replicas of two trading posts. It's well worth a stop to learn about the Plains Indians, the history of the fort and how the West was "tamed."

The small community on Elkwater Lake, 21 miles (34 kilometers) south of the Trans-

Canada on Highway 41, is also the administrative center of the Alberta section of the park. The village offers a range of facilities, from boat and bike rentals to a sandy beach and visitor's center where you can pick up maps and hiking brochures. Guided walks are offered throughout the summer. There is motel and campground accommodation in Elkwater, and 12 other campgrounds scattered throughout the park.

A number of trails from half a mile to 5 miles (1 to 8 kilometers) long offer a variety of hiking experiences. You can stroll along the shoreline of Elkwater Lake or climb up to the plateau for striking views over the hills toward Montana. Mountain biking is also popular, and bikes are permitted on three trails.

During the winter, the park grooms 25 miles (40 kilometers) of trails for cross-country skiing. In Saskatchewan's Centre Block, a further 15 miles (24 kilometers) of trails are available. Both sections offer snowshoeing and ice fishing.

Grasslands National Park

You are surrounded. There's no escape from the endless sky, the boundless prairie and the longest horizon you've ever seen bisecting the two. You are a flag on the landscape, sticking out like the proverbial sore thumb. And you are likely the only person for miles.

Grasslands National Park in southwestern Saskatchewan is not a place to go for human company. The land seems vast and empty, perhaps a bit lonely. But patience and a keen eye will reward you with a surprising amount of activity on the subtle prairie landscape.

Grasslands is a park in progress.

In 1984 the federal government began acquiring land to preserve one of the largest areas of virtually undisturbed mixed shortgrass prairie in North America. On a willing-seller basis, and with Crown land donated by the provincial government, the land accumulated has grown to over half of the park's 350-square-mile (900-square-kilometer) objective.

The park is divided into two distinct sections. The West Block, accessed near the village of Val Marie, takes in a portion of the Frenchman River Valley. In what was once a glacial meltwater channel, the receding ice left deeply dissected plateaus, coulees and buttes. The East Block, accessed near the town of Wood Mountain, features the prehistoric Killdeer Badlands. Untouched by glaciation, multi-colored layers of bedrock reveal 60,000 years of eroded strata. It was here, in 1874, that the first dinosaur

Grasslands National Park is home to more than 50 species of grasses.

Indian teepee ring, Grasslands National Park.

remains in Canada were found and recorded.

Plains Indians once hunted bison in the grasslands, and you can still see remnant teepee rings, medicine wheels and vision-quest sites on the hilltops. Today, pronghorn antelope and white-tailed deer gallop across the grassy ridges where bison once grazed. By the late 1800s, cattle replaced the bison, ranching prospered, and homesteading was encouraged. The semi-arid environment has taken its toll, however, and derelict buildings attest to the abandoned dreams of early settlers.

But a different kind of community thrives in this desert-like region: the black-tailed prairie dog towns. These are Canada's only colonies of this small mammal. Standing on their haunches, guarding their burrows, they chirp out warnings of danger – when coyotes approach, or ferruginous hawks circle above. These and many other rare or endangered species are found throughout Grasslands. The burrowing owl, sage

When you go

Grasslands National Park
PO Box 150
Val Marie, SK S0N 2T0
Tel: (306) 298-2257
Fax: (306) 298-2042

grouse and the noisy long-billed curlew all make their homes in the short grasses, sage brush and wide open spaces of the prairies.

As might be expected, there are many species of grasses in the park – more than 50 in all. Their growth depends on the slope, aspect and soil type, and many birds and animals depend on the grasses for food and shelter. The lush valley bottoms and moist coulees support trembling aspen, Manitoba maple, wolf willow and thorny buffalo berry. Where it's drier, sage mosses, lichens and cacti take hold.

Grasslands is largely a do-it-yourself park. Visitors can start by driving the self-guided Frenchman River Valley Ecotour in the West Block, or by hiking the Two Trees

Interpretive Trail (1 mile/ 1.5 kilometers), the only designated trail in the park. Horseback riding is an excellent way to cover large areas, and local outfitters can arrange pack trips or shorter trail rides. You can hike anywhere, but be sure you have sturdy hiking boots with ankle coverage to protect you from prickly cactus spines. You may also want to carry a stick to brush through the grass as you walk – prairie rattlesnakes aren't overly common, but it would be best to avoid an encounter.

A stop at the Visitor Reception Centre in Val Marie is absolutely essential. Not only will they provide you with maps and self-guiding brochures, you'll be able to fill up on water. Once you're in the park, there are no facilities, no toilets and no water; you must carry at least two pints (two liters) of water per person per day. There's a campground in Val Marie if you plan to make day trips to the park; otherwise, random camping is permitted in the park.

Last Mountain Lake National Wildlife Area

Many of Canada's best wetlands have been lost forever, drained and plowed under for crops or filled in for building developments. Fortunately, over a century ago, in 1887, a handful of concerned individuals convinced the federal government to set aside a 3.8-square-mile (10-square-kilometer) area as a migratory bird sanctuary. Thus, the site became the first wildlife sanctuary in North America. Located at the northern end of Last Mountain Lake about 90 miles (150 kilometers) north of Regina, the protected area was expanded in the 1960s and now occupies over 60 square miles (156 square kilometers) of wetlands and grasslands strictly devoted to birds and other wildlife.

Situated in the heart of North America's central flyway, Last Mountain Lake is an important migratory stopover for an astounding number of birds traveling between northern breeding grounds and southern wintering grounds. They've been coming to the north end of the lake for centuries, attracted to the warm, shallow bays, islands and neighboring marshes for the opportunity to rest and feed.

The statistics are mind-boggling: 50,000 cranes, 450,000 geese, several hundred thousand ducks, scores of songbirds, shore birds and birds of prey – in all over 280 species have been recorded during migration. Some travel incredible distances. The sandhill crane, for example, flies 3,600 miles (5,800 kilometers) from Alaska to Mexico, stopping for a month in the autumn to rest and feed at the wildlife area in preparation for the rest of the journey south. Even more remarkable is the distance covered by the lesser golden plover – more than 9,300 miles (15,000 kilometers) from the high Arctic islands to its winter home in Argentina.

Equally significant are the thousands of birds that spend the summer at Last Mountain Lake to nest and raise their young. It's an important breeding ground for over a hundred species such as western grebe, American white pelican, American avocet and Wilson's phalarope. Nine of Canada's 36 vulnerable, threatened and endangered birds find appropriate habitat here, including peregrine falcon, piping plover, whooping crane, burrowing owl, ferruginous hawk, loggerhead shrike, Baird's sparrow, Caspian tern and Cooper's hawk.

Here in the wetlands and on the mixed-grass prairie that borders the lake, every species finds a habitat that's just right. The wetlands are the most complex and most productive of bird habitats. Wet meadows, ponds, marshes, sloughs, mudflats and streams are rich with small plants, insects and animals that provide food for the birds. The marshy edges supply nesting material, shelter and hiding places. Cattails and sedges are homes for species such as the yellow-headed blackbird, while red-winged blackbirds prefer shallow marshes. American bitterns and herons live in the marshes and canals where they feast on minnows, snails and frogs.

Bordering the wetlands is

Aerial view of Last Mountain Lake National Wildlife Area.

Pelicans, Last Mountain Lake.

mixed-grass prairie, dotted with aspen groves and dense clumps of shrubs. The birds and animals that live here have adapted to the environment. Coloring, nesting habits, songs and food sources are quite different from those of their cousins living in the wetlands. The gray-brown color of savannah sparrows and the sharp-tailed grouse, for example, blends well with the grassland. Clay-colored sparrows nest in shrubs, while vesper sparrows nest on the ground and use the shrubs as singing perches. All have adapted to different environments, thereby spreading out the competition for food.

Farmland, too, plays a valuable part. Local farmers are contracted to seed "lure" crops to attract migrant birds and reduce crop damage on nearby farms. They also adjust their swathing of hay to avoid disturbing duck nests. It's a cooperative effort between humans and avians. The raucous sandhill cranes, which feed on the lure crops, do their part for the farmer by keeping grasshoppers

and other insects at bay. Over 50,000 ducks and several thousand geese and cranes may feed on a single lure crop at one time.

Humans have further intervened by building islands and platforms to encourage birds to nest. These isolated homes keep birds safe from predators such as coyotes, foxes and skunks. Dams built by Ducks Unlimited hold water in the wetlands during the summer, encouraging birds to remain in the protected environment of Last Mountain Lake.

Although the area has been set aside for wildlife, many outdoor activities are offered during daylight hours. Stop at the information kiosk and pick up a map and brochures on the wildlife area, and check the

When you go

Canadian Wildlife Service
PO Box 280
Simpson, SK S0G 4M0
Tel: (306) 836-2022
Fax: (306) 836-2010

notice board for current information. A 10-mile (16-kilometer) driving tour and two short nature trails, one through mixed-grass prairie, the other along a boardwalk through a marsh, provide amazing opportunities to learn about the interdependence of habitat, birds, animals and humans. Of course you'll have your binoculars, but wear a hat and carry some water as well on these walks — the summer temperatures can reach a parching 104°F (40°C). Late September and early October are the best times to observe migrating birds, but there is still plenty to see during the spring and summer as well.

There is no overnight camping permitted in the wildlife area, but the nearby Last Mountain Regional Park has sites and a boat launch. Always remember that your actions can disturb the birds; if you're canoeing or boating on Last Mountain Lake, stay clear of its northern shore and the nesting islands from May until the end of October.

Athabasca Sand Dunes

Northern Saskatchewan is probably the least likely place in Canada where you might expect to find sand dunes that would make any Bedouin feel at home. Yet there they are, stretching for 60 miles (100 kilometers) on the south shore of Lake Athabasca, the result of a unique interplay of climatic and geologic forces.

The dune fields, the largest in Canada, were formed some 8,000 years ago when the shoreline of glacial Lake Athabasca began to recede. Lake-bottom sediments, mostly sand scraped from areas of bedrock south of the lake, were exposed, dried and reworked into dunes by powerful winds. In fact, the areas of sand that are not stabilized by vegetation are still being reworked into an ever-changing dunescape.

In order to protect the fragile vegetation and unique plant species that fight for survival in this harsh environment, the 775-square-mile (2,000-square-kilometer) area

encompassing the dunes was declared a provincial wildlife park in 1992.

There is no road access to the park, but visitors can charter floatplanes or boats from communities near Lake Athabasca to reach various areas of the park. Guided nature-based tours are also available.

The best examples of active dunes are in the western section of the park, along the William River and at Thomson Bay. These dune fields cover 64 and 37 square miles (166 and 97 square kilometers) respectively. In some areas shifting sands have exhumed buried trees and exposed tree root systems, leaving behind bizarre landscapes. In

other areas the sand is encroaching on live vegetation, slowly burying it.

The William River dunes can be accessed by canoe or on foot. Canoeists usually fly in to Carswell Lake and paddle downstream about 35 miles (60 kilometers) to the start of the dunes. The river is challenging because of shallow water, rock gardens and ledges, and a maze of channels between the dunes and the lake. It is best paddled in June to take advantage of the highest water levels.

After four or five days of paddling and portaging, the first dunes appear as massive, 65-foot-high (20-meter-high) banks of white sand lining the west bank of the river. Boreal forest lines the opposite bank, creating a surreal scene. The largest dunes, some up to 100 feet (30 meters) high and half a mile (a kilometer) long, are set back from the river but can be reached on foot in an hour or so. The steep dune faces and sinuous ridges form a desert landscape of raw beauty. The dune field continues for about 15 miles (25 kilometers) to the William River delta, where it abruptly ends. Here the sand-choked river braids into countless shallow channels before flowing into Lake Athabasca.

Alternatively, you can hike to the dunes from Thomson Bay, a 17-mile (28-kilometer) stretch of raised sandy beaches on the south shore of Lake Athabasca. A 3-mile (5-kilometer) hike from the designated primitive campsite on the bay, one of six campsites in the park, brings you to the William River delta, which you must cross by wading the shallow, braided channels. The main dune field is to the south. This is a day-use area only; no camping or fires are allowed.

Despite their appearance, parts of the dune fields are very delicate, especially the desert pavement or

Aerial photo of the Athabasca Sand Dunes.

The Athabasca Sand Dunes.

gobi, a thin layer of stones and pebbles on top of the sand that can be permanently damaged by hikers. Take care to walk only on loose sand. The dunes also harbor ten endemic plant species that are found nowhere else in the world. These range from the relatively abundant felt-leaved willow and sea lime-grass (supposedly used in the past for both food and as padding in boots!) to the rare and beautiful inland sea-thrift. Pink wintergreen, yellow sand heather and purple fireweed create islands of color in the dune slacks, the more moist sheltered areas between the bigger dunes. Avoid disturbing any vegetation in the dune areas.

The eastern edge of the park is roughly defined by the course of the

When you go

Saskatchewan Environment and Resource Management
General Delivery
Stoney Rapids, SK S0J 2R0
Tel: (306) 439-2062
Fax: (306) 439-2036

Recommended Reading

Karpan, Robin, and Arlene Karpan. *Northern Sandscapes: Exploring Saskatchewan's Athabasca Sand Dunes.* Saskatoon: Parkland Publishing, 1998.

MacFarlane River, a very technical and demanding river for paddlers. It should be attempted only by experienced canoeists with good whitewater skills. However, the river does flow through some spectacular scenery before encountering the Yakow Lake dune field close to Lake

Athabasca. These dunes can also be reached on foot from the lakeshore.

It's possible to paddle the entire length of the lakeshore from William River to the MacFarlane River, a distance of about 60 miles (100 kilometers). However, this is a serious undertaking because of Lake Athabasca's notorious wind and waves. You could well be shorebound for days at a time waiting out a storm.

The Athabasca sand dunes are not easy to reach and travel through, but your efforts and perseverance will be rewarded with a unique experience. Nowhere else in Canada will you see desert landscapes such as these and endemic plants that are found nowhere else in the world.

Prince Albert National Park

Right smack dab in the middle of Saskatchewan, where you might expect to see combines cutting swaths of golden grain on plains as flat as glass, you find instead a landscape in transition. The wide-open prairie and parkland to the south gradually give way to the boreal forest and lakes of the north. Bridging the two worlds is Prince Albert National Park.

Less than an hour's drive north of the city of Prince Albert, this 1,496-square-mile (3,875-square-kilometer) expanse encompasses more than 1,500 lakes, numerous rivers, varied forests and huge areas of inaccessible muskeg. Sitting as it does between two different environments, the park is home to a wide variety of bird and animal life, including parkland residents such as deer, elk and fox, and those who prefer the boreal forest – moose, black bear and wolves. Beaver, otter, fisher and marten live near lakes and ponds, and over 200 species of birds take to the skies above. The park

protects a herd of about 175 plains bison that roam the southwestern part of the park, where a pocket of Canada's last remaining fescue grassland is preserved. More than 15,000 white pelicans nest at Lavallée Lake in the north end of the park, and although the area is closed to the public, you can often see these odd-looking birds feeding on other lakes throughout the park.

Many visitors to Prince Albert come specifically to hike or paddle to Beaver Lodge, home of the legendary Grey Owl. Both routes start at Kingsmere River at the end of Kingsmere Road, about 20 miles (32 kilometers) from the town of

Waskesiu, the park's main center. Hikers follow the east bank of the Kingsmere River; paddlers canoe up the shallow river then portage 440 yards (400 meters) into Kingsmere Lake. It's a 9-mile (15-kilometer) paddle up the lake, and an equal distance on land, to the Northend Campground, situated on a wide bay with a long, sandy beach. Then it's a 1.8-mile (3-kilometer) hike to Grey Owl's cabin on Ajawaan Lake. It was here that the well known conservationist wrote three of his books, two of which were inspired by the antics of Rawhide and Jellyroll, orphaned beaver kits raised by Grey Owl.

There are a number of other hiking trails, accessible from Highways 2 and 263, the main arteries leading into the park. Short walking trails such as the Treebeard Trail, Waskesiu River Trail, Amiskowan Trail, Narrows Peninsula, Mud Creek Trail, and Boundary Bog are good introductions to the park's variety of habitat and take less than a few hours to hike. You can follow lakeshore trails along sandy beaches, walk through cool aspen forest or white spruce and balsam fir forests shading luxurious fern beds. You'll be delighted with the sedge meadows and black spruce bogs, always lively with birds and aquatic life.

The 5.3-mile (8.5-kilometer) Spruce River Highlands Trail is short and steep in parts, with panoramic views of rolling glacial hills and aspen stands. In the spring and early summer, the hillside meadows are covered in wildflowers, while autumn turns the trees a golden hue. The historic Freight Trail, 16.8 miles (27 kilometers) in its entirety, may be

Mud creek in winter, Prince Albert National Park.

Prince Albert National Park in summer.

broken into three smaller chunks. Late in the 19th century, the road was used to haul furs and logging supplies between Prince Albert and La Ronge.

In all, the park offers about 90 miles (150 kilometers) of hiking trails; six trails are open to mountain biking. These are located primarily in the southern section of the park and range in length from 3 to 38 miles (5 to 61.5 kilometers). Three short trails take you to Anglin, Fish and Hunters lakes, where you can camp and fish. The Freight Trail is open to cyclists, as is the 24-mile (39-kilometer) Elk Trail, a challenging route through long grass and over rolling hills. The Westside Boundary Trail covers some of the most interesting parts of the park, including the Sturgeon River Valley and the fescue grasslands where the plains bison roam.

Horseback riding is permitted on a number of trails in the southern portion of the park, notably those leading to Fish, Camp and Hunters lakes, and other trails accessed from the Cookson Road. Information on commercially guided horse trips is available from the park.

Canoeing is one of the best ways to see the park. There are a number of small, quiet lakes to explore, including the Hanging Heart Lakes, Trapper's Lake, Shady Lake and Sandy Lake. The Narrows on Waskesiu Lake is an ideal place for bird watching, and all the lakes are good for fishing and swimming.

The Bagwa canoe route is one of the finest short trips in the park. It can be paddled in a day, but taking two days would allow more time to explore. It begins at Pease Point on Kingsmere Lake and connects with Bagwa, Lily and Clare lakes, ending again on Kingsmere. Great blue herons, blue-winged teal and red-necked grebe nest and feed on these small, shallow lakes, and white pelicans are often seen throughout the route.

The Bladebone canoe route is something of an epic, taking nearly a week to complete, and traveling through a chain of remote lakes. From Bladebone Bay at the northwest end of Kingsmere Lake, it's a 30-mile (50-kilometer) loop with up to 14 miles (22 kilometers) of portaging. This demanding trip is rewarded with good fishing and plenty of opportunities for wildlife viewing.

Prince Albert has a very active winter season. When the snow flies, the hiking trails are packed and groomed for all levels of cross-country skier; the frozen Waskesiu Lake is available for ice fishing; and snowshoers have the run of the park.

At any time of the year, backcountry camping is administered on a first-come, first-served basis, but all visitors must register first for their backcountry outing.

When you go

Prince Albert National Park
PO Box 100
Waskesiu Lake, SK S0J 2Y0
Tel: (306) 663-4522
Fax: (306) 663-5424

Recommended Reading

Grey Owl. *Pilgrims of the Wild.* Toronto. Macmillan, 1968.

Grey Owl. *Sajo and the Beaver People.* Toronto: Macmillan, 1987.

Grey Owl. *Tales of an Empty Cabin.* London: L. Dickson, 1936.

Moose Mountain Provincial Park

One of Saskatchewan's largest parks is the perfect outdoor playground for families. Located in the southeast corner of the province about two hours from Regina, Moose Mountain Provincial Park offers a full range of amenities and activities on a scale manageable for the novice outdoor enthusiast or families with young children.

Situated on a plateau some 500 feet (150 meters) high and covering 150 square miles (388 square kilometers), Moose Mountain is a treasured height of land in an area dominated by the prairie landscape. The rolling hills, covered in lush aspen forest, were shaped by the receding glaciers after the last Ice Age. Deposits of ice embedded in the land eventually melted to form more than 400 ponds and "potholes" that today support a variety of wetland plants and creatures.

The main center is on Kenosee Lake, where you can choose from a wide assortment of accommodation, including cabins, modest motels and a full-blown resort. As well, restaurants, stores, a riding stable, mini-golf and a waterslide park provide plenty of diversions for family fun. Kenosee Lake is often packed with summer vacationers, but it's not hard to escape the crowds.

Kenosee Lake, Moose Mountain Provincial Park.

A Victorian Dream

Cannington Manor, 16 miles (26 kilometers) southeast of the park, provides an interesting destination for a day trip. In the 1890s, English settlers attempted to create a Victorian society here, complete with fox hunting, cricket matches and croquet. The harsh prairie, however, proved too much for the tea-and-crumpet crowd, and the village slowly died. A few homes, a carpenter's shop and a log church are all that remain, but guides in period costume and interpretive displays tell the story of a faded dream.

Two easy hiking trails have been established in the park; both are suitable for children and seniors. Wuche Sakaw Trail forms a one-and-a-quarter-mile (2-kilometer) loop exploring the birch and aspen forests of Pickerel Point on Kenosee Lake. For kids, the marshy lakeshore is full of exciting things to discover. Blue-winged teal and pintail ducks and a whole host of other waterfowl are attracted to the wetlands, and great blue herons nest near the lake. In the early evening, you might see one of these beauties taking flight from the marsh, their enormous gray-blue wings carrying them slowly into the forest.

Beaver Lake Trail is 2.8 miles (4.5 kilometers) long and is open to cyclists as well. The self-guiding nature trail passes stations along the way that explain the park's flora and fauna. In the early morning or cool of the evening, moose feed on tender green shoots sprouting from the lake bottom. Animals such as the beaver and the porcupine are seldom seen during the day, preferring instead to go about their lives at night and in the early hours of the morning. You may, however, catch a glimpse of a white-tailed deer, elk or coyote, especially along the road.

When you go

Moose Mountain Provincial Park
PO Box 100
Carlyle, SK S0C 0R0
Tel: (306) 577-2600

The beach on Kenosee Lake is always a hub of activity. Swimming, sailing, sailboarding and canoeing are all popular on this warm lake. There is also one canoe trip that is suitable for novice paddlers. The trip is divided into two loops. The smaller loop is about 4 miles (7 kilometers) long and is a good five-hour trip. The second loop continues from the first for a total of 10 miles (16 kilometers). This trip can be done in a long day, but for those who'd like to try a night out, there's a primitive campsite about two-thirds along the way.

During the winter, the park offers 35 miles (57 kilometers) of groomed cross-country ski trails for beginner to expert skiers. Five warm-up shelters are well spaced along the trails. There's also an outdoor skating rink in the village of Kenosee and 75 miles (120 kilometers) of snowmobile trails in a section designated for motorized activity.

Hiking in Moose Mountain Provincial Park.

Spruce Woods Provincial Heritage Park

Ten thousand years ago, what is now mostly agricultural land in Manitoba was flooded by a vast inland sea, the prehistoric Lake Agassiz. In the southwest corner of the province, an area of sand dunes two square miles (5 square kilometers) in size is all that is left of the extensive sandy delta that once covered this region.

The desert-like dunes are only part of Spruce Woods, an area 95 square miles (250 square kilometers) in size that was protected as

a provincial heritage park in 1964. In fact, the park encompasses an amazing variety of landscapes, from the forests of white spruce that stabilize the sands and give the park its name, to marsh wetlands, pots of quicksand and mixed-grass prairie. All this is cut through by the fast-flowing Assiniboine River, which loops from the southwest boundary to the eastern edge of the park on its journey to Lake Winnipeg.

From the city of Winnipeg, it's about a two-hour drive west to Spruce Woods via Highway 5, which dips into the park's western portion, providing access to the Visitor's Centre and the Kiche Manitou Campground. There's a full range of facilities here, including restaurants, stores, canoe rentals and a supervised swimming beach on nearby Kiche Manitou Lake. The crescent-shaped lake is an oxbow, one of many that have been cut off from the Assiniboine River.

You can explore the sand dunes by hiking a short 1.5-mile (2.5-kilometer) trail that takes you across mixed-grass prairie and up onto the dunes of Manitoba's only desert. A further 2.2-mile (3.5-kilometer) trail continues through the Spirit Sands, where pincushion and prickly pear cacti blossom in the spring. The native people considered the dunes sacred, thus the name Spirit Sands. It's easy to feel reverence for these great shifting mountains of sand, towering 100 feet (30 meters) above the surrounding prairie. Another option is to see the dunes as many pioneers did, from a horse-drawn covered wagon. Scheduled wagon rides leave the trailhead two or three times a day during July and August and take about an hour and a half.

A longer trail of 5.3 miles (8.5 kilometers) combines the sand

Sand hill at Spruce Woods Provincial Heritage Park.

dunes with another unique feature, the Devil's Punch Bowl. Surrounded by hundred-year-old spruce, the spring-fed, blue-green pond seems like a mirage – an oasis in the midst of an arid expanse.

North of the sand dunes, the Epinette Creek area offers a system of trails, ranging from 1.8 miles to 15 miles (3 kilometers to 24.2 kilometers), that can be hiked in a few hours or several days. Several campsites are located along the trails, and an overnight cabin at Jackfish Lake can be reserved. Trail riders and mountain bikers also use the trail system.

On various trails throughout the park, you might catch a glimpse of several unique creatures. The Northern prairie skink, the province's only lizard, and the rare Western hognosed snake are both endangered species and are protected in Manitoba. Because of the variety of habitats in the park, over 150 species of birds have been noted. In the wetlands, you're likely to see hooded merganser, while boreal chickadees keep to the spruce forests, and sharp-tailed grouse make their home on the prairie grass-

When you go

Spruce Woods Provincial Heritage Park
PO Box 900
Carberry, MB R0K 0H0
Tel: (204) 834-3223

Visitor Services Centre (May to September)
Tel: (204) 827-2543

lands. On the dunes, you may see the tracks of red fox, white-tailed deer, varying hare and wolf.

During the summer, daytime temperatures can rise to over 86°F (30°C). On hot, sunny days, be sure to wear a hat and sunscreen and carry drinking water. Always keep to the trail; it's easy to lose your bearings, and besides, the dunes especially are very fragile ecosystems.

In the winter, 43 miles (70 kilometers) of groomed trails offer cross-country skiing for novice and intermediate skiers. The Jackfish Lake cabin is available for overnight stays. Other snow-weather activities include tobogganing, skating, snowshoeing and snowmobiling.

Spirit Sands at Spruce Woods Provincial Heritage Park.

Northern prairie skink, Spruce Woods Provincial Heritage Park.

Riding Mountain National Park

When early explorers and fur traders struck out for western Canada, they did so by canoe, one of the least difficult ways to travel in a land crisscrossed by lakes and rivers. Imagine their chagrin when they reached an escarpment abruptly rising 1,300 feet (400 meters) above the surrounding plains of what is now western Manitoba farmland. Beyond the escarpment stretched a plateau over 1,150 square miles (3,000 square kilometers) in size. Because their progress by canoe was effectively blocked, horseback became the only sensible way to proceed.

It was part of the Manitoba Escarpment they encountered, a band of hard shale that has resisted erosion longer than the surrounding bedrock. The vast plateau is now a national park, whose isolation above the prairie landscape offers a sanctuary for wildlife and a wilderness retreat for outdoor enthusiasts.

The escarpment is also the remnant shoreline of ancient glacial Lake Agassiz, which once covered much of Manitoba. Some of the greatest natural diversity in the country occurs on the plateau at the top of the escarpment. Riding Mountain National Park lies at the crossroads of three different vegetative regions. Eastern hardwood forest, native prairie grasslands and northern boreal forest support plant and animal communities that account for Riding Mountain's wide diversity of species. On any of the 250 miles (400 kilometers) of trails throughout the park you might see elk, deer, moose, black bear and coyote, or even signs of the Canada lynx and timber wolf.

Seven interpretive trails, all less than 2.5 miles (4 kilometers) long, lead through various landscapes with unique features. Signage en route or self-guiding pamphlets explain the effect of fire, or demonstrate how glaciers shaped the land thousands of years ago. Some trails lead through the heart of the boreal forest, where "prairie potholes" – kettle ponds formed by chunks of melting glaciers – are home to a wide range of waterfowl such as canvasbacks and hooded mergansers.

Several longer trails will take the better part of a day to complete. The 4-mile (6.4-kilometer) Gorge Creek Trail affords impressive views over the checkered farmland below. If you can arrange a vehicle at the Birches picnic site, you'll avoid doubling the distance – and the steep 1,050-foot (320-meter) climb back up the escarpment.

The 11-mile (17.5-kilometer) (round trip) Grey Owl Trail leads to the cabin occupied by this famous conservationist during the summer of 1931, before he transferred to Prince Albert National Park. This is an excellent mountain biking route through aspen and spruce forests, past small lakes and ponds. The trail is easily negotiated, even by novice cyclists.

Several overnight trails explore the eastern edge of the park. These include the 15.5-mile (24.9-kilometer) Ochre River Trail, the South Escarpment Trail (14.4 miles/23.2 kilometers) and the North Escarpment Trail, which links up with Jet, Packhorse and Bald Hill trails to form different loops of varying lengths. Backcountry campsites are situated along each route.

The Central Road from Lake

Horseback riding through wildflower meadows, Riding Mountain National Park.

Audy to the westernmost portion of the park extends 45 miles (73 kilometers) through rough fescue grassland, rolling hills and meadows, aspen forest, ponds and marshes. Most suitable for cycling or trail riding, many trails branch off from the Central Road, providing endless opportunities for exploration.

In 1930 when Riding Mountain National Park was established, it was named for the use of horses as the traditional mode of transportation through the park. Early park wardens patrolled Riding Mountain on horseback, a practice that continues even now. Today, trail riding is a very popular activity, and one of the easiest ways to cover long distances. A number of outfitters are licensed to operate in the park, providing a variety of services from one-hour rides to overnight pack trips. If you have your own horses, you can book the horse corrals at Lake Audy, where there's ample parking for trucks and trailers.

The community of Wasagaming, located just inside the south entrance on Clear Lake, is the park's center for facilities and services. Besides offering a variety of accommodation, the community also has shops, restaurants and the park's Visitor Centre. The swimming beach on Clear Lake is popular on a hot, sunny day, as are canoeing and fishing.

East of the townsite on Highway 19 is the Shawenequanape Kipichewin (formerly Lake Katherine) Campground, operated independently by the Anishinabe First Nation. Forty teepees are available for rent, and the camp offers interpretive programs, cultural experiences and day tours – a wonderful opportunity to become immersed in Anishinabe culture.

Winter on Riding Mountain is a very active time, with reliable snowpack from January to March. The park offers trails to suit all levels of ability. Over 150 miles (250 kilometers) on 30 trackset trails range from the easy 1-mile (1.5-kilometer) loop at Wasagaming Campground to the long and difficult 16-mile (25.6-kilometer) Crawford Creek route. Most of the trackset trails are graded easy or moderate, and many of these are located in and around the townsite of Wasagaming.

If you're looking for a little more rugged experience, a further 15.5 miles (25 kilometers) of trails are regularly packed but not trackset, and over 25 miles (40 kilometers) are rated "wilderness" trails. These include the North and South Escarpment routes, both approximately 11 miles (18 kilometers) long, and the 4.8-mile (7.8-kilometer) Cowan Lake Trail. Winter camping is allowed at any of the designated campsites on the wilderness trails, provided you obtain a backcountry permit. A comfortable backcountry shelter, the Cairns Cabin on the Ochre River Trail, is available for overnight use for a fee of $10 per person per night. The cabin sleeps eight people and is equipped with a stove for heat and cooking.

When you go

Riding Mountain National Park
Wasagaming, MB R0J 2H0
Tel: 1-800-707-8480
Tel: (204) 848-7275/7272
Fax: (204) 848-2866

Grey Owl's cabin, Riding Mountain National Park.

Seal River

Northern Manitoba is a region of nearly 2,000 miles (3,200 kilometers) of wilderness waterways that offer a lifetime of canoeing opportunities. One of the wildest and most pristine rivers is the Seal, with its headwaters at Shethanei Lake, 620 miles (1,000 kilometers) north of Winnipeg, and its finish at Hudson Bay. The 12- to 14-day journey down the river takes you through some incredible northern landscapes and is a wildlife watcher's Eden. In 1992 a 160-mile (260-kilometer) section from the junction of the North and South Seal rivers to Hudson Bay was designated a Heritage River.

The trip is for experienced canoeists only, but less experienced paddlers can raft the river in safety with an outfitter. (Travel Manitoba will provide names of recommended outfitters.) Most trips start at Tadoule Lake, 185 miles (300 kilometers) by air north of Thompson. From here until journey's end at Churchill you won't see a road or bridge. The first few days involve lake paddling through superb subarctic boreal forest, with unusually large white spruce and tamarack. But even the first few days can be exciting when strong winds whip up whitecaps on the sizable lakes.

Downstream from Shethanei Lake the pace of the river starts to pick up. For the next 150 miles (240 kilometers) the current is strong and there are numerous Class II and III rapids. It's here that you might start to see harbor seals that have made their way upstream from Hudson Bay.

The most striking features along the upper stretch of the river are the eskers. These north–south serpentine ridges of sand and gravel, some up to 100 feet (30 meters) high, are remnants of under-ice rivers that carried meltwater from the

Riding the rapids at Seal River.

Camping at Seal River.

retreating glaciers. They extend for long distances, sometimes hundreds of miles, and are used as travel corridors by caribou, wolf, moose and black bear. In places, wind-eroded eskers have the appearance of desert dunes.

At about the halfway point, Great Island splits the Seal into a north and a south channel. The rapids at Bastion Rock and Nine-Bar Rapids in the south channel are the highlight of this section of river. Skilled canoe-ists and rafters can run the 1.8-mile-long (3-kilometer-long) Nine-Bar Rapids at some water levels, but a spill can have serious consequences.

As the river flows east toward Hudson Bay, or *Tu Cho* to the Dene – "the great body of water"– the boreal forest gives way to tundra, almost treeless terrain with dwarf shrubs and tiny subarctic wildflowers. A close inspection will reveal dwarf rhododendron, marsh ragwort and numerous

lichens and mosses. This is the area favored by caribou that cross the river on their annual migration. The sighting of more birds such as snow geese, Canada geese, Arctic terns, eider ducks and jaegers hint at a large body of water not too far away.

Too soon, the rocky shoreline of Hudson Bay appears, but there is a final treat in store in the form of Deaf Rapids on the Seal River estuary. Because of isostatic rebound – the uplifting of the land after the removal of the vast weight of glaciers – the shoreline has risen almost 65 feet (20 meters) over the centuries. The long, boulder-strewn rapids to tidewater are a technical Class III and make a thrilling finale to an exciting trip.

The estuary is also a place for polar bear sightings. These magnificent creatures must be treated with respect and considered potentially dangerous.

Most groups arrange for air or boat taxi pick-up at the estuary to take them to Churchill. When you travel by boat, another thrill is in store – the opportunity to see beluga whales, narwhal and more harbor seals. Any attempt to paddle down the shoreline is considered quite dangerous because of the vagaries of weather and the presence of polar bears.

Because of the short-lived northern summer, July and August are the best months to paddle the Seal River. You can expect warm, dry, but buggy weather at this time but be prepared for cool, windy and wet conditions. An advantage of the northern summer is that you can take a hike at midnight if the notion appeals to you.

When you go

For free information and personalized travel counseling, call Travel Manitoba, 1-800-665-0040.

Whiteshell Provincial Park

In the beginning, the Creator breathed into a small, white seashell, the *megis*, giving life to the first humans. These people became hunters, fishers and gatherers, nomadic groups that followed the movements of wildlife from place to place throughout the year. Eight thousand years later, the descendants of these first nations, the Anishinabe, follow the path of life set out for them.

Whiteshell Provincial Park, named for the sacred *megis*, has a strong link to native spirituality and

tradition. Within its borders a number of "petroform" sites are preserved. These are rock mosaics that Algonkian people built on the bedrock in various locations

throughout the park. A variety of forms such as snakes, birds and humans were used as sources of healing, instruction and initiation.

Following the natives were fur traders and French explorers such as La Vérendrye, whose 1733 expedition down the Red River was an important event in the development of the West. Later, the railway opened the region to mining, homesteading and, by 1920, recreation. Cottages soon lined the shores of half a dozen lakes, but it wasn't until 1961 that Whiteshell became Manitoba's first provincial park.

Located about a two-hour drive east of Winnipeg, Whiteshell is a large, 1,050-square-mile (2,719-square-kilometer) park dotted with more than 130 lakes. Sport fishing has always been very popular here. Walleye, northern pike, perch and smallmouth bass are found in most of the park's lakes and rivers, and lake trout in West Hawk Lake.

The roads and highways have opened up the park, and Whiteshell is now easily accessible to families out for a few days of camping, picnicking and swimming, as well as to hikers, backpackers and canoe trippers.

The Trans-Canada Highway cuts through the southern corner of the park, past the major resorts at Falcon Lake and West Hawk Lake. You can choose from a huge variety of activities here: for some easy exercise, you can launch your canoe from your campground, or walk along the 1.3-mile (2.2-kilometer) Falcon Creek Trail to a sphagnum bog.

This is one of ten easily accessed short hiking trails – each less than 3 miles (5 kilometers) long and taking from two to four hours to hike. Most require that you wear good hiking boots with solid ankle support; rocky sections can be very slippery when wet. A few are self-

Whiteshell Provincial Park.

guiding trails with excellent pamphlets that give background information about natural and cultural history.

A longer, more difficult trail begins at the Manitoba–Ontario border near West Hawk Lake. The 7.8-mile (12.6-kilometer) Hunt Lake Trail leads north to Indian Bay and returns along the east shore of West Hawk Lake. There are some steep climbs on this trail, but spectacular views as well.

Highway 44, also known as La Vérendrye Trail, leads northwest from the Trans-Canada. On the western edge of the park near the village of Rennie, a short, 1.5-mile (2.5-kilometer) trail makes a loop to Goose Pond at the Alfred Hole Goose Sanctuary. In May and June, the goslings have just hatched and will be busy scurrying after their parents in endless lines on the pond. In September and October, more than a thousand geese come to stage in preparation for migration south. A viewing area inside the sanctuary's Visitor Centre allows you to watch the geese without disturbing them.

Just east of Rennie, La Vérendrye Trail (now Highway 307) turns north. Trails at Brereton Lake and Jessica Lake lead to beaver dams and falls, along rocky ridges

and through boreal forest. At Betula Lake, the short Forester's Footsteps Trail leads through jack pine and red pine plantations where purple crocuses bloom in early May and, a few weeks later, western red lilies and the rare moccasin-flower are a

When you go

Whiteshell Provincial Park
PO Box 4000
Lac de Bonnet, MB R0E 1A0
Tel: (204) 345-1444

delight to find. (A 2.6-mile/ 4.2-kilometer mountain bike loop links with this trail.)

Farther along the highway are the petroform sites at Bannock Point. The Anishinabe still follow tradition here, leaving offerings of cloth or tobacco at the sites. The petroforms and the area surrounding these features are sacred places – please do not disturb them. Continue to Nutimik Lake and visit the Whiteshell Natural History Museum to learn about the boreal forest, Winnipeg River history, and First Nations' culture in the area.

Whiteshell offers one long-distance trail for experienced backpackers. The Mantario Trail is a 41-mile (66-kilometer) route between Caddy Lake in the park's

southern portion and Big Whiteshell Lake in the north. This is a true wilderness hike, leading past pristine lakes and through thick forests of jack pine, tamarack, black spruce and aspen. It takes from three to six days to complete the trek, staying at any of nine primitive campsites along the way. The best time to hike the trail is in August, when it's likely to be driest, but even then hikers will cross wet spots.

With so many lakes to choose from, canoeing is a popular activity. A dozen lakes suitable for casual paddling are also easily accessible from the road. A variety of short sections on the Whiteshell Canoe Route are ideal for novice paddlers. Beginning at Caddy Lake, the route follows part of La Vérendrye's 1733 expedition to the Red River. Another easy paddle – but a fair bit longer – is the 22.5-mile (36-kilometer) route along Hanson's Creek to Frances Lake. Four short portages are required, more depending on the amount of beaver activity.

The park does not provide descriptions of the more involved canoe routes but will gladly review your plans, offer advice and help with specific details. Trip itineraries should be registered with the park before you head out.

American bittern, a popular bird species.

Quetico Provincial Park

The haunting cry of a loon, echoing across a glassy lake. A cow moose and calf standing in a bog, munching on tender shoots. The howl of a lone wolf on a distant hillside. These are the pleasures of a wilderness canoe trip, and there is no better place in Canada to experience them than Quetico Provincial Park.

Located in northwestern Ontario, this enormous wilderness park encompasses 1,837 square miles (4,758 square kilometers) of Canadian Shield country pocked with hundreds of lakes and bogs separated by spruce and pine forests. A maze of interconnecting waterways offers over 900 miles (1,500 kilometers) of canoe routes – a paradise for paddlers looking for peace and solitude.

Quetico has been used as a transportation corridor for thousands of years. Paleo-Indians first lived in the region more than 9,000 years ago, leaving evidence of their existence in the form of stone points, tools and pictographs. More than 30 sites of the red-ocher paintings can be seen on cliff faces bordering numerous lakes. Images of animals, canoes and people, faded over time, tell a story of ancient people.

The Ojibwa lived here when explorers and fur traders such as La Vérendrye, Pierre Radisson, Alexander Mackenzie and Simon Fraser passed through during the 1700s, looking for a route to the West. They were followed two centuries later by settlers, looking for a new life beyond Upper Canada. When the railway was built in 1885, logging the great white and red pines became a lucrative industry. Initially set aside as a forest reserve in 1909, Quetico became a provincial park in 1913. But it wasn't until 1973, when it received its wilderness designation, that resource extraction ceased.

There are six entry points to the park, only one of which can be accessed by car. The Dawson Trail Campground on French Lake, just off the Trans-Canada Highway, provides camping on 106 sites, as well as showers, a laundromat and other amenities. The Information Pavilion here is an important stop for canoe trippers. You can pick up a copy of the park map, discuss your route with knowledgeable staff, bone up on current conditions and pay a visit to the resource library. Slide shows,

Blue sky and calm water in a rocky cove, Quetico Provincial Park.

Photography Tips

- Take a basic course in photography to learn what your camera can do and how to operate it properly.

- Slow down! You'll see more potential photo subjects if you slow your pace and take the time to observe your surroundings.

- The best times of day for shooting are dawn and dusk; the light is best at these times, and wildlife are most active.

- Shoot lots of film! Number your rolls and take detailed notes about exposure, speed, time of day, cloud cover, etc. You'll learn not only from your mistakes, but from your successes as well.

- Use a tripod to avoid blurred photos.

- Travel alone or with a very patient friend who's willing to stop while you set up shots. A quiet friend is essential if you're photographing wildlife.

- If you're photographing wildlife, don't compromise your safety, or that of people around you. Use at least a 300 mm lens to shoot potentially dangerous subjects such as bears, moose and elk. There's no shame in taking wildlife shots from the safety of your car. Minimize disturbance to wildlife, including nesting birds. Get shots from a safe and respectful distance.

---

talks, displays and other programs are offered throughout the summer. Although most people come to Quetico for the canoeing, there are a few hiking trails, one of which can be stretched out to a two- or three-day trip, for those staying at the Dawson Trail Campground.

In Quetico, you can paddle for a day, a week or much longer. With such a large area to explore, you could spend a lifetime of summers visiting the park and still not cover every inch of it. July and August are the peak periods, but even during these months it's possible to have a lake all to yourself if you choose a route off the beaten path. There are approximately 2,200 backcountry campsites, on small rocky islands, in sheltered coves and inlets, or set back in the shelter of the pines where you can enjoy the quiet seclusion. Sand beaches

When you go

Quetico Provincial Park
Ministry of Natural Resources
Atikokan, ON P0T 1C0
Tel: (807) 597-2735

Peace and solitude on Quetico's waters.

and clear water invite a refreshing dip in the heat of the afternoon.

Anyone with wilderness tripping experience will find something suitable in Quetico. With marked portages around all rapids and falls (albeit those less frequently used may be quite overgrown), whitewater skills are not necessary. In the town of Atikokan, a half-hour drive north of French Lake, you can rent or purchase canoeing and camping equipment and stock up on supplies. If a self-organized trip is too daunting, however, you can leave the logistics to the professionals. A number of companies offer fully outfitted trips, or they can drive or fly your party in to remote entry points. A complete list of outfitters and other local services is available from the park office.

Sleeping Giant Provincial Park

From the city of Thunder Bay looking east across the bay to Sibley Peninsula, you can clearly make out the form of a reclining figure – head, shoulders, chest, knees. Poor Nanabosho. The giant was only trying to protect the Ojibwa people from the white man who sought their silver-laden land. He raised a great storm, sank their canoe and drowned the intruders. The Great Spirit, Gitchi Manitou, punished Nanabosho for doing this, turning him to stone.

Nanabosho rests at the tip of Sibley Peninsula, with the cold, tempestuous Lake Superior lapping his feet on one side, and the warmer, calmer waters of Thunder Bay on the other. The white man, who found Nanabosho's secret stash of silver anyway, has honored the legendary figure with a park.

From Thunder Bay, take the Trans-Canada Highway 20 miles (32 kilometers) to the Sleeping Giant Provincial Park turnoff. Highway 587 runs the entire length of the Sibley Peninsula, ending at the little village of Silver Islet. Just offshore is the tiny island where all the fuss began, the discovery of what would prove to

Aerial view of the peninsula at Sleeping Giant Provincial Park.

View of Sleeping Giant Provincial Park.

be the world's richest silver mine. The mine started operations in 1872, but obtaining the mineral was so difficult and hazardous, it eventually closed at the turn of the century. All that is left of the community is a general store, jail, customs house and a number of miners' cabins now used as cottages.

Logging became the major industry – and the reason for protecting the remaining red and white pines in 1944 as Sibley Provincial Park. In 1988, the park was renamed after the giant Nanabosho, whose backbone is formed by a series of five flat topped mesas. Composed of sedimentary rock and capped with a volcanic erosion-resistant

diabase, the mesas rise above Lake Superior, with cliffs at the tip of the peninsula reaching as high as 820 feet (250 meters).

Although there are 50 miles (80 kilometers) of hiking trails throughout the park, the majority of these – and perhaps the most spectacular – are concentrated at the tip of the peninsula. But start your exploration first with a stop at the Visitor Centre at the south end of Marie Louise Lake, about 12.5 miles (20 kilometers) from the park entrance. There are displays on native legends, arctic plants and wetland habitats, and a model mine shaft where you can watch a video on the history of the Silver Islet Mine. Next door at the gate-

house you'll find maps and brochures about the hiking trails.

The ever-present form of Nanabosho draws you to explore the giant's contours, and several trails lead to various parts of his "body." The park's most difficult route is the spectacular 25-mile (40-kilometer) Kabeyun Trail. The full hike takes four days to complete, and you stay at any of 11 back-country campsites along the route. Numerous trails intersecting with the Kabeyun, however, allow you to pare it down into day hikes.

One recommended day trip begins at the Kabeyun South Trailhead just north of the village of Silver Islet. Walk or bike along the old logging road to Lehtinen's Bay,

White-tail deer grazing.

with detours to see the diabase dike formations at Sea Lion and Tee Harbour. Both are examples of differential erosion, in which the softer sedimentary rock has been eaten away, leaving the more resistant volcanic rock exposed – the same process that created the Sleeping Giant mesas.

At Lehtinen's Bay, leave your bike behind and continue to the Chimney. Be very careful along this section – walking across the boulders becomes especially treacherous in wet weather. The grinding climb up the steep, boulder-strewn talus slope, through the Chimney to the Sleeping Giant's knees, is for fit hikers only. In half a mile (1 kilometer) you

gain over 800 feet (250 meters), a strenuous effort even for experienced hikers. At the top, the views east over Lake Superior are spectacular, and an extra scramble will take

When you go

Sleeping Giant Provincial Park
General Delivery
Pass Lake, ON P0T 2M0
Tel: (807) 977-2526

you to an equally impressive panorama of Thunder Bay.

Another great day trip takes you to the Nanabosho Lookout via the Sawyer Bay Trail. You can bike along the abandoned logging road as far as the bay, then hike up the steep trail to the giant's chest and the lookout. You're now standing atop the highest vertical cliffs in Ontario, 820 feet (250 meters) above Lake Superior. Views in every direction are breathtaking.

For those looking for a tamer outing, eight short nature trails are suitable for a morning or afternoon's outing. Interpretive signs on all but two routes describe the features along the way. Apart from visiting picturesque lakes and pretty waterfalls, you'll be traveling through surprisingly diverse terrain: shaded cedar groves; stands of white, red and jack pine; marshes, swamps and barren, glacier-scoured rock. Plants such as cloudberry, bistort and butterwort grow hundreds of miles south of their usual Arctic habitat. The deep, moist ravines on the Sleeping Giant host an amazing 38 species of ferns, and in the bogs and woodlands, 30 species of orchid, two of them rare in Ontario, grow in abundance.

The short Piney Wood Hills Trail leads to a lookout above Joeboy Lake, typically a favorite spot for moose. Yet wildlife patterns in the park have changed over time. The shape of the Sibley Peninsula – narrower at the "neck" – essentially funnels wildlife into the park. Trapped on three sides by water, they tend to remain, resulting in high concentrations of certain species. Demand for

food causes alterations in the plant environment of the park, which in turn affects the wildlife populations. Over many decades, what once were abundant, such as woodland caribou, are now scarce, replaced by moose and white-tailed deer. Another change is occurring, however, and moose numbers are dwindling significantly.

Bird watchers can look for the nearly 200 species of birds that have been recorded in the park along the marshy shores of Pickerel Lake, the southern outlet of Marie Louise Lake and Silver Islet's rocky coast. The 7-mile (11.4-kilometer) Burma Trail, which skirts a number of small inland lakes, is especially good for bird watching.

A visit to the Thunder Cape Bird Observatory situated at the tip of the peninsula is a must for bird enthusiasts. Staff and volunteers there have banded thousands of birds to track their migration routes and patterns. The annual fall migration of three species is particularly interesting; golden eagles, the red-throated loon and the harlequin duck are normally found in the Rocky Mountains, the high Arctic, or on the north Atlantic and north Pacific coasts, not here in Lake Superior country.

There are no overnight canoe routes, but canoeing is permitted on lakes Marie Louise, Lizard, Pickerel and Pounsford. You can rely on a good catch of bass, perch and pike on the lakes, and, in the spring, head to the streams entering Lake Superior for the rainbow trout. Hiking into the smaller inland lakes and streams might land you a dinner of brook trout.

From early January to late March the park is open for winter fun. Thirty miles (50 kilometers) of groomed trails are graded for novice to expert skiers and an additional 9 miles (15 kilometers) of ungroomed snowshoeing trails are open. The annual Sibley Ski Tour, held the first Saturday in March, draws over a thousand participants to join in the family fun and competitive races on circuits of 6, 12 or 30 miles (10, 20 or 50 kilometers).

Voyageur Trail

For a country whose trail-building is in its infancy – especially when compared to Britain and Europe – Canada is developing a bit of a reputation for hiking trails. And long hiking trails at that. Across the country, trail groups everywhere are busy planning, building and maintaining hiking trails. All are volunteers who willingly spend their weekends and holidays clearing brush, flagging trails and organizing events to make their communities aware of these precious corridors.

Ontario now has five long-distance hiking trails, and more are on the drawing board. Over 25 years ago, in 1973, a handful of hikers started to build a trail they dreamed would eventually stretch from South Baymouth on Manitoulin Island, along the north shore of Lake Huron to Sault Ste.

Blackburnian Warbler.

Marie, and around the top of Lake Superior to Thunder Bay. They called it the Voyageur Trail. Striving to become the longest trail in Ontario, it currently boasts over 400 miles (650 kilometers) of completed trails of its proposed 680-mile (1,100-kilometer) route.

The completed portion of the Voyageur Trail is divided into 15 sections with local trail clubs responsible for each area. Except for two sections, one through Lake Superior Provincial Park and the other

through Pukaskwa National Park, that are maintained by park staff, the Voyageur Trail was cleared, blazed, built and is now maintained by volunteers. Many segments are located on private land, where landowners' permission had to be sought, an often long and involved process. When permission was given, the arrangement was sealed with a handshake, a practice that continues today.

Every part of the trail has its attractions. The Casque Isles section, from Rossport to Terrace Bay, is one of the most scenic and in places one of the most difficult. It involves 32.5 miles (52.4 kilometers) of rugged hiking along the Lake Superior shoreline that fortunately can be reduced to bite-sized day hikes. The route is divided into five distinct segments, with ten access points along the way.

This part of the Voyageur Trail follows Superior's immensely varied coastline. At times, you'll hike past glacial erratics, or boulders, to a raised cobble beach, 1 mile (1.6 kilometers) from the present shoreline, an indication of once higher water levels on Lake Superior. In other spots, you'll clamber over enormous lichen-covered boulders on gigantic raised terrace beaches. Still other areas offer fine sand beaches. Heart-thumping ascents to rocky ridges bring their rewards – the superb views overlooking Lake Superior.

Human history is evident in the remains of a 1930s mining camp and gold mill, as well as Indian pictographs on a granite cliff. And ancient life has also been observed, on a rocky outcrop known as the Gunflint Formation. This was found to contain microscopic algae and fossil remains that are believed to be among the earliest forms of life discovered on earth. Radioactive dating

Skiing along the Voyageur Trail.

has placed the deposition of these 1.6 to 2 billion years ago.

The Casque Isles section gives just a taste of what the Voyageur Trail has to offer – beautiful scenery and the feeling of solitude. The Voyageur Trail Association produces a guidebook with detailed

When you go

Voyageur Trail Association
Box 20040, 150 Churchill Blvd.
Sault Ste. Marie, ON P6A 6W3
Tel: (705) 942-1891
E-mail: voyageur.trail@sympatico.ca
Website: www3.sympatico.ca/voyageur.trail

route descriptions and maps of each section. Because trail conditions can change quickly, contact the Voyageur Trail Association for current information, or ask about joining one of the guided hikes offered to the public.

Lake Superior Provincial Park

The Trans-Canada Highway bisects the park from border to border. It's so easy to drive straight through, yet difficult to keep your eyes on the road – look at those views! You may as well at least stop for a picnic and a swim at one of the many lakes en route. And since there are half a dozen short trails, you may as well spend a couple of hours checking out some of the park's features. What the heck! With several campgrounds to choose from, why not pitch a tent? It may be days before you can pull yourself away.

Lake Superior Provincial Park is one of Ontario's largest parks and is situated on the world's largest body of fresh water. Originally accessible only by water, the Trans-Canada

Highway now provides easy access for visitors and a wide variety of activities to please every ambition.

The park was established in 1944 to preserve 600 square miles (1,556 square kilometers) of rugged Superior shoreline and Canadian Shield country. Hiking is the easiest way to explore the park, and there are several trails of varying difficulty. The park's showpiece – Agawa

Rock – is a short but rugged 15- to 20-minute walk from the highway. Ojibwa images more than 25 centuries old are depicted on the rock, among them an Indian chief, caribou and Misshepezhieu, the mythical spirit of the lake, or Gitchee Gumee. To see the images up close, you must walk about 300 feet (100 meters) out onto a sloping ledge below the rock, right on the edge of Superior. Take care, as the ledge can be slippery, and the lake is cold and unforgiving.

Other short walks include Trapper's Trail, an easy, 1-mile (1.5-kilometer) loop around Rustle Lake. The area supports a variety of wildlife such as beaver, otter and marten. The 3.7-mile (6-kilometer) Pinguisibi Trail (meaning "river of

Canoeing along the shoreline of Lake Superior Provincial Park.

fine white sand") follows the Sand River, past a series of waterfalls and rapids.

Nokomis Trail is a moderate 3-mile (5-kilometer) loop that leads through the Old Woman River valley and across ancient cobble beaches. A steep climb takes you to a lookout over Lake Superior and a view of Old Woman Bay cliff.

Orphan Lake Trail is one of the most diverse in the park. This moderate 5-mile (8-kilometer) loop ascends through a forest of sugar maple, yellow birch and conifers to lookouts over Orphan Lake and Superior. The trail then descends to the coast and returns along the Baldhead River to Orphan Lake.

The 15-mile (24-kilometer) Towab Trail is a demanding hike leading to a ridge above the Agawa River and a spectacular view of 82-feet-high (25-meter-high) Agawa Falls. If you're visiting the park in the fall, the Towab Trail is particularly beautiful. Spending the night at a campsite below the falls splits the trail distance over two days, making it a more manageable hike. A short alternative is to hike 2 miles (3.5 kilometers) to Burnt Rock Pool, where you can swim and fish for trout.

The 6-mile (10-kilometer) Awausee Lookout Trail features four lookouts on a loop trail. It starts at the base of Agawa Mountain and climbs 650 feet (200 meters) above the Agawa Valley, through mixed forest, up a steep ravine to a ridge overlooking the Agawa River mouth and delta on Lake Superior.

The Coastal Hiking Trail is the longest and most demanding in the park, although it can be broken up into shorter segments. It follows the Lake Superior shoreline for 34 miles (55 kilometers) between Sinclair Cove and Chalfant Cove north of Cape Gargantua. Fit and experienced hikers only should attempt the five- to seven-day trip.

Canoeing is another obvious way to explore the park, and canoe rentals at Rabbit Blanket Lake and Crescent Lake campgrounds enable even novice paddlers

Ice-covered cliff face, Lake Superior Provincial Park.

to get out for a short excursion. Lake Superior itself is cold and volatile, and anyone venturing onto its waters must be highly skilled. There are eight routes, however, ranging from easy to challenging, that stretch into the interior. Two are suitable for day paddles or short overnight trips – an 8-mile (13-kilometer) return route to Belanger Lake and a 10-mile (16-kilometer) loop to Treeby Lake.

The remote Sand River route begins with a train ride on the Algoma Central Railway to the start point at Sand Lake. The 35-mile (56-kilometer) trip takes four or five days to complete and is best done in high water, usually in spring. There are 29 portages, each about half a mile (one kilometer) long, that enable canoeists to avoid all rapids and other obstacles. If you

have whitewater skills, some of the rapids can be run.

Whether you stop for a short hike or intend to backpack the Coastal Hiking Trail, the park's dramatic features and variety of landscapes will impress you – from ancient glacier-worn hills to volcanic diabase dikes to magnificent canyons created by earthquakes. The mix of vegetation provides a home to bear, moose, timber wolf, Canada lynx and many smaller mammals. More than 250 species of birds have been spotted in the park, and over 120 species nest there.

The park has three campgrounds close to the highway, as well as 175 backcountry sites accessible only on foot or by canoe. Proximity to the chilly waters of Lake Superior moderates the park's temperatures, which average about 70°F (20°C) during the summer. Nighttime temperatures drop considerably. No matter what the season, always be prepared for cold, fog, wind and rain. And enjoy the sun on those warmer days!

When you go

Lake Superior Provincial Park
PO Box 267
Wawa, ON P0S 1K0
Tel: (705) 856-2284
Fax: (705) 856-1333

Pukaskwa National Park

Superior: a sea of superlatives. Nothing comes in small, dainty doses here. The world's largest freshwater lake, deep, dark and deathly cold, behaves at times like a wild, unruly giant. Although it's gentle-looking while asleep, gusts of westerly winds can whip it into a fury, smashing ancient shorelines with its anger.

On its rugged northeast coast, a remote area preserves the primitive landscape bordering this tempestuous character. Set aside in 1978 and opened to the public in 1983, Pukaskwa National Park (pronounced *puck-a-saw*) encompasses 725 square miles (1,878 square kilometers) of Canadian Shield, boreal forest and untamed waters.

Hattie Cove, in the northwest corner of the park, is the end of the road and the beginning of exploration by foot or boat into this wilderness park. Located 250 miles (400 kilometers) northwest of Sault Ste. Marie, a short drive off the Trans-Canada Highway, Hattie Cove is the center of park activities.

Three self-guided, interpretive trails start near the Hattie Cove campground. Although you can walk each one in an hour or two (all are less than 2.5 miles/4 kilometers long), you can easily spend half a day exploring the beaches and rocky headland. For a good introduction to Pukaskwa, follow the Southern Headland Trail to a rocky point overlooking Lake Superior. Stunted black spruce, hardy arctic-alpine plants, and dramatic surf pounding rocks pocked with potholes epitomize the park's theme, "Wild Shore of an Inland Sea."

The Beach Trail, an extension of the Headland Trail, wanders along three sand beaches connected by boreal forest. Bleached boom logs on middle beach are remnants of the log drives on the Pic River that took place until the early 1980s. On north beach, boardwalks allow a close-up view of the park's dune complexes without disturbing the fragile environment.

The 2-mile (3.5-kilometer) Halfway Lake Trail skirts a small inland lake surrounded by boreal forest. At the north end of the lake, a boardwalk extends over a shallow, marshy area where great blue herons, white-throated sparrows, black-throated green warblers, buffleheads and goldeneyes are commonly spotted.

Besides the rocky headlands and stretches of fine sand, Superior's shores are dotted with cobble beaches, where an intriguing discovery has been made – the "Pukaskwa Pits." These shallow rock structures were built by aboriginal people who lived in the area for thousands of years. The purpose of the pits, which are up to 8 feet (2.5 meters) long and with walls 5 feet (1.5 meters) high, is unclear. They may have been used as shelters for fishing or hunting, or possibly as vision-quest sites. Whatever their purpose, they've been in existence for perhaps 7,000 years, and today they're important spiritual sites for the local Ojibwa. Because these sites are difficult to identify, visitors should avoid walking on cobble beaches, and backcountry campers should seek sandy beaches on which to pitch their tents.

Apart from the short hikes around Hattie Cove, Pukaskwa offers a long, challenging day hike to and from the White River Suspension Bridge. This 10-mile (16-kilometer) hike covers quite rugged terrain and requires about six to eight hours for the round trip. The steadily increasing roar of the White River thundering over

Challenging the wilderness of Pukaskwa National Park.

White River, Pukaskwa National Park.

Bird's Eye primrose, Pukaskwa National Park.

Chigamiwinigum Falls and through the narrow gorge announces the trail's turn-around point at the suspension bridge. But don't stop there! Walk out to the middle of the bridge and stare down at the giant standing waves – a dizzying sensation!

From here, hardy, experienced backpackers can continue on the Coastal Hiking Trail, a 37-mile (60-kilometer) trek from Hattie Cove to the North Swallow River. The round trip takes 10 to 14 days, but most hikers do it one way, or divide it into smaller portions, using pre-arranged boat shuttles to a starting point, then hiking back to Hattie Cove. The Coastal Trail is a superb but arduous hike through boreal forest blanketed with thick, spongy moss and arctic-

alpine plants. The forest is home to moose, wolf, black bear and many other smaller animals, as well as a small, precious herd of woodland caribou.

For those who love to be on the water, the inlets and islands in Hattie Cove are suitable for families and casual paddlers to explore; more experienced paddlers can venture out into Pulpwood Harbour, although caution is still advised. For experienced paddlers, the White and Pukaskwa are challenging wilderness rivers, with many portages around rapids, dams and falls, and plenty of exciting whitewater to run. The White is easily accessible, and from White Lake Provincial Park it's a 45-mile (72-kilometer), four- to six-day adventure to Hattie Cove. The Pukaskwa River is more difficult and remote, with 38 portages over its 69-mile (111-kilometer) length. It takes eight to ten days starting from Sagina Lake on Highway 17 and can only be run during spring flood, from May to early June.

Paddling the Lake Superior coastline is akin to paddling an ocean, with giant swells, dangerous winds, dense fogs and abrupt weather changes. Highly experienced paddlers may tackle the 10- to 14-day Coastal Canoe Route, which starts at Hattie Cove and terminates at Michipicoten Harbour, 100 miles (160 kilometers) distant.

Anyone paddling or hiking in the backcountry must register in and out with park staff. The number and size of parties permitted in the backcountry is limited, so call well in advance to book your trip.

When you go

Pukaskwa National Park
Heron Bay, ON P0T 1R0
Tel: (807) 229-0801
Fax: (807) 229-2097

Maps, charts and guides are available from:
The Friends of Pukaskwa
General Delivery
Heron Bay, ON P0T 1R0

Algoma Central Railway

When you travel on holidays, is it usually by car? Plane? Bus? How about the train? In a country whose history is closely linked with the railway, it seems a natural choice. In Northern Ontario, the Algoma Central Railway not only makes it easy to travel by train, it opens up a vast area to outdoor recreationists.

Algoma Central Railway has been operating since 1899, hauling timber and iron ore from the northern hinterland to the busy port city of Sault Ste. Marie on Lake Superior. Laying track through dense forests, over rocky hills, across rivers and over deep ravines was a monumental task. The result of all this effort is an awesome ride through one of the wildest landscapes in the country.

Algoma Central provides two services. The one-day Agawa Canyon Train Tour begins in "The Soo"; final destination, Mile 114 of the line. The views are impressive at any point, but the highlight is definitely Agawa Canyon. Here, the train descends 500 feet (150 meters) to the canyon floor, with sheer granite walls on either side reaching up to 575 feet (175 meters). Passengers disembark for two hours to hike short trails leading to scenic lookouts and cascading waterfalls before returning to Sault Ste. Marie.

Not just a scenic train ride, though, the Algoma Central Railway is a passenger service as well, providing recreational access to hikers, backpackers, mountain bikers, canoeists, skiers, snowmobilers and anyone else looking for a remote backcountry experience. Smoothing out some of the rough edges of the Algoma wilderness are more than a dozen secluded lodges and resorts, all accessible by train, some only by train. True, you can fly in by floatplane to some of the resorts, but nothing beats the railway. Where else can you flag down a train, throw your pack, canoe, bike, skis and snowshoes into a baggage car and settle back for a breathtaking ride?

Every resort offers something different, from rustic to first class. You can be pampered with home-cooked meals, or rent a cottage and cook your own in a fully equipped kitchen. Your hosts will know where you're likely to spot a moose or can

Historic train at the Algoma Central Railway.

An aerial view of dense forests and Agawa Canyon.

point out the best fishing spots. They know the trails and what condition they're in, and they can even set you up with a guide.

The countryside is harsh and rugged, typical Canadian Shield terrain that gradually shifts to boreal forest north of Agawa Canyon. Pristine lakes and rivers offer superb fishing opportunities for northern pike, perch, walleye, lake trout and whitefish. Loons, mergansers, great blue herons, eagles and osprey are frequently sighted on the lakes and, less often, sandhill cranes and belted kingfishers. In the forests, you might see or hear pileated woodpeckers or Wilson's warblers. Moose are common in the boreal forest, and you might be fortunate enough to hear the

When you go

For train schedules and information about the tours and lodges, contact:
Algoma Central Railway Inc.
129 Bay Street, Box 130
Sault Ste. Marie, ON P6A 6Y2
Tel: (705) 946-7300
Fax: (705) 541-2989

Boxcar Art

Between 1918 and 1923, several members of the Group of Seven rented a boxcar outfitted like a cabin and had it shunted to locations along the line. From there, they hiked and canoed to remote spots to paint the beautiful Algoma wilderness.

haunting howl of timber wolves or coyotes.

During the winter, you can ride the rails to two year-round resorts on Windy Lake and Kwagama Lake. Both are open in the snow season, from about the first of December to the end of March. Cross-country skiing, snowshoeing and ice fishing consume your days, while evenings are spent in the comfort of a warm cabin or lodge.

The Algoma Central Railway passenger service runs three or four times per week, depending on the season. Advance reservations are not accepted, but there is never a shortage of space. Be sure to call for an updated schedule before you leave home.

Georgian Bay Islands National Park

You'd never think that the 30,000 islands of Georgian Bay were once towering mountains, higher and more rugged than the Rockies. Of course, that was a billion years ago, and time has a way of wearing things down. *Way* down, in this case – almost to sea level. Among the 30,000 islands is a tiny national park, established in 1929 to protect a portion of this intriguing landscape from private ownership.

Georgian Bay at dusk.

Just 4.5 square miles (12 square kilometers) in size, Georgian Bay Islands National Park takes in all or parts of 59 islands spread out along the southeast shore of the bay. Only four are accessible to the public – Beausoleil, Centennial, Bone and "Island 95." Of these, Beausoleil Island is the largest and the focal point of activities and services. It's just a stone's throw from the mainland and the town of Honey Harbour, where the park administration office is located. Visitors to Beausoleil, which is accessible only by water, may rent a boat from the local marinas in Midland, Penetanguishene or Honey Harbour, or take advantage of the water taxi service.

Upon reaching Beausoleil Island, stop in at the Visitor Centre, where videos, slide shows and interpretive displays will acquaint you with the park. Most intriguing of its features is the mix of vegetation. The national park sits at the edge of the Canadian Shield in the transition zone between Northern and Southern Ontario forests. On Beausoleil, the transition is remarkably abrupt. The northern part of the island is barren, glacier-scraped rock, with lonely, windswept pines bent and twisted on the exposed shorelines. Yet the southern part of Beausoleil is dominated by tall hardwood forests and thick, rich soil.

In this dual landscape live over

Rocky Waters

There are close to 90,000 islands in the region known as The 30,000 Islands. Many of them are little more than big rocks, some barely breaking the surface of the water.

700 species of plants and animals and a variety of reptiles and amphibians. The park is one of the last remaining natural habitats in the world for the Eastern Massasauga rattlesnake, a threatened species protected in Ontario. Small and timid, this poisonous snake is best seen at the Visitor Centre, where a captive-bred specimen is on view. Though you're unlikely to come across one of these potentially dangerous snakes, it's wise to wear boots and long pants while hiking.

There are 11 easy hiking trails on Beausoleil Island, covering over 16 miles (27 kilometers) of varied terrain. The trails range from about 200 yards to 3.7 miles (300 meters to 6 kilometers) and can be combined in any number of ways to make a pleasant day's outing. Two are open to bicycles.

The 3.7-mile (6-kilometer) Huron Trail traverses three-quarters of the length of Beausoleil, leading from thick, stately stands of maple and beech in the south to the glacially sculpted terrain of the north. This is pure Shield country, made famous by the Group of Seven. Other trails in the northern part lead to warm inland lakes, perfect for a refreshing dip in the heat of the summer. Or through wetlands and past remnant beaver ponds, noisy with frogs and toads. Back to the southern part of the island, the short Firetower Trail leads from an open meadow to the highest point in the park (689 feet/210 meters above sea level) and wonderful views of the bay.

Because the park is surrounded by so much water, it's only natural that it is a boater's paradise. Sheltered in Georgian Bay from the fearsome power of Lake Huron, the many channels, coves and inlets are ideal for sea kayaking. If you're heading to Cedar Spring around the south end of Roberts Island, be sure you can paddle the 3 miles (5 kilometers) of open water from the mainland. This is the longest crossing and is recommended for confident paddlers only. It's also the main campground and docking area and large boat traffic is

Glaciated red granite of Canadian Shield landscape, Georgian Bay Islands National Park.

heavy – best avoided in peak summer months. The many sheltered inlets and small islands around the northern edge of Beausoleil Island are much quieter, and perfect for sea kayakers to explore. To reach this area and the six campsites there, paddle northwest from Honey Harbour through the Main Channel or Little Dog Channel. Alternatively, you can paddle through Big Dog Channel and camp on Tonch Point. At the southern end of the island, Beausoleil Point and Christian Beach provide two campsites on sandy beaches, where it's easy to pull up your boats.

During the winter, the park is open when ice conditions on the bay are safe, usually from mid-January to early March. Before you travel, contact the park for current conditions. Cross-country skiing, snowshoeing and snowmobiling are all popular activities. Winter camping is especially good at two sites on Beausoleil Island where the enclosed picnic shelters provide added comfort.

At any time of the year, be sure you have everything you need for the length of your stay before you leave the mainland. There are no stores or restaurants of any kind on the islands – you must be completely self-sufficient! There are 12 semi-primitive campgrounds on Beausoleil (and one each on Island 95 and Centennial Island), available on a first-come, first-served basis. The campsites at Cedar Spring Campground can be reserved from May to September.

When you go

Georgian Bay Islands National Park
PO Box 28
Honey Harbour, ON P0E 1E0
Tel: (705) 756-2415
Campground reservations:
Tel: (705) 756-5909

Bruce Peninsula

Separating Lake Huron from Georgian Bay is a jagged finger of land 60 miles (100 kilometers) long called the Bruce Peninsula. Commanding the eastern half of the peninsula is the rugged Niagara Escarpment, which extends south to Niagara Falls and north off the tip of the Bruce, later reappearing as a chain of islands. This scenic region, named a World Biosphere Reserve in 1990, draws over half a million visitors every year to two national parks, Bruce Peninsula and Fathom Five.

Highway 6 slices down the middle of the Bruce Peninsula, ending at the little fishing village of Tobermory where the parks' Visitor Centre is located. Stop for information, then head back to the Cyprus Lake Campground, and leave your car in the Head of the Trails parking lot. From here, you can choose from three hiking trails leading to three inland lakes: Marr, Horse and Cyprus.

All are easy trails with sections on the boulder beaches and cliffs that require sturdy boots and some

caution. The 3-mile (5-kilometer) Georgian Bay Trail leads past Horse Lake through sheltered woods and over ridges of ancient coral reefs to the Georgian Bay shoreline. Heading west, you follow the Bruce Trail to Indian Head Cove, a beautiful spot for swimming and snorkeling. Farther west you'll come to The Grotto, one of the most photographed spots on the peninsula, and certainly the most visited of the caves. Carved into the steep limestone cliffs by wave action, The Grotto is a huge, echoing chamber, cool and light inside. You can climb down to explore the cave, and watch the scuba divers who swim in from the bay via an underwater entrance.

From here, tiered limestone ledges lead past the cobble beach at Marr Lake to Overhanging Point, a slab of resilient dolomite that has been left unsupported as the weaker limestone layers beneath were worn away. The cap-rock juts out 100 feet (30 meters) above the water – an unnerving sensation for those brave enough to step out onto the slab.

Return to the parking lot via the Marr Lake Trail. This and the 4-mile (7-kilometer) Cyprus Lake Trail wander through sheltered woods brimming with rare and delicate wildflowers. The Bruce Peninsula is well known for its variety of orchids – over 40 species – and you may see coral root, rattlesnake plantain and purple-fringed varieties along these and the Horse Lake trails. Spring and early summer are the best times to catch these wonders in bloom.

Dorcas Bay, on the west side of the peninsula, is a landscape dominated by marshy lowlands, woodlands and the cobble shores of Lake Huron. This is an even better environment for rare plants to flourish. You can follow a short trail through wet meadows and fens and spot rose pogonia and the showy lady's slipper orchids, as well as the insectivorous sundew and pitcher plant. The trail leads through an area of low sand dunes, covered with dwarf lake irises in May and yellow lady's slipper in early June. The access parking lot is at Singing Sands, a small, sandy beach that is great for families with kids – you can swim a third of a mile (half a kilometer) out from shore in the warm, shallow water.

The second half of the Bruce Peninsula experience is Fathom Five National Marine Park. Established in 1987, Canada's first national marine park encompasses 19 islands, rugged limestone pearls that are an exten-

Sea kayaking at Flowerpot Rocks, Fathom Five National Marine Park, Bruce Peninsula.

A Calypso orchid, one of over 40 species of orchids found in Bruce Peninsula National Park.

sion of the Niagara Escarpment, and 43 square miles (112 square kilometers) of cold, clear Lake Huron water. The lake is the watery grave for 21 sunken ships that met their demise on treacherous offshore shoals in the late 19th and early 20th centuries.

These shipwrecks make Fathom Five one of the best freshwater scuba diving sites in the world. But you needn't be a diver to investigate the wrecks. Hop aboard one of the many tour boats that operate from Little Tub Harbour near Tobermory. Some of the wrecks lie very close to the surface and are easily seen through the clear water.

The tour boats will let you off at Beachy Cove on Flowerpot Island, where you can spend a few hours exploring. A 1.8-mile (3-kilometer) loop trail leads to the island's landmarks, the most popular being the

When you go

Bruce Peninsula National Park
PO Box 189
Tobermory, ON N0H 2R0
Tel: (519) 596-2233
Fax: (519) 596-2298

The Bruce Trail Association
PO Box 857
Hamilton, ON L8N 3N9
Tel: (905) 529-6821

"flowerpots" for which the island is named. Two huge dolomite pillars, 39 feet and 23 feet (12 meters and 7 meters) high, stand isolated from the limestone bluffs, where wave action continues to form sea stacks.

Just past the large flowerpot, stairs lead up the bluff to a platform in a "hanging" cave. Perched 100 feet (30 meters) above the shore, this former sea cave is evidence that water levels were once much higher.

The trail continues to the Coast-guard's Flowerpot Island Light Station, then heads inland through a cool, moist forest where ferns and mosses grow. In May, you'll see the dainty calypso orchid in bloom. You may also spot some slithery creatures in the woods. Cut off from mainland predators, the island has become a haven for snakes, all of them harmless to humans.

If you're heading back to the mainland, make sure you get to the dock in time to catch your prearranged tour boat. If you're prepared to camp, Flowerpot has six sites perched on wooden platforms above the shoreline, available on a first-come, first-served basis. When the last boat has spirited the crowds away, hike up to Castle Bluff and enjoy a tranquil evening watching the sun sink into the water.

Mansfield Outdoor Centre

Just over an hour's drive north of Toronto, set in the forested Mulmur Hills, is an educational facility well known to school boards and youth groups in the Toronto area. What some people don't realize is that it's a great little escape for a day of mountain biking or cross-country skiing in a wilderness setting.

Located on 300 beautifully wooded acres, including part of the Dufferin County Forest, the property was a working farm up until 1967. John Caisley bought the land and opened it up to snowmobiling, utilizing the original 1908 farmhouse as the main lodge. In the mid-1970s, cross-country skiing replaced snowmobiling, and by 1983 when Ken Mikoliew took over, more and more educational programs were being offered.

During the summer, Mansfield Outdoor Centre offers a network of mountain biking trails that wind and grind over nearly 20 miles (30 kilometers) on a thousand acres of land.

When you go

Mansfield Outdoor Centre
PO Box 95
Mansfield, ON L0N 1M0
Tel: (705) 435-4479
Fax: (705) 435-3370
E-mail: mansfield@sympatico.ca
Website: www.mansfield-outdoors.com

Five trails range from 2 to 4 miles (3.3 to 6.6 kilometers) in length, rated from novice to expert. If you're a little shy off-road, you can start on the double-track trails. Smooth and wide, they have just enough ups and downs to get you puffing. At the other end of the scale, a tougher double track and some gnarly single track with sharp drop-offs, gut-busting climbs and awesome technical challenges will test even the most seasoned rider.

The center takes its educational role seriously and has utilized low-impact trail design and construction in the making of their mountain biking trails. The network is constantly monitored for eroded or heavily worn areas, and mountain bikers are required to wear helmets. Mountain bike races and clinics for men and women are held throughout the summer.

When the snow flies, the center grooms 25 miles (40 kilometers) of trails for cross-country skiing. Eight well marked routes are graded from novice to expert. Seven trails are double-tracked for the kick-and-glide crowd, and one 4-mile (7-kilometer) trail is dedicated to skating enthusiasts.

Set on the edge of a fault, all trails but the easiest begin by climbing up onto the ridge. On top, the terrain is gently rolling, with some wonderful vistas over the Pine River valley. The trails intertwine in such a way that you can ski as much or as little as you like, and maps at every intersection mean you'll always know where you are. All the trails on the escarpment are intermediate, with the exception of the White Trail. If you venture onto this trail, be

Bunchberry, a common sight in the forest.

sure you can handle the steep and winding downhills – an expert run to be sure!

After a day on the trails, you can warm up in the center with a bowl of delicious homemade soup or chili, or prop your feet up in front of a wood-burning stove and sip a steaming mug of hot chocolate. On weekends, depending on availability, groups of four or more can be accommodated either at the Main Lodge or the Field Centre. The Field Centre is a country-style inn with all the amenities under one roof. The Main Lodge and cabins are a little more rustic, with washrooms and showers in adjacent buildings.

Bicycling along one of the trails at the Mansfield Outdoor Centre.

Saugeen River

Ontario is quite rightly known for its wilderness waterways: lakes, rivers and portage routes that once carried native peoples and intrepid voyageurs to and from their fur trading grounds. Nowadays, these routes are plied by outdoor adventurers who spend weeks planning their forays into Ontario's backcountry, transporting canoes, food and equipment by car, train and floatplane to reach these far-flung destinations.

But for those with little inclination to expend such time, energy and money to paddle these out-of-the-way watercourses, there is another option. The Saugeen River in south-central Ontario offers a not-too-daunting destination that's still steeped in history and passes through some surprisingly "wild" countryside. The icing on the cake: it's only a short drive away from Ontario's major urban centers.

The Saugeen is a great summer getaway for novices, families or weekend warriors looking for a quiet canoe route close to home and easily accessible. In the mid-1800s, many a

pioneer family and their possessions were transported down the river on log rafts or flat-bottomed scows, en route to the fertile farmland of Bruce County. As towns and villages developed along the river, railways, roads and bridges aided the flow of traffic, and dams tamed the wilder sections of the mighty Saugeen.

Canoeists have a much easier time navigating the river now. After the spring floods and high water levels during April and early May, when experienced whitewater paddlers find plenty to challenge their skills, the Saugeen slows to a level suitable for novices and families. By late summer, low water levels in some sections may have you cooling your heels as you guide your canoe over the shallows.

With the aid of a road map, you can put in and take out at dozens of points along the length of the river below Hanover. The full 63-mile (102-kilometer) route from there to Southampton takes three to four days to complete. There are plenty of private or conservation area campgrounds along the banks, or you can camp on a sandy island in midstream (poison ivy alert!). Alternatively, B&Bs in Hanover, Walkerton, Paisley and Southampton mean you can easily split up your paddling days to spend the night in comfort.

The 12.5-mile (20-kilometer) stretch from Hanover to Walkerton is easily paddled in a day. Three short portages bypassing three dams are the only carries you'll have to do. It's a relaxing five-hour day, meandering through the lowland flats west of Hanover, past wooded hillsides and along a glacial spillway.

Day two is a long 24-mile (39-kilometer) stretch between Walkerton and Paisley that will take seven to ten hours to complete. This is the most challenging part of the river, with several fun rapids to negotiate where the river bisects the Walkerton Moraine. Just past the bluffs, a glacial sand plain is home to colonies of swallows and kingfishers.

From the historic town of Paisley, a final section of 27 miles (43 kilometers) carries you to the take-out at Denny's Dam near Southampton. The broad and winding Saugeen Valley is now primarily pasture and farmland, where beef and dairy cattle drink from the river and go about their ruminating business as you float by.

You can take out at Denny's Dam, or, if you have good whitewater skills, continue the final 5.5-mile (9-kilometer) leg to Lake Huron. Across the lake from the mouth of

Canoeing on the Saugeen River.

Cape May warbler.

the river is a federal wildlife sanctuary on Chantry Island. Although the island is closed to anyone lacking feathers, the mouth of the Saugeen River is an excellent spot for bird watching. During the spring, you may see great blue herons, great egrets, double-crested cormorants and flotillas of waterfowl, including hooded mergansers, wood ducks, grebes and loons. In May, warblers and other woodland songbirds move through the river valley, many on their way to their northern nesting grounds.

The Saugeen River has plenty to offer the casual paddler and budding naturalist. Pockets of wilderness support a wide range of wildlife, including herons, ducks and geese, beaver, muskrat, mink, turtles and snakes. Fishing is very good for bass, pike, rainbow trout and brown trout in season.

When you go

Saugeen Valley Conservation Authority
RR 1
Hanover, ON N4N 3B8
Tel: 1-888-301-4268
Tel: (519) 364-1255
Fax: (519) 364-6990
E-mail: naturetours@svca.on.ca
Website: www.svca.on.ca

For information on Conservation Nature Tours, contact the Saugeen Valley Conservation Authority.

Recommended Reading

Armitage, Andrew. *Sweetwater Explorer: Paddling in Grey and Bruce Counties*. Owen Sound: The Ginger Press, 1995.

Several companies operate canoe trips on the Saugeen River, and various outdoor shops in the area rent canoes, paddles, lifejackets and other equipment. Conservation Nature Tours, under the auspices of Saugeen and Grey Sauble conservation authorities, offers a unique two-day trip that combines history with the paddling experience. You canoe down a 17-mile (27-kilometer) section of the Saugeen River in an authentic 25-foot Voyageur Canoe, sleep out in a teepee in the Saugeen Bluffs Conservation Area, and basically experience life as it would have been for the *coureurs de bois* 400 years ago. You'll learn to identify edible wild plants (then eat them!), make leather sashes, start fires with flint and steel, and hear stories of the pioneer days. Who said you need to go to Northern Ontario to experience a bit of the past in a wilderness setting?

Grand River

When the first explorers came to Canada, they set out by canoe on a veritable highway of lakes and rivers that linked the country from sea to sea. For centuries, these waterways have been at our disposal, and many have been altered to suit our civilized purposes. Today, a pressing need has arisen to protect our once wild rivers. In 1984, a cooperative program involving provincial, federal and territorial governments was formed to give national recognition to some of Canada's most important rivers. Called the Canadian Heritage Rivers System, the program is seeking to conserve the natural and human heritage of our precious rivers.

In 1994, the entire Grand River watershed, covering 2,688 square miles (6,965 square kilometers), was designated a Canadian Heritage River. The valley, the river and its four major tributaries – the Nith, Eramosa, Speed and Conestogo rivers – are recognized for their outstanding natural, cultural and recreational value. Twelve conservation areas operated by the Grand River Conservation Authority (GRCA) preserve everything from rare Carolinian forest to important wetlands to awe-inspiring geological features. Through it all, the Grand River is a common thread, linking natural and cultural landscapes of the past and present.

Native cultures were the first to prosper from the Grand's rich agricultural valley. They thrived along its banks for over 10,000 years, before French explorers and missionaries arrived in the 1600s. Later, Irish, Scottish and English immigrants came to settle, as did Mennonites from the U.S. who were looking for religious freedom. When you're traveling through the region, don't be surprised to see Old Order Mennonites and Amish dressed in traditional clothing and still using horse-drawn buggies for transportation.

Canoeing is perhaps the most logical and most enjoyable way of exploring this heritage river. The Grand begins near Dundalk, just south of Georgian Bay, and curls through quaint villages, towns and cities on its way to Lake Erie, 180 miles (290 kilometers) distant. Its source is north of the Luther Marsh, a large and diverse wetland that supports a great number of nesting birds and some provincially rare reptiles. Canoeing is not advised in the

A swan on a tranquil section of the Grand River.

Luther Marsh Wildlife Management Area (bugs!), but an easy trail and observation towers along the shores of Luther Lake provide the opportunity to observe marsh life.

From the Luther Marsh to the town of Elora, canoeing is limited by very low water levels, except during spring run-off. At Elora, however, the Grand River plunges over a 50-foot (15-meter) limestone cliff on the Niagara Escarpment and rushes through the 2-mile-long (3-kilometer-long) Elora Gorge. Sheer limestone walls some 80 feet (25 meters) high line the gorge on either side. This is one of the most beautiful sites in Southern Ontario, and a busy summer attraction. In the Elora Gorge Conservation Area, camping, hiking and swimming in the spring-fed lake are all popular activities. Just be careful near the edge of the gorge, where a slip could be fatal! The torrential flow through the gorge makes for superb whitewater canoeing and kayaking, and for a thrill of a different sort, the Conservation Authority rents inner tubes (with helmets and lifejackets!).

From here, the Grand is fast and shallow, meandering from side to side across the rocky bed. A few hours downstream, the river flows

Eastern meadowlark.

When you go

The Conservation Authority's guidebook to canoeing the Grand River provides essential information about access, river flow, portages, shuttle services and camping. The Authority also produces a number of books and videos highlighting the Grand River, including a map of the entire watershed and a guide to hiking trails along the Grand. These and other information are available from:

Grand River Conservation Authority
400 Clyde Road, Box 729
Cambridge, ON N1R 5W6
Tel: (519) 621-2761
Fax: (519) 621-4844

For information about the Canadian Heritage Rivers System contact:
Canadian Heritage Rivers Board
25 Eddy Street, 4th Floor
Hull, QC K1A 0M5
Tel: (819) 997-4930
Fax: (819) 994-5140

under the West Montrose Covered Bridge, the last of only five of its kind in Ontario. The wooden heritage structure, also known as the "Kissing Bridge," was built in 1881 and is still in use today. Beyond the bridge, the river becomes deeper and wider, winding through a broad alluvial valley and floodplain.

One of the most remarkable modern-day developments along the Grand is the flood-protection wall on both sides of the river through

the city of Cambridge. The walls are over 16 feet (5 meters) high, slightly higher than the water levels reached during the flood of May 1974.

From Cambridge to Paris, a 12-mile (20-kilometer) stretch called the Grand River Forest contains Carolinian forest species rare to Canada. This is the most popular day trip for canoeists, with views of high bluffs, sprawling floodplains and the flora and fauna of the forest. The river cuts through sand hills, gravelly moraines, farmland and charming towns and villages. Some heritage buildings now house markets, restaurants, ice cream shops and art galleries.

The Grand has much to offer in the way of fishing, too. Carp, rock bass and yellow perch are found all along its length, but other species such as large and smallmouth bass, black crappie, pike, walleye, salmon and trout occur in some sites. The Grand River draws enthusiasts from all over North America for its world-class brown-trout fishing.

Besides canoeing and fishing, the Grand River Valley offers access to an immense network of superb hiking trails. Three of these – the Cambridge to Paris Rail Trail, Elora Cataract Trailway and Hamilton to Brantford Rail Trail – are part of the Trans Canada Trail system. And the Grand Valley Trail links to several others, including the Avon Trail, the Guelph-Speed Trail, the Bruce Trail and the Thames Valley Trail. Cycling, horseback riding, cross-country skiing and snowmobiling are popular on many of these routes.

Whatever the activity, the Grand River continues to play an important role not only for the communities that line its banks, but also for the birds, wildlife and landscapes that feed upon it. And now, as a protected heritage river, its future is guaranteed.

Rouge Park

Quick! Describe an urban park. Carefully tended lawns with picnic tables under shade trees? A paved pathway for cycling and in-line skating? Pony rides and paddle boats? Jammed parking lots and refreshment-stand line-ups? Would you be surprised to learn that North America's largest urban park has none of these?

Rouge Park, on the east side of Toronto, is a unique wilderness surrounded by high-rises, expressways and the fast pace of a big city. The slogan "Wild in the City" captures

The Rouge Valley.

the essence of this urban park, where wildlife, forests and wetlands exist in a peaceful oasis, and people can retreat for a quiet moment.

Opened in 1995, the 17-square-mile (45-square-kilometer) park stretches from Lake Ontario north to Steeles Avenue. The focal point is the 22-mile-long (35-kilometer-long) Rouge River, named for its red clay banks. North of Steeles Avenue, the Rouge and its tributaries rise from the Oak Ridges Moraine, and small strips of land adjacent to the waterways are also preserved as park. They are the only green links between the Oak Ridges Moraine and Lake Ontario, providing a corridor for wildlife to move freely. And that is what makes Rouge Park so special.

Even though it is accessible to millions of people, the Rouge River has remained almost entirely in its natural state. Sitting on the edge of the Carolinian Forest Zone, the park supports an incredible diversity of plants, animals, birds and reptiles. Thick maple, oak, hemlock and poplar forests and stands of white pines occupy the upper slopes of the valley, but there's a very different feel along the banks and in the marshlands. Black maple and sycamore trees, dense thickets and lush ostrich ferns give the feeling of a southern U.S. old-growth forest.

On any given day, you might see white-tailed deer or raccoons, or the tracks of coyote and fox imprinted on a muddy trail. A wide range of bird species nest and feed along the Rouge. If you're patient, you might see or hear such rare birds as pileated woodpecker, Carolina wren, scarlet tanager or Cooper's hawk. Along the river banks, you're almost certain to see great blue herons, swans and coots.

Bird watching is especially good in the Rouge Marsh at the mouth of the river. These wetlands are an important stopover for migrating waterfowl and are a nesting site for the rare least bittern, Virginia rail and blue-gray gnat catcher. A

Saw-whet owl.

nesting platform has been erected in the marsh in the hopes of drawing a pair of the few osprey that are slowly returning to the Rouge Valley.

You can hike into the marsh, but a drier alternative would be to paddle up the mouth of the river a short way. You can launch your canoe or kayak from Rouge Beach Park – also a great place for swimming and family outings. The fishing is good too, as it is all along the river. Just be careful not to disturb any nesting birds while you're on the water.

Farther up the river, three short hiking trails lead through the floodplain along the valley bottom or up to the thickly forested tops of the tablelands

between the Rouge River and Little Rouge Creek. Sturdy shoes are required, especially in spring when the trails are wet and muddy, or in the winter when it can get slick with ice.

Besides the natural attractions, there are a number of historical sites. The ruins of a sawmill – one of fourteen on the river in 1850 – and the remains of houses, a Mennonite

farmstead and a Gothic-style church tell the story of the pioneer days when logging and farming were the major industries on the Rouge. Two very significant archaeological sites – a 14th-century Iroquoian village and a 17th-century Seneca village – take you even further back in time, when the First Nations farmed, fished and hunted along the Rouge Valley.

People have never been far from the river, using it wisely and sometimes abusing it unwittingly. These days, people are banding together to help nurture the park, so it can remain a sanctuary for wildlife and nature lovers for many centuries to come.

When you go

Rouge Park
361A Old Finch Avenue
Scarborough, ON M1B 5K7
Tel: (416) 287-6843
Fax: (416) 287-2425

The Waterfront Trail

*R*egeneration. It means renewal, restoration, bringing back to life. For Lake Ontario, it means the reversal of a death sentence. And for Southern Ontarians, it means a rediscovery of this once "sparkling water."

Regeneration is also the word used to describe the process to stop the decline of Lake Ontario's water and shoreline. The Waterfront Regeneration Trust was established in 1992 by the Ontario government on the recommendation of the Royal

Commission on the Future of the Toronto Waterfront, chaired by former mayor David Crombie. With the help of governments,

municipalities, communities and concerned individuals, the Trust is breathing new life into Lake Ontario's waterfront.

People all over Southern Ontario are finding new potential in a lake once avoided because it was smelly and ugly. Who, after all, would want to visit a lake lined with commercial and industrial sites that spilled toxic waste into the water? Yet pockets of wilderness still existed where wildlife thrived, and urban centers began to realize the value of a greenbelt along the waterfront. There seemed to be hope for the lake's recovery.

Communities all along the lakeshore have taken up the cause, setting aside parkland previously slated for industrial use, providing recreational space for stressed-out urbanites and conserving ecosystems for birds and animals. Called the Waterfront Trail, approximately 215 miles (350 kilometers) of discontinuous trail has been established between Niagara-on-the-Lake in the west, through Toronto, to Trenton in the east.

The route connects 28 cities, towns and villages using many existing parks, pathways and natural areas along the waterfront. About 5 million people are within easy reach of the trail and the limitless variety of activities it provides access to. In the more built-up areas, you can visit museums, art galleries, festivals, vegetable markets and antique fairs or relax at a sidewalk café. You can jog, swim, sail, or rent a canoe and explore the shoreline. Hundreds of archaeological and historical sites, preserving a link to the past, are there for you to investigate. Because the path is paved in many places, it's great for bikes, in-line skates, strollers or wheelchairs.

Least bittern, one of many species found along the Waterfront Trail.

The best news for outdoor enthusiasts is the number of green spaces for hiking, cycling, canoeing, cross-country skiing, birding and wildlife viewing: the trail links 177 natural areas and 143 parks. From the regenerated wetland of Nawautin Nature Sanctuary near Grafton to Oshawa's Second Marsh, an important stopover for more than 250 species of migratory birds, to Burlington's 30 miles (50 kilometers) of hiking trails in the Royal Botanical

When you go

Lake Ontario Waterfront Trail
Waterfront Regeneration Trust
207 Queen's Quay West, Suite 580
Toronto, ON M5J 1A7
Tel: (416) 314-8572
Fax: (416) 314-9497

Hike Ontario
Walking Centre
Tel: 1-800-422-0552

Recommended Reading

The Waterfront Trail Guidebook. Toronto: Waterfront Trail Regeneration Trust, 1995.

Gardens, there is no end to the outdoor activity possibilities.

The Trust's goal is to link all the communities from Niagara-on-the-Lake to Gananoque and eventually connect at each end with the Seaway Trail in New York State. With accommodation readily available at campgrounds, B&Bs, motels or hotels, and buses and GO trains connecting each community, a circumnavigation of the new, improved Lake Ontario is just a step away.

A view of Lake Ontario along the western tip of the Waterfront Trail.

Ganaraska Trail

When you hear the phrase "long-distance trail," do you think expedition? Do you think heavy loads, blisters, aching muscles? Do you think – *Not me*! Yet "long distance" doesn't have to mean difficult, or that you have to go the whole nine yards! The Ganaraska Hiking Trail – over 300 miles (500 kilometers) long – offers nearly 280 miles (450 kilometers) of easy, scenic walking through some of the prettiest countryside in Ontario.

Completed in 1989, the Ganaraska Trail was built and is now maintained entirely by volunteers. Beginning in Port Hope on Lake Ontario, the trail travels north along the Ganaraska River, through the Ganaraska Forest to the picturesque Kawartha Lakes. From here it crosses the Trent Canal and heads west, skirting the northern shore of Lake Simcoe and ending at Glen Huron on the edge of the Niagara Escarpment. Two spur trails connect to Wasaga Beach on Georgian Bay and to the city of Midland.

For most of its length, the Ganaraska Trail can be divided into day hikes. You could, however, link several day trips by camping at any number of provincial parks and private campgrounds along the way. Another alternative allows you to leave the tent and camping gear at home and still spend a week hiking different parts of the Ganaraska Trail. The Ganaraska Trail Inn-to-Inn is a network of six B&Bs in the Lake Simcoe area that caters specifically to hikers. The B&Bs are spaced a pleasant day hike apart between Orillia and Midland. Every night you can look forward to a delicious dinner, comfortable bed and a hot shower, and be sent on your way in the morning with a hearty breakfast and a packed lunch. Your hosts help coordinate your itinerary, and shuttle your bags or car to your next day's destination.

Like much of the "civilized" sections of the Ganaraska Trail, the route passes through a variety of gentle terrain, on country lanes, over forested paths and grassy meadows, past farmland, lakes, rivers and marshes. Periodically, the trail passes through towns and villages, where you can stop for a snack or take in some local history. Ontario's smallest jail, in Creemore, is one such stop. Built in 1892, the stone building measures roughly 16 by 23 feet (5 by 7 meters) and holds three "guests" in separate cells.

The western terminus of the Ganaraska Hiking Trail.

Rapids seen from the Ganaraska Hiking Trail.

Closed in the early 1940s, it's now open to the public, and the picnic table on the property is a favorite lunch-time stop for hikers.

Each season along the trail has its delights: a sea of trilliums in the spring before the leaves of the forest unfurl; wild strawberries and raspberries during the summer; and breathtaking fall colors. Situated in the heart of Ontario's snowbelt, a long season of cross-country skiing and snowshoeing is virtually guaranteed, and the Ganaraska Trail is always open.

If an expedition is what you're looking for, one section of the Ganaraska Trail will fill the bill. Linking the Peterborough and Orillia sections is a long, 40-mile (65-kilometer) stretch of strenuous backpacking in the appropriately named Wilderness section. Even very experienced hikers are advised not to hike this rugged part without a leader from the Ganaraska Trail Association. There is no visible trail on this route, only blazes on rocks and trees – and these are often rearranged by the very active resident beavers!

The Ganaraska Trail Association, formed in 1970, now claims more than 500 members in nine separate trail clubs. A guidebook, including detailed maps and trail descriptions, is available from the association.

When you go

Ganaraska Trail Association
PO Box 19, 12 King St.
Orillia, ON L3V 1R1
Website: www3.sympatico.ca/hikers.net

For information on the Ganaraska Trail Inn-to-Inn:
Trail's End B&B
Tel: (705) 835-2158
Website: www.barint.on.ca/~siberinn/inntoinn

Haliburton Highlands

Just two hours north of Toronto, you can escape the mad rush of the city and retreat to the small-town feel of Haliburton County. The transition from "that other world" is made all the more complete as you cross the county line and enter the rolling, rugged landscape of the Canadian Shield. Here, the roads dip and weave, following the contours of the land and water.

More than 600 lakes, picturesque rivers and secluded forests have attracted cottagers to Haliburton for nearly a century. During the summer, the resident population of 15,000 swells to 130,000. Yet the county is considered "not quite discovered," and the tourism industry has not swelled the heads of the Highlanders.

The same attractions have lured canoeists, hikers and cross-country skiers seeking an accessible wilderness experience in a friendly atmosphere. And the county delivers: endless waterways to explore by canoe or kayak, hundreds of miles of trails to investigate on foot, and innovative facilities promoting environmental education to stimulate the mind.

The Leslie M. Frost Centre, situated on 926 square miles (2,400 square kilometers) of forested lands 7 miles (12 kilometers) south of Dorset, is well worth checking out. Run by the Ministry of Natural Resources, the center is primarily an outdoor education facility, offering a variety of public programs during the summer. Birding, geology, forest ecology – even painting! – are just a few of the courses. They also offer canoeing classes and other outdoor-skills

Waterfall in the Haliburton Highlands.

Goldenrod and white asters.

workshops. A network of canoe routes, portages and campsites has been established throughout the property, 95 percent of it on publicly accessible Crown land. Only a handful of the 60 lakes are decorated with cottages, leaving plenty of pristine wilderness to seekers of solitude. Closer to the Frost campus, marked walking trails and 15 miles (25 kilometers) of groomed cross-country skiing trails are maintained for public use.

East of the Frost Centre is the privately owned Haliburton Forest and Wildlife Reserve. It's also an outdoor education facility with a 775-square-mile (2,000-square-kilometer) playground for a variety of activities. During the summer, over 180 miles (300 kilometers) of rough roads and trails are maintained for mountain biking. You can spend an afternoon or a week riding to any of 50 lakes on the property and dozens of rivers, streams and creeks. Just keep your eyes peeled for wildlife – deer, beaver, bear or moose are commonly seen, and you may come across signs of the wild wolves that live in the forest.

The Wolf Centre provides another opportunity

for viewing these intelligent creatures. Opened in July 1996, this unique center features a pack of timber wolves. Captive, yet untamed and unsocialized, the pack lives in a 15-acre (6-hectare) natural-forest compound. At one end of the enclosure is an indoor observatory with one-way windows overlooking the feeding area. At meal times, you can observe the wolves without your presence being known to them. It's an incredible opportunity to see this elusive creature, seldom seen in the wild.

Educational programs are high on the list of priorities at Haliburton Forest, and one particular activity will really get you high – off the ground, that is. The canopy board-walk tour involves a drive deep into the forest, a hike along a creek, and a

boat ride across an isolated lake to a stand of old-growth white pine. You quickly gain 65 feet (20 meters) as you're hoisted above the forest floor to a suspended boardwalk that winds through the treetops to a platform, where interpretive guides discuss the forest environment.

Though summer is the busiest time in the county, winter has quite a reputation among the cross-country ski crowd. The Haliburton Nordic Trails Association grooms, maintains and patrols approximately 180 miles (300 kilometers) of trails throughout the Highlands. Of particular note is the 90-mile (150-kilometer) trail network in the Central Area around Lake Kashagawigamog. Fifteen resorts, some of which are involved in a lodge-to-lodge ski operation, share access to the system. You can stay at a different lodge every night and ski new terrain every day.

This is just a taste of what Haliburton Highlands has to offer. If you're traveling there for the first time, you'd be wise to stop at the Chamber of Commerce in Minden, or contact them prior to your visit. They'll provide maps and information on dozens of different activities in the county.

When you go

Haliburton Highlands
Chamber of Commerce
PO Box 147
Minden, ON K0M 2K0
Tel: 1-800-461-7677
Tel: (705) 286-1760
Fax: (705) 286-6016
E-mail: hhcc@cybernet.on.ca
Website: www.cybernet.on.ca/~hhcc

Algonquin Provincial Park (Summer)

If you examine a map of Algonquin Provincial Park, you'll see hundreds of squiggly dark blue lines and an equal number of irregular light blue blobs. And except for a fat red line representing a highway that cuts through the southwest portion of the park, the rest is green.

These colors are much sought after – the blue maze of lakes, rivers and streams, the vast green forested tracts. This raw, beautiful terrain, a combination of ancient bedrock and recent glaciation, may be Ontario's pride and joy, but it has also captured the hearts of millions of people the world over.

Yet Ontario's first provincial park was not established to preserve a virgin landscape. In fact, logging the region's great white and red pines had been going on for 60 years before a park was even proposed. With all the development rapidly taking place in other parts of Southern Ontario, clearing the land for settlement and agriculture was greatly feared, especially by the timber barons. Thus, an area encompassing 18 townships was set aside in 1893 to protect the forests, the watersheds of the five major rivers that flow from the highlands, and the wildlife. Over the years, the park has doubled in size with subsequent additions.

Almost immediately, visitors began coming to Algonquin, first by train and later by car to cottages, resorts and summer camps. Many of them gained their first apprecia-tion for the peace and solitude of the natural world at Algonquin, which led to a lifelong affection for the park's lakes and forests.

Leaving the blues and greens aside, it is the park's stunning reds, golds and yellows that are its primary inspiration, especially to artists like Tom Thomson, who captured the essence of the landscape in his paintings. When people think of Canada's wilderness, it is his images that most come to mind.

Late September and early October is the time most recom-mended for a visit to Algonquin. The crowds have disappeared, as have the pesky mosquitoes, and the forest palette is rich and varied. The days are still sunny and warm, and the nights are not too cool. You can drive along Highway 60, which cuts through the southern corner of the park, and have your pick of quiet campsites on glassy smooth lakes.

If it's your first visit to Algonquin, a stop at the Visitor Centre, 27 miles (43 kilometers) east of the West Gate, is highly rec-ommended. Overlooking Sunday Creek valley, this modern facility

Moose in Algonquin Park.

Tom Thomson

Tom Thomson, whose paintings of Algonquin have shaped our apprecia-tion of Canada's wilder-ness, drowned mysteri-ously in Canoe Lake in 1917. He is considered a member of the Group of Seven, although the group wasn't officially formed until 1920.

was opened during the park's centennial in 1993. It houses world-class exhibits depicting the park history and wildlife habitats, as well as a bookstore where you can pick up maps and booklets on the hiking and canoeing routes, and dozens of other publications featuring Algonquin park. The Logging Museum, just inside the East Gate, is another interesting stop, with displays of the early logging days, including a re-created camboose camp, a steam-powered log tug called an "alligator," and a working log dam and chute.

Private cottages, campgrounds and picnic areas line the 35-mile (56-kilometer) length of Highway 60 (also known as the Parkway Corridor), the busiest part of the park. Thirteen interpretive hiking trails are readily accessible from the highway, varying in length from half a mile (1 kilometer) to 7 miles (11 kilometers). Interpretive brochures are available at each trailhead, explaining the ecology of the park's lakes, rivers, bogs and forests, and how humans have altered it. In the fall, you'll want to head for higher ground – more effort is required, but you can let your pulse settle while you drink in the colorful views of Algonquin's forests.

In July and August, it might seem like half the population of Southern Ontario has joined you in Algonquin for a quiet, "wilderness" experience, but there are ways to escape the crowds along Highway 60. The eastern portion of the park, at Achray Campground, is a little off the beaten path, and two interpretive trails start from here. The scenic Berm Lake Trail is an enjoyable 2.8-mile (4.5-kilo-meter) loop around Berm Lake, through fragrant pine and oak forests. The 1-mile (1.5-kilometer) Barron Canyon Trail leads to the highlight of this area, the north rim of the 330-foot-deep (100-meter-deep) Barron Canyon.

Wolf Howl

Every fall, hundreds of people travel to Algonquin to join public wolf howls. Park staff give an interpretive talk on wolves then lead visitors by car to a site where they send out a wolf howl and wait for a response.

The longer Eastern Pines Trail has 3.7- and 9-mile (6- and 15-kilometer) loops that can be completed in a day, but campsites along each provide an easily accessible getaway. Two other overnight backpacking trails, accessed from the highway, are available for the serious hiker. The Highlands and the Western Upland trails loop into the interior of the park on circuits of 12 to 55 miles (19 to 88 kilometers) in length.

Algonquin Park.

But to really get away from it all, you'll have to launch your canoe in several of the myriad lakes, rivers and streams in the backcountry. There are nearly 1,500 miles (2,400 kilometers) of canoe and portage routes to choose from, starting at any of 29 access points. Some of these are located along Highway 60, others around the perimeter of the park.

With 100,000 people heading into the interior every summer, you still won't be alone in the backcountry, especially a day or two away from an access point. But there are plenty of nooks and crannies to explore – just use a little imagination and some sage advice from park staff in planning your route, and that precious Algonquin tranquility won't evade you.

One of the highlights of any canoe trip into the park is the opportunity to see – and hear – wildlife. Moose, which can be seen along the populated Parkway Corridor and on a number of the hiking trails, seem to be more in their element here. Hug the shoreline of the lakes and rivers and you're bound to see a cow and calves nibbling the tender young vegetation in the shallows. Perhaps you'll see a bull moose standing at the edge of the forest, feigning a lack of interest in your paddling progress before he turns and crashes through the brush. Come

Canoeing Tips

- Choose the correct canoe for the type of paddling you expect to be doing. There are different designs, materials and sizes for lakes, rivers, whitewater and expedition paddling. Consider the weight of the canoe if you plan to do a lot of portaging. Ask a specialized dealer.

- Getting wet is a given. Wear synthetic clothing instead of cotton, which dries slowly and can chill you quickly.

- Quick-drying nylon pants are much better than cotton jeans, and much more comfortable. Make sure they're roomy enough to allow kneeling in the canoe.

- Always wear a Personal Flotation Device (PFD). Choose carefully. It needs to be comfortable while paddling so you won't be tempted to take it off. For kids, purchase a PFD that has a crotch strap and grab loop on the collar. Kids should wear their PFD at all times, even around camp.

- Remember that children's clothing and gear have to be adequate as well. Rig a seat in the middle of the canoe so they can sit comfortably, and let them paddle at leisure with their own blade.

- The weight and design of your paddle depend on the type of canoeing you do. For example, a narrow, small blade moves better in lakes. In general, the paddle should come up to your chin when standing, but it will depend on your seat position – you'll need a longer paddle if you sit high in the boat.

- For cold-water paddling, neoprene booties and gloves help keep you warm and more comfortable.

- A spray cover will protect your gear from wind, water and rain.

- Choose a destination that won't over-stretch your abilities on the water. This is especially true when traveling with kids – you must be able to come to their aid in an emergency.

- Canoes allow you the luxury of carrying extras you wouldn't carry on a backpacking trip: camp chairs, a tarp for cooking under, a roomy tent, fresh food and a bottle of wine to have with dinner.

- If your trip involves portaging, think "backpacking" when you're loading the canoe and leave the luxuries at home! Take a pack that will hold a large amount of gear rather than trying to carry a dozen items in your arms. Remember to take along a good pair of walking or hiking boots.

- Use dry bags for waterproof packing. Protect camera and binoculars in Pelican containers.

- Tie your gear into the canoe firmly.

- Attach a length of rope (called a painter) to each end of your boat.

- Cut out the bottom of a plastic bleach bottle to use as a bailer and attach it to your boat. Carry a sponge to soak up the dregs.

- Outfit your canoe with knee pads for greater comfort in a kneeling position.

September, the sound of his bugling will echo throughout the park.

Black bears, white-tailed deer and raccoons are often seen, but it is the wolf you've come to hear. Much research has been conducted on Algonquin's wolf population, and an estimated 175 to 200 of them in 35 to 40 packs wander throughout the park. Once you've heard their spine-tingling howls, the sound will never leave you.

Have your binoculars ready to zoom in on rose-breasted grosbeak, brown thrasher or scarlet tanager, common residents of the hardwood forests. Or gray jay and spruce grouse that prefer the spruce and pines. On many lakes, in the evening

When you go

Algonquin Provincial Park
Ministry of Natural Resources
PO Box 219
Whitney, ON K0J 2M0
Tel: (705) 633-5572
Tel: (705) 633-5538 (reservations)
Fax: (705) 633-5581

Maps and publications may be ordered from:
The Friends of Algonquin
PO Box 248
Whitney, ON K0J 2M0
Tel: (705) 637-2828
Fax: (705) 637-2138
Website: www.algonquinpark.on.ca

as you watch the sun setting behind a rounded hill, you'll hear the laugh of the loon – the epitome of any Algonquin experience.

Though some people claim

you cannot have a true wilderness experience in Algonquin, the park can still swallow a large number of canoeists. However, all backcountry campsites on your route must be reserved either at the point of access or, preferably, well in advance of your departure. This avoids over-burdening popular campsites and ensures everyone the experience they're seeking. There are also a number of refurbished historic ranger cabins available for rent.

There are more than a dozen outfitters offering canoe trips into the park's interior. Consider taking one of these if you're at all unsure of your abilities. They'll make sure your visit is a memorable one – pleasantly so!

Fall in Algonquin Park.

Algonquin Provincial Park (Winter)

Perhaps a winter trip is not what immediately comes to mind when you think of Algonquin park, but then, why not? Ontario's oldest and most beloved provincial park is still only three or four hours from the rest of Southern Ontario, and if you're looking for peace and solitude, the snow season guarantees it.

The park has developed three major cross-country ski areas accessible from Highway 60, the main corridor cutting through the southwest corner. Together they offer over 50 miles (80 kilometers) of groomed, trackset trails ranging in length from about a mile to 15 miles (1.3 to 24 kilometers).

The Fen Lake Ski Trail, at the West Gate, is the smallest of the three areas. About 11 miles (18 kilometers) on four trails loop through stands of sugar maple, birch, beech and hemlock frequented by

moose. Watch out for gaping holes in the snow – moose tracks are common on the trails! An easy trail follows Gateway Creek to Fen Lake, a good spot for lunch or a hot drink before you tackle the intermediate

When you go

For a map of the ski trails and a list of winter outfitters, contact:
Algonquin Provincial Park
Ministry of Natural Resources
PO Box 219
Whitney, ON K0J 2M0
Tel: (705) 633-5572

section on the return portion. A difficult trail branches off from this and climbs a ridge overlooking Heron Lake, and a very easy trail, just over half a mile (a kilometer) long, loops around the west edge of the lake.

The Minnesing Ski Trail near Canisbay Lake on the north side of the highway offers 17 miles (28 kilometers) of trails on four stacked loops. Three loops are rated easy, with distances of 3, 6 and 10.5 miles (5, 10 and 17 kilometers); one loop of 15 miles (24 kilometers) is more difficult. Part of the trail follows the Minnesing Road, which once ran from the Highland Inn on Cache Lake to Minnesing Lodge on Burnt Island Lake. Minnesing Lodge was billed as a "luxury" wilderness resort for visitors in the early part of the century, but it was eventually torn down in the 1950s.

Leaf Lake Ski Trail at the East Gate is the most extensive and most varied of the ski trail systems, with more than 30 miles (50 kilometers) of trails and three warming shelters. The Pine Tree Loop is one of the most scenic routes, with beautiful vistas overlooking Pinetree Lake and exhilarating downhill runs. Groomed but not trackset, it provides a little more of a backcountry feel. Every year, the Algonquin Park Wilderness Ski Marathon and Loppet is held on the Leaf Lake system, with events for families and children as well as a full 25-mile (40-kilometer) marathon.

Apart from the groomed

Snowshoeing in Algonquin Provincial Park.

cross-country ski trails, experienced winter enthusiasts can make their own tracks, whether on skis or snowshoes, in many other areas of the park. Following summer backpacking routes is one possibility if you have solid map-reading skills or you're already familiar with the trails. Another possibility is to follow the frozen waterways. Barron Canyon – a spectacular summer canoe route – is also impressive in the winter, with its stark cliffs rising 330 feet (100 meters) above the smooth, snow-covered surface of the river.

Three dog-sledding outfitters are licensed to operate in three different locations in the park. The Sunday Lake, Brûlé Lake and Chocpaw trails, totaling over 90 miles (150 kilometers), are maintained by the outfitters, but

Mew Lake birch tree, Algonquin Provincial Park.

open for public use. Each outfitter offers day trips or multi-day outings from their rustic tent camps.

There are plenty of services and accommodation just outside the park gates, in Oxtongue Lake and Dwight on the west side, and in Whitney on the east side. But for a unique winter experience, try renting one of two refurbished ranger cabins (ski or snowshoe in), one at Kitty Lake, the other at McKaskill Lake. Or rent one of the "yurts" at Mew Lake Campground. These spacious tent structures have basic furniture and electric heat. Mew Lake Campground is also open for winter camping, but be sure you know what you're doing before setting out. Winds and temperatures can be bitterly cold in the winter, causing serious frostbite in a matter of minutes.

Lake of Two Rivers, Algonquin Provincial Park.

Bon Echo Provincial Park

Mishipashoo, the Great Water Lynx, lived in the deep waters of Mazinaw Lake, or so the Ojibwa believed. Before crossing the lake, they would offer tobacco to the water spirit so it wouldn't whip up its great spiked tail and overturn their canoes.

The image of Mishipashoo, and more than 260 other mythical beings, animals, birds and people, is painted in red ocher on Bon Echo Rock, the star attraction of Bon Echo Provincial Park in central Ontario. The imposing mile-long (1.5-kilometer-long) sheer cliff, which rises 300 feet (90 meters) above Mazinaw Lake, is the drawing board for one of the largest concentrations of native pictographs in North America.

Every year, more than 170,000 visitors come to explore Bon Echo's lakes and forests, and to examine the intriguing rock paintings. A close-up view is best achieved by canoe, launching at the lagoon on Mazinaw Lake across the narrows from the rock face. While you focus on the drawings just above the waterline, your gaze may be drawn to the eastern white cedars that cling to the rock. Up to a thousand years old, these twisted, dwarf evergreens survive in tiny pockets of soil in cracks and ledges on the rock.

There are two alternatives to visiting the pictographs by canoe. The Friends of Bon Echo Park offer hour-long tours on the *Wanderer Too* that include a stop at the cliff and a discussion of the spiritual significance of the images to the Algonkian people. The Friends also operate a ferry service on the *Mugwump*, shuttling park visitors across the narrows to the base of the cliff and the start of the Cliff Top Trail. This mile-long (1.5-kilometer-long) interpretive trail leads to the top of Bon Echo Rock.

Not just a pretty cliff, Bon Echo Rock is home to several remarkable bird species. Prairie warblers nest here in the summer on the rock barrens. Huge, blue-black ravens soar above the lake, or perch high up, mocking you with their raucous call. Turkey vultures are also seen around Bon Echo Rock, though they nest in the boulders at the base of the cliff. But if you're really lucky, you may see a peregrine falcon, one of 33 birds that were released between 1994 and 1998 as part of a re-introduction program for this endangered species.

Although Bon Echo Rock is the park's centerpiece, there are several hiking trails and over a dozen lakes to explore. The 3-mile (4.8-kilometer) Shield Trail follows for a short distance the long-abandoned Addington Road, built in the 1850s to encourage colonization of the area. Farming and mining efforts failed, but some economic benefit was gained through logging of the great white pines.

The Bon Echo Creek Trail is a birder's paradise, leading through wonderfully varied habitats where warblers, yellow-bellied sapsuckers, belted kingfishers, ducks, vireos, thrushes and a host of other species can be spotted within its half-mile (one-kilometer) length. Another easy loop, the mile-long (1.4-kilometer-long) High Pines Trail, features the ecology of the mixed forest and wetland communities, and an opportunity to see a white-tailed deer or a five-lined skink.

The most strenuous of the park's hiking routes is the Abes and Essens Trail System, a series of three stacked loops covering 2.5, 5.5 and 10.5 miles (4, 9 and 17 kilometers). The longest loop can be hiked in a

The cliff face at Bon Echo Provincial Park.

Bon Echo Provincial Park.

full day, but for a special treat, camp at one of five hike-in sites. Each one is situated on a tranquil lake, where the only sounds are the call of the loon or the slap of a beaver tail.

There are excellent canoeing opportunities within the park, well suited to the whole family. The Kishkebus route is a leisurely five- or six-hour loop of 13 miles (21 kilometers) starting in Mazinaw Lake. Don't be put off by the mile-long (1.5-kilometer-long) portage into Kishkebus Lake – the trail is well maintained and there are plenty of rest stops. No camping or fires are allowed on this route, so take a picnic lunch. Take your rod and reel, too, for a chance to hook into some bass or lake trout. The circuit continues through Shabomeka and Semicircle lakes, and back to Mazinaw Lake,

with three very short portages linking the lakes.

Nestled in the western portion of Bon Echo, Joeperry and Pearson lakes offer a tranquil backcountry experience for day trippers or overnight canoe campers. Scattered

When you go

Bon Echo Provincial Park
RR 1
Cloyne, ON K0H 1K0
Tel: (613) 336-2228

along the shores of these two lakes are 25 interior campsites accessible only by canoe. You can spend quiet days paddling on the lake, swimming, fishing and watching for wildlife. You might see moose in the shallows, or a family of curious otters. In the narrows between the two lakes, you'll see great blue herons, ducks, loons and all other

manner of waterfowl and shore birds that nest and feed in the marshes.

For car-campers, the park offers 500 sites in two large campgrounds at Mazinaw Lake and the more secluded Hardwood Hill.

Adjacent to the lake campground, the Friends of Bon Echo Park provide boat tours and operate a concession where canoes, kayaks, paddle boats and surf bikes can be rented. Be sure to stop at the Visitor Centre and Museum for information and a peekpreview of the park's special features, then head next door to Greystones Gifts and Bookstore to pick up some of the excellent interpretive brochures published by the Friends, available for a small fee. The park is open for camping from mid-May to Thanksgiving weekend, and reservations are strongly recommended.

Ottawa River

The mighty Ottawa River. Once it was the conveyor of native people in their fragile birchbark canoes. Then legendary explorers and voyageurs tackled the raging waters in their *canots de maître*. And when logging replaced the fur trade, huge rafts of great white pines were floated down the dangerous Ottawa River to the St. Lawrence River. Now, the foaming waters are speckled with blue, yellow and orange rubber rafts filled with today's intrepid adventurers – whitewater rafters.

The Ottawa River is Ontario's premier whitewater rafting destination, and OWL Rafting is the premier outfitter to take you on this exciting ride. The company was started in 1981 by the Kerckhoff family, who'd already established a successful whitewater kayak and canoe school on the Madawaska River. With the family's reputation firmly in place, whitewater rafting on the Ottawa River seemed a natural offshoot. Today, the company is owned and operated by Claudia Kerckhoff and Dirk Van Wijk.

The rafting experience begins about 90 minutes north of Ottawa at the OWL Centre, a large complex on the bank of the river. After a briefing session, participants are outfitted with paddles, helmets and lifejackets, then shuttled off to the put-in a short drive upstream.

This is where the action really begins – rapid action that is! Depending on the trip you've signed up for, you'll take the Main Channel all the way down a 7.5-mile (12-kilometer) section of the river. Or, after running McCoy's, the first set of Class III rapids, you might split off and take the Middle Channel. Either way, it's a rough-and-tumble ride through Class I to IV rapids such as the deceptively named Little Trickle, the playful Angel's Kiss, and the formidable, technically demanding Garvin's Chute, ending with the Grand Canyonesque Coliseum rapids.

If splooshing through the rapids doesn't get you wet enough, try

Whitewater rafting on the Ottawa River.

The Ottawa River in winter.

body surfing through some of the milder rapids. With toes pointed downstream and arms outstretched, it's quite a feeling to bounce along with the river rippling and bubbling all around you. Whatever you do, a grin will be plastered across your face for the duration, an indication of the high-risk-of-fun factor.

After about six hours on the river, you'll finish off with a barbecue lunch aboard OWL's Cruise Diner, which meets you after the last rapid and ferries you 2.5 miles (4 kilometers) downstream to the OWL Centre and the trip's end. Located right on the banks of the Ottawa River, the center has its own beach, campground, cabins and pavilion, plus outdoor sports facilities, pedal-boats and other toys to keep you amused.

OWL offers different strokes for different folks. Their family float trips are a wonderful introduction to whitewater for young and old alike. The 3.7-mile (6-kilometer) trip follows a gentler route down the river, still with lots of whitewater and plenty of thrills, but without the worry. All you do is hang on, have fun and let the guide do all the work. Children must weigh 50 pounds (22 kilograms) or more to take this trip.

The regular raft trip involves a 12-person raft with one guide using a stern-mounted oar to steer the boat through the rapids. Guests help paddle – it's part of the fun! – but the guide maintains full control. For experienced paddlers, or those looking for more adventure, smaller seven-person sport rafts provide plenty of challenge. All guests and the guide work as a team to successfully negotiate each set of rapids. And for the thrill of whitewater playboating, OWL offers the "sportyak" experience. You and your partner test your skills in one of these inflatable kayaks while a guide coaches you through the rapids from his own kayak.

Two-day packages combine whitewater fun and beach activities at the center, plus meals and accommodation either in tents or in cabins. The season begins in mid-May and goes right through to the end of September, seven days a week, rain or shine (you'll get wet regardless!). A one-day excursion starts at $85 (weekday rate); the two-day vacation starts at $180; and the family float trip is $55 for adults and $35 for children 12 and under.

When you go

OWL Rafting
PO Box 29
Foresters Falls, ON K0J 1V0
Tel: (613) 646-2263
Fax: (613) 646-2307
Reservations: 1-800-461-7238
Website: www.owl-mkc.ca

Prince Edward County

For rural Ontario charm, nothing quite compares to this delightful county on the north shore of Lake Ontario. Just a two-hour drive east of Toronto, Prince Edward County – or Quinte's Isle as it's also known – is an "almost island," a small balloon connected to the north shore of Lake Ontario by a narrow bridge of land at Carrying Place. It was here that fur traders bound for Montreal once portaged their voyageur canoes. But it is the heritage left by the United Empire Loyalists that is most evident in Quinte – in its architecture, history, industry and culture. And there's no better way to step back into history and enjoy the isle's natural features than at the leisurely pace of a bicycle.

Prince Edward County Chamber of Commerce has mapped out six bicycle trips, all circle routes ranging in length from 22 to 35 miles (36 to 56.5 kilometers). Each can be completed in a day and still allow time for exploration on foot.

And there's plenty of that to do! The region is brimming with museums, antique shops and art galleries. No need to pack a lunch either; the many roadside markets, cozy cafés, noisy pubs and ice cream shops you'll pass along the way are perfect for afternoon rest stops.

Long a vacationer's paradise, people flock to the county for summer recreation. It may be more enjoyable, then, to cycle Quinte's Isle before the Victoria Day weekend in May and after Labor Day in September, when the traffic isn't as heavy. Using the route maps provided by the Chamber of Commerce, you can develop your own itinerary to include some of Quinte's natural highlights.

Lake on the Mountain Provincial Park, part of the Route #1 cycling circuit, is one you won't want to miss. The existence of the lake, perched nearly 200 feet (60 meters) above the Bay of Quinte and with no apparent source, has had people scratching their heads since the days of the pioneers. Once a spiritual site for the Mohawk people, the mystery of the lake is now rather dully explained by modern-day scientists as a "collapsed doline" – basically a giant sinkhole in the limestone escarpment that filled with water. Regardless, it's an intriguing and beautiful spot. After grunting to the top of the hill, park your bike under one of the broad trees and admire the view over the Bay of Quinte and the town of Glenora, Sir John A. Macdonald's boyhood home. A pretty little ferry shuttles back and forth from Glenora to the "mainland" free of charge.

After leaving the park, the route takes you past stately homes, antique shops and pioneer farmland that parallels Adolphus Reach. From your slightly elevated perspective, you get occasional views of the reach and the shores of the mainland opposite. Further along on the Smith Bay side of the peninsula, the road is steeper and winding. You may as well give in to the temptation to stop for a break at the Duke of Marysburgh Pub and General Store, or the Travellers' Tales bookstore. Another must-see is the Macaulay Heritage Park, the site of the Prince Edward County Museum and Macaulay House in Picton, where this bike route begins and ends.

Again setting out from Picton, bike Route #2 leads in the opposite direction to the spectacular

Prince Edward County.

Sandbanks Provincial Park. Once there, cycle to the West Lake section, lock your bike and strike out for the dunes. The provincial park protects two bay-mouth and sand-dune systems battered into shape over the centuries by the prevailing westerly winds and waves crashing onto the southwest shores of Quinte's Isle. The West Lake system is the largest fresh-water sand dune system in the world, with dunes reaching as high as 80 feet (25 meters); the East Lake system, known locally as "The Outlet," is smaller but still impressive.

You'll find a remarkable diversity of plants and birdlife in this desert-like region – juniper heaths on the open dunes, forests of pine, maple and cedar, sand dune wetlands (called "pannes") and marshes. During spring and fall migration, uncommon birds such as yellow-breasted chat, Kentucky warbler, blue-gray gnatcatcher, hawks, saw-whet owls and turkey vultures have been spotted in the park.

Retrieve your bike and continue on bike Route #2. At Milford, you can continue on to Picton to complete the tour, or take a long detour

When you go

Prince Edward County
Chamber of Tourism & Commerce
Box 50, 116 Main St.
Picton, ON K0K 2T0
Tel: (613) 476-2421

Sandbanks Provincial Park
RR 1
Picton, ON K0K 2T0
Tel: (613) 393-3319

For rentals and guided off-road rides:
Bloomfield Bicycle Company
Box 78, 225 Main St.
Bloomfield, ON K0K 1G0
Tel: (613) 393-1060

to the Mariners' Museum in South Bay. This is a fascinating museum, filled with memorabilia retrieved from offshore shipwrecks. South Bay itself has an exciting history: rum-runners from the United States came here to load up on the county's major crop – barley – and later returned with illegal rum.

It might be more reasonable to make a full day trip of this loop, to allow time to visit Little Bluff Conservation Area and the Prince Edward Point National Wildlife Area at the southeastern tip of the Long Point, rivalled only by Point Pelee on Lake Erie as a major stopover for migrating birds. More than 300 bird species have been recorded here during the spring and fall migration. These are perfect spots for birding, and the quiet, scenic route will round out your county experience.

Walking through the forest along the open dunes.

Gatineau Park

One of the joys of visiting the nation's capital is that it's easy to escape to nearby Gatineau Park! About a 15-minute drive north of the Parliament Buildings, this gem of wilderness has been the playground of Ottawa Valley residents for over a century. Once threatened by logging and other industries, the 135-square-mile (356-square-kilometer) region was established as a park in 1938 and is now a treasured refuge for wildlife and enjoyed by hikers, skiers and sightseers alike.

Abruptly separated from the plains of the Ottawa River Valley, the park's western boundary is formed by the remarkable Eardley Escarpment, a 1000-foot (300-meter) cliff stretching 18 miles (30 kilometers) from north to south. Looking west from the escarpment, you see a fertile valley, once primarily farmland, now encroaching urban sprawl. To the east as far as the Gatineau River are the rolling hills, forests and lakes of the park, a landscape scoured by glacial action. This is Canadian Shield country.

Every season in Gatineau is a delight. In spring, the trees aren't fully in leaf, allowing unimpeded views of the countryside and easier sightings of north-migrating birds. Masses of trilliums bloom early, blanketing the forest. Canoeing is good on Fortune Lake at this time of the year, when the marshy shoreline is bustling with birds, beavers, muskrats and a myriad of other pond creatures busy feeding and raising their young.

In summer, there are 75 miles (125 kilometers) of hiking trails to explore, most of which can be done in less than a day. They range from short strolls to more arduous and challenging hikes on a maze of interconnecting forest trails. Of these,

55 miles (90 kilometers) are accessible to mountain bikes from May 15 through the end of November.

Part of Canada's National Trail goes through the park, passing some major highlights along the way. The backpacking trail starts in Wakefield, Québec, and ends at the Parliament Buildings in Ottawa, for a total distance of 28 miles (45 kilometers). From there, it links up with the Rideau Trail. The National Trail can be hiked in two sections, with a stop overnight at a B&B in the charming town of Old Chelsea.

Pink Lake is one of the many highlights on the National Trail. This unique lake, where weekenders from the Ottawa Valley once went to swim, hike and dive from the cliffs, is now a protected environment. Because only the top layer of the water circulates, the bottom layer of Pink Lake is completely without oxygen, preserving rather than decomposing any vegetable matter and providing valuable information about the natural history here. You can learn all about the green, "meromictic" waters and their significance on interpretive signs on a boardwalk around the lake.

In late September and October, Gatineau's forests of maple, beech, birch and oak are bursting with color. At this time of year, a visit to Mackenzie King's Estate is a favorite outing. The former prime minister collected and relocated the ruins of stately buildings, among them a fireplace from the Parliament Buildings, which were destroyed by fire in 1916. Stories of seances and other-worldly goings-on at this site feed the imagination. In the fall, the ruins are set against a stunning backdrop of gold, orange and flaming red trees.

After the last fallen leaf has been generously doused with snow, Gatineau really sparkles. Winter is

Trees overlooking Pink Lake in Gatineau Park.

Autumn leaves overlooking Gatineau River.

the time to dust off your skinny skis for four months of excellent cross-country skiing in the Gatineau Hills. Once the snow flies, the 125-mile (200-kilometer) trail network is maintained for both classic ("glide and stride") and skate skiing. On weekends, the park is alive with brightly colored, Lycra-clad skiers charging up and down hills or going flat out on "Highway One." Novice, intermediate or expert; classic or skate-skiers; families with babies in pulks (sleds) and children shuffling alongside – all come to Gatineau to play on one of the largest trail networks in North America.

The snow season normally lasts from mid-December to the end of March. About 90 miles (150 kilometers) of trail are trackset for classic; 50 miles (80 kilometers) of these are groomed for skate skiing as well; and an additional 30 miles (50 kilometers) of trails are marked but not groomed. Approximately 18 miles (30 kilometers) of trails are designed specifically for winter hiking and

snowshoeing, although snowshoeing is permitted anywhere in the park other than on ski trails.

The park maintains a variety of accommodations suitable for overnight or multi-night ski or snowshoe touring. Four cabins and two yurts are available for the do-it-yourself crowd. These cozy tent shelters sleep from 6 to 16 people and are equipped with wood-burning stoves, bunk beds with mattresses and cooking gear. Bring only your sleeping bag, food and eating utensils. More luxurious accommo-

dation is offered at the Camp Gatineau Outdoor Centre and the Carman Trails International Youth Hostel. Trails to the shelters vary in length and difficulty and are suitable for intermediate or better skiers.

Gatineau is the perfect wilderness area for trying winter camping. There are five sites at Philippe Lake, just a short ski-in 1.8 miles (3 kilometers) from Parking Lot 19. You can ski in, set up your tents, dump your overnight gear and strike out on any number of day trips from your base camp. (If you need to bail out, you're not far from civilization and a warm car!)

Gatineau Park's less-maintained trails provide a real backcountry experience. The Richard Lake Yurt and the Camp Gatineau Outdoor Centre in the northwestern sector of the park are the most remote, but are still easily accessed by strong skiers. Swap your skinny skis for wider, heavier backcountry skis, and revel in blazing your own way.

When you go

Gatineau Park Visitor Centre
318 Meech Lake Road
Chelsea, QC
Tel: (819) 827-2020

National Capital Commission
Tel: 1-800-465-1867
Tel: (613) 239-5000

Recommended Reading

Fletcher, Katharine. *Historical Walks: The Gatineau Park Story.* Quyon: Chelsea House Publications, 1997.

Parc du Mont-Tremblant

You're driving north from Montréal, destination Parc du Mont-Tremblant. The stretch of highway between this vibrant international city and Québec's oldest park is a veritable playground, full of exciting distractions. Saint-Jérôme, Saint-Sauveur, Saint-Hippolyte, Morin-Heights, Val-Morin, Val-David, Sainte-Agathe, Saint-Jovite. Pretty little resort towns just a quick turn off the highway, or snuggled up to a round, forested mountain. Green-, orange-, or red-roofed houses with tiny dormers and flowers spilling from window boxes. Outdoor cafés, art galleries, craft shops, festivals, health spas, waterslide parks, safari parks...

And then there are the recreational diversions. The Québécois have an active, lively society and are always looking for fun and new adventures. Winter is a time for sleigh rides, dog sledding, skating, snowshoeing, snow rafting, inner tube sliding, downhill skiing (no fewer than 18 ski resorts in the region!) and snowboarding. And

in the warmer months, walking, cycling, swimming, water skiing, boating, whitewater rafting, climbing, fishing...

You'd be lucky to ever make it to the park at all!

But Parc du Mont-Tremblant is a place of retreat, of getting away from the bustle of the resort towns. The frantic pace of life gradually calms as the tranquility of the mountains and waterways creeps under your skin. Leave the excitement of the resorts behind and enter a wilderness experience.

Set aside as a forest reserve in 1895, the area became known as the park of the *montagne tremblante* – trembling mountain – to the early French settlers. The name originated

with a native legend in which the great spirit, the manitou, caused the mountain to tremble if the sacred laws of nature were breached. There's nothing earth-shattering

Snowshoeing

What did the *coureurs de bois* do when they hung up their paddles for the winter? Strapped on their snowshoes! Here are a few things to keep in mind.

- Before you buy a pair, rent different models to see which fits best for your weight (including pack) and the terrain you'll be traveling in.
- A narrow shoe allows a fairly natural stride, is easy to maneuver and gives good edging.
- A long "tail" acts as a rudder, which helps you track a straight line, but can hinder movement in technical or bushy terrain.
- If you're traveling in deep powder, steep terrain and with an overnight pack, you'll need fairly wide, long snowshoes for better flotation, and shorter toe length for uphills.
- Backcountry beginners should try a smaller snowshoe to aid balance and turning and let a more experienced person do the trail-breaking!
- A turned-up toe keeps the tip up and prevents excessive snow build-up.

Chutes Croches, Parc du Mont-Tremblant.

about Mont-Tremblant now except the endless possibilities it offers to nature buffs. It was officially designated a provincial park in 1981, and the logging that once took place has been excluded, to the delight of recreationists.

Parc du Mont-Tremblant encompasses 575 square miles (1,490 square kilometers) of the vast Laurentian Highlands, an ancient mountain range stretching along the north shore of the St. Lawrence River, of which Mont-Tremblant itself is the highest peak (3,067 feet/935 meters). Located 85 miles (140 kilometers) northwest of Montréal, it's easily accessible – once you've jostled your way onto the highways. The landscape is one of rolling, rounded hills and soft peaks, of streams spilling through deep gorges and lakes sprawling through wide valleys. Maple, beech, birch and evergreens transform the forests into outrageously beautiful scenes in the autumn, making it the best time to visit the park.

Mont-Tremblant park is divided into three sectors roughly following three different watersheds: La Diable, La Pimbina and L'Assomption. Three main entrances access the park from the south, with three additional access roads from the north.

Four self-guided nature trails, from 1 mile to 2 miles (1.5 to 3.4 kilometers) in length, will ease you into the delights of the park. In the L'Assomption sector, for example, take the Lac-de-L'Assomption Nature Trail to an observation point overlooking a delta teeming with waterfowl. Information brochures (French only) are available at all four trailheads. For those with a little more time and ambition, six hiking trails totaling 13 miles (21 kilometers) wind through the forest to some of the many waterfalls (called *chutes*) and panoramic views of lake-studded countryside.

Longer hiking trails vary from 6 to 12 miles (10 to 20 kilometers); some can be combined to make a 53-mile (85-kilometer) circuit bisecting the park from east to west. Those who like to be self-sufficient can settle into one of four shelters along the route. Two of the backpacking

trails, Toit-des-Laurentides and Centenaire, make up part of Québec's link to the Trans Canada Trail.

Mountain biking is a very popular activity in the park, either along the gravel roads or on woodland trails. A family favorite is the 8-mile (13-kilometer) route to Chutes Croches in La Diable sector. From the Ménagerie campground on the west shore of Lac Monroe, the trail follows Rivière du Diable to the 25-foot-high (7-meter-high) cascade that gushes through a narrow gorge. Several other trails are suitable for "relaxed" cycling, and thrill seekers will enjoy the more challenging 10.5-mile (17-kilometer) Lac-Cassagne trail in La Pimbina sector.

There are 6 rivers and 400 lakes in Parc du Mont-Tremblant, and dozens of them are accessible to canoeists and anglers. Two rivers and three lakes are particularly noteworthy. Rivière du Diable is a superb two- to four-day trip from Lac aux Herbes to the Vache-Noire campground, a total distance of 28 miles (45 kilometers). Ten campgrounds between Lac aux Herbes and Lac

Cross-country skiing at Parc du Mont-Tremblant.

Laplante make it an ideal wilderness trip. A lengthy portage of over 4 miles (7 kilometers) is required around the Chute du Diable, but transportation can be arranged by the park for a small fee. Paddlers will encounter Class I and II rapids on the river, all of which can be run or portaged, depending on your skill and comfort level. If you don't want to do the entire trip or tackle any swift water, the stretch between Lac Chat and Mont de la Vache Noire takes about three hours, placidly winding through spectacular scenery.

Rivière L'Assomption is a two- to three-day trip from Lac de L'Assomption to the Saint-Côme reception center on the park's southern boundary. The 9-mile (15-kilometer) route is a favorite with novice paddlers who can float idly down the river or test their mettle in a variety of small rapids.

The Armand–Rossi–Draper lakes circuit, far removed from the park's busier areas, provides a true wilderness experience on quiet, isolated lakes. With a little patience and luck you might see moose, white-tailed deer or black bears as you silently paddle along. Keep your binoculars handy – you never know when you'll come across herons, loons, woodpeckers, warblers or any of the other 180 species of birds found in the park. Anglers can try wetting a line for speckled trout, northern pike, walleye and brown trout, some of the 30 different fish species in the lakes. Fishing permits are awarded on a daily draw; be sure to check with the park for details.

Winter is a special time in the Laurentians. Many people head for the lively alpine resorts, while others seek out the quiet corners to ski or snowshoe under the snowy forest canopy. There's no lack of such places, and, with an average of 140 inches (350 centimeters) of snowfall from December to March, no lack of the fluffy stuff.

Parc du Mont-Tremblant maintains two networks of marked, patrolled and groomed trails, rated

Winter beauty at Parc du Mont-Tremblant.

easy to challenging. In La Diable sector, 35 miles (56 kilometers) on nine circuits range from 2.5 to 12.5 miles (4 to 20 kilometers) in length. Five wood-heated shelters, strategically placed, give you an opportunity to warm up and eat your lunch in comfort. La Pimbina sector, with two warming huts, has seven trails that cover 18 miles (30 kilometers) from half a mile to 9 miles (1 to 15 kilometers) long.

The backcountry skier has three long trails to choose from, and a total of 58 miles (94 kilometers) to traverse. Unlike the cross-country ski trails, the backcountry routes are marked but not mechanically groomed or patrolled. Four bunk-houses, each

Cross-country skiing.

Backpacking

Progressing from day hiking to overnight trips can be daunting—there's so much to carry!
Here are some hints to make the transition a bit easier.

- Develop your outdoor skills while car camping and/or on your day hikes. You need to know how to pitch your tent (every tent is different), light a small one-burner stove (and be able to cook a meal on it!) and bearproof your food.

- Start by hiking into a campsite that's within a reasonable walking distance of your car — say, two or three hours. Then, if you have to bail out, you'll be able to reach civilization quickly.

- Set up a comfortable base camp from which you can take day trips farther afield. That way you avoid lugging a heavy backpack every day.

- Because you've hiked only a short distance to your base camp, you can afford to take luxuries that you might otherwise leave behind: a good book to read, fresh pasta instead of a freeze-dried meal, a carton of wine (pull out the plastic liner and leave the cardboard container at home), a chair converter for your sleeping pad, and a pair of booties or sandals to wear around camp.

- Carry a pocket knife, whistle and lighter or waterproof matches on your person in case of an emergency.

- Take your friends! More people means less weight, as food and equipment can be divvied up.

- Most backpacks are not waterproof. Take along a large plastic garbage bag to line your pack in case of rain. An orange bag lets you see the contents of your pack and also acts as a signaling device in an emergency. You may also prefer to wear a brightly colored poncho that covers your pack.

- Package all food in plastic bags or plastic containers. Take about 32 ounces (900 grams) of food per person per day, more if you're playing hard in a cold climate.

- To pack, put items you don't need during the day at the bottom: sleeping bag and mattress, headlamp, spare socks and underwear, stove and fuel (allow 3 ounces [75 grams] per person per day), cooking pot, bowl and spoon, toilet kit, food. Keep closer to the top your first aid kit, rain jacket and pants, tent, lunch and water bottle. In the pack lid carry your sunscreen, insect repellent, maps, compass and blister kit.

- Choose the correct size of backpack: too small and you'll end up attaching things to the outside (which can get wet or lost); too large and you'll be tempted to take more than you need or can carry. You shouldn't carry more than 30 percent of your body weight.

- In general, put the heaviest items close to your back. One person should carry the tent, another the fly so each will have emergency shelter if separated.

---

accommodating 16 to 20 people, allow you to plan a trip of two to five days. Bunkhouses are equipped with wood stoves, firewood, a shovel and an ax. You bring your sleeping bag, pad, dishes, pots, matches and food.

If you'd like to try winter camping, five sites in La Diable sector are located just a third of a mile (half a kilometer) from the Lac-Monroe service center (where you can retreat to a warm building and washrooms!).

When you go

Parc du Mont-Tremblant
Chemin du Lac-Supérieur
Lac-Supérieur, QC J0T 1P0
Tel: (819) 688-2281
(information and reservations)
E-mail: meftremblant@cil.qc.ca

Instead of setting up your tent, try sleeping in one of the lean-tos, complete with straw, open fireplace and firewood, for a cozy night in the open air. After a night or two of Mont-Tremblant's magic, you'll be sufficiently refreshed to tackle civilization once again!

The Charlevoix Traverse

Ask any avid backcountry skier to name the "classic" traverses and they'll rhyme off half a dozen in the Coast Mountains and the Rockies of B.C. and Alberta, and one that may surprise you: La Traversée de Charlevoix in Québec. Though not a high mountain traverse, Charlevoix's version is long, rugged and beautiful, truly earning the "classic" designation.

Québec's premier ski traverse involves 60 miles (100 kilometers) of trails through the Charlevoix Mountains in the heart of a UNESCO World Biosphere Reserve.

These are some of the oldest mountains in the world, with rounded tops and deep river gorges that look deceptively gentle. Although the panoramic views along the traverse are outstanding, reaching them is no small matter. With a total elevation gain and loss of approximately 6,500 feet (2,000 meters), and six or seven days to complete the route, this is not an outing to be taken lightly!

The traverse was the brainchild of Eudore Fortin, who, with the help of the Fédération québécoise de la montagne, built the first log cabin in 1977. The climbers who frequented the nearby cliffs put the cabin to good use, yet Eudore wanted to share his beloved Charlevoix wilderness with other outdoor enthusiasts. He set about clearing a ski trail, bridging streams and rivers, and building five more cabins along the route for comfort and safety.

Now the president of the nonprofit La Traversée de Charlevoix Inc., Eudore is responsible for the development and maintenance of the trail network. In 1991, six beautiful log cottages were built adjacent to the six cabins, more than doubling the sleeping capacity to its current 140 limit, and providing a little more comfort than the small, rustic cabins.

The traverse starts 15 miles (24 kilometers) northwest of St. Urbain near Parc des Grands-Jardins, about a two-hour drive northeast of Québec City. The route dips and rises through the majestic Hautes-Gorges of the Malbaie River, and ends near the Mont Grand-Fonds ski resort just north of La Malbaie. From December through mid-March, skiers can book the cabins or the cottages, each spaced 9 to 12 miles (15 to 20 kilometers) apart. The cabins are fairly rustic, with wood stoves for heat and room for eight skiers. The cottages sleep up to 15; they also have wood stoves and propane, but are a little more comfortable and spacious than the cabins.

Hardy souls may wish to load up and carry their own food and

Backcountry ski hut on the Charlevoix Traverse.

supplies for the week-long trip, but the option of leaving behind a heavy backpack and carrying just a day pack is far more appealing. Food and baggage are transported by snowmobile to the next cabin or cottage – which means you don't have to skimp on the wine! Guides and shuttle services are also available, and Eudore's staff will even pick you up at the airport in Montréal or Québec City.

Don't let all these conveniences lull you into a false sense of security, however. You still must be prepared for hard days on the trail. While you can, enjoy the downhill runs that snake through spruce and hardwood forests, and revel in the views from the summit plateaus. And on the uphill days, just think of how fit you're getting! Fortunately, there's a warm, dry place at the end of the day, and French-Canadian comrades to share it with.

While most of western

Canada's classic ski traverses can be hiked in the summer, none is open to hiking and mountain biking. For years a dedicated cross-country ski route, the Charlevoix Traverse was opened to mountain biking in 1994. But what was covered by a soft, deep layer of snow in the winter becomes

When you go

La Traversée de Charlevoix Inc
841 St-Edouard
St-Urbain, QC G0A 4K0
Tel: (418) 639-2284
Fax: (418) 639-2777
E-mail: traverse@charlevoix.net
Website: www.charlevoix.net/traverse

exposed in the summer, making this a grueling route fit for fearless mountain bikers.

The trail varies from root-and-rutted single track to gravelly logging roads, with numerous stream crossings thrown in for good measure.

Some sections are smooth – fast and easy sailing. Others require skillful maneuvering down a slalom course of erosion gullies and jagged rocks; either pick your way through slowly or risk a head-over-heels descent (no loose helmet straps please!). Rewards await, however; after every river valley ascent to a broad summit plateau is the subsequent downhill run into the next valley.

It takes a few days to complete the traverse by bike, depending on how hard you ride. But if all this sounds too much to handle, you can also hike the traverse or simply stay in the Dôme cottage and take day trips to the surrounding summits. The summer season begins in June, but the best time for hiking and biking is late August through the end of September, when the bugs are less buggy, and the mountains are splashed with reds, oranges and yellows.

Mountain bikers on the Charlevoix Traverse.

La Vérendrye Wildlife Reserve

Ontario has Algonquin Provincial Park; Québec has La Vérendrye Wildlife Reserve. Algonquin has 1,500 lakes and about 1,500 miles (2,400 kilometers) of canoe routes, La Vérendrye over 4,000 lakes, 500 miles (800 kilometers) of marked routes and 870 miles (1,400 kilometers) of unmarked routes. Algonquin is crowded, La Vérendrye virtually unknown. If you prefer a true wilderness paddling experience, the choice is obvious.

The 5,255-square-mile (13,615-square-kilometer) La Vérendrye Wildlife Reserve is located in the vast fin of land between Ottawa, Montréal and Val d'Or. Le Domaine, the jumping-off point for most canoe trips, is about 150 miles (250 kilometers) north of Ottawa and 217 miles (350 kilometers) northwest of Montréal. Highway 117 to Val d'Or bisects the reserve. All of the campgrounds, hunting and fishing lodges, day-use areas and interpretive centers are concentrated along this 110-mile (180-kilometer) corridor. Powerboats use the larger lakes near the highway, but you will not encounter them on the backcountry circuits.

Given the large number of lakes and interconnecting streams and rivers, it is no problem to find a canoe route that suits you, from day trips to 30-day wilderness circuits. Canot-camping La Vérendrye, based in Le Domaine, will help you plan a trip and will even provide equipment, supplies and instruction at a reasonable cost. The facility operates from mid-May to mid-September.

One of the disadvantages of La Vérendrye over Algonquin Park is that the lesser-used portages may be overgrown, rough and sometimes hard to find. Be prepared for some difficult portages on extended trips. In addition, during periods of high water, some of the portages may be submerged; check with Canot-camping La Vérendrye for current conditions. However, an advantage of La Vérendrye over Algonquin Park is that the portages are shorter: the longest is a mile (1.5 kilometers) and the average is about 330 yards (300 meters).

A good introductory trip is the 15-mile (24-kilometer), two-day Jean-Péré loop that starts at Le Domaine and involves just one

Canoeing on the Chochocouane River, Parc de la Vérendrye.

short portage of 450 yards (410 meters). The route travels through island-studded lakes fringed with dense forest of black spruce, white spruce, jack pine and balsam fir. This short trip will allow you to capture the essence of canoe camping: a chance to set up a comfortable camp and stargaze while listening to the haunting cry of the loon.

A longer and more challenging route is the Petite Boucle Chochocouane, a five-day backcountry circuit in the northern part of the reserve that covers 40 miles (65 kilometers) and follows part of the wild Chochocouane River. The route follows the tea-colored Canimiti River upstream for about 18 miles (30 kilometers), with portages bypassing the occasional rapids. Beaver dams, the bane of canoeists, block the river in at least two spots and leeches add to the fun. On the positive side, the opportunity for wildlife viewing is excellent. Moose, deer, loons and mergansers are just some of the 40 land mammals and 150 bird species you might see in the reserve.

The reward for your upstream toil is an exciting descent of the Chochocouane River that includes rapids up to Class V, and numerous ledges and falls that must be portaged around. It's along this river that you realize you are not in an untouched wilderness: rusting cables, skids and overgrown tracks are a reminder that this area was once logged for its white and red pines.

The Chochocouane empties into the Dozois Reservoir, but to complete the circuit it's necessary to leave the river before this and rejoin the Canimiti River for a final upstream pull to the start point. This difficult trip will either whet your appetite for more or convince you to return to gentler routes for your next trips.

When you go

Canot-camping La Vérendrye
4545 avenue Pierre-de-Coubertin
CP 1000, Succ. M
Montréal, QC H1V 3R2
Tel: (514) 252-3001 (Sept. to mid-May)
Tel: (819) 435-2331 (mid-May to Sept.)

La Vérendrye at dusk.

La Mauricie National Park

Heartbreaking. When you think of the 400-year-old pines that once covered much of the Canadian Shield, then read about the logging practices that denuded its rounded hills, it's simply heartbreaking. The myth of inexhaustible timber resources caused a logging craze in much of Ontario, Québec and the Maritimes in the mid-1800s. Almost too late, Canadians realized how precious and vulnerable our forests are and set aside small pockets of land to protect some of the remnants.

In the case of La Mauricie, the government designated 210 square miles (536 square kilometers) of Québec's Laurentian landscape as a national park in 1970. By then, logging had been carried out for 120 years, and hunting and fishing for the last 70 of those. The new-growth forest and the wildlife are now protected, and fishing is strictly regulated, but it'll take at least a hundred years for the land to return to anything like its former splendor.

Controlled tourism is much kinder to the park, and over the past several decades, the forests have begun to recover and the moose populations have increased. Although it's well used by Québécois, more and more people from outside the province are discovering the pleasures of La Mauricie. Its gently rolling terrain, lakes, cooling cascades, and location (125 miles/ 200 kilometers north of Montréal) attract families, nature lovers and outdoor enthusiasts seeking a retreat from the city.

The park is shaped somewhat like a lumpy horseshoe, with two major drainages in its tines. A 40-mile (63-kilometer) parkway bisects the southern edge of La Mauricie, providing an accessible corridor to three major campgrounds, scenic viewpoints, picnic areas, lakes, rivers and hiking trails. The Visitor Centre at Saint-Jean-des-Piles on the eastern boundary is a good place to begin your discovery of La Mauricie. It houses extensive interpretive exhibits on the natural and human history of the park and a unique 3D slide show.

With more than 150 lakes and ponds in La Mauricie, many within a short distance of the parkway, it makes sense that canoeing is a popular summer activity. Long and narrow, Lac Wapizagonke in the southwest part of the park is one of the busiest paddling lakes. Canoes can be rented by the hour or the day, and many routes begin from here. A great outing for families with older children is the interpretive tour on Lac Wapizagonke led by parks staff. You set out in a large canoe, called a *Rabaska*, to learn

Sunset on Lac Wapizagonke, La Mauricie National Park.

Common loon, La Mauricie National Park.

about how glaciation shaped the terrain, about wildlife, flora and fauna in the park's waterways, and about the Attikamek, an Algonkian tribe that hunted and fished here 300 years ago.

There are almost limitless possibilities for longer canoe trips, combining lakes, rivers and portages. About 175 backcountry campsites on a dozen lakes are accessible only by canoe or on foot. Lac Anticagamac is an easy overnight extension from Lac Wapizagonke, and you can even continue through to the Matawin River on the northern boundary of the park. In the park's southeast sector, you can link Lac Édouard, Lac-à-la-Pêche and Lac Isaïc through a series of lakes and short portages. Canoeists are not permitted to land on any Islands, to protect moose calving grounds and nesting birds.

The visit to Waber Falls combines canoeing and hiking. You paddle 2.5 miles (4 kilometers) to the northern end of Lac Wapizagonke, where you beach your canoe, and take the Waber portage to the falls, 1.8 miles (3 kilometers) distant. You could easily while away an afternoon cooling off under the cascade. When you're ready to leave, take a quick detour to the viewpoint overlooking Lac Anticagamac; you might see a moose along its reedy shores.

Hikers have not been neglected in La Mauricie. There are a number of one- to two-hour interpretive hikes. (They're conducted in French – a good chance to brush up on your hand signals!) Trails range from less than a mile to 75 miles (up to 120 kilometers), leading to waterfalls, through maple tree stands and over rocky escarpments. On the Tourbière Trail, you can explore the Esker Bog. A boardwalk takes you out on the peat bog, where the insectivorous sundew and pitcher plants grow alongside delicate orchids. The 10.5-mile (17-kilometer) Les Deux-Criques Trail will provide a good workout for strong hikers and reward you with the scenic Ruisseau du Fou falls.

Mountain bikers have the run of an 18.5-mile (30-kilometer) circuit in the Rivière-à-la-Pêche sector in the southeast area of the park – skirting the lakeshores or winding through maple forests, primarily on old logging roads or paths that once led to hunting and fishing camps. These trails are also shared with hikers, so caution is necessary!

During winter, 50 miles (80 kilometers) of cross-country ski trails are kept groomed, including some for skate skiers and a 2.5-mile (4-kilometer) loop specially designated for snowshoeing. Trails are numbered and rated for difficulty for novices and experts alike. The Rivière-à-la-Pêche Centre, just inside the east gate, is the focus of the network; there are eight warm-up shelters along the trails.

You can camp at the Lac-à-la-Pêche Campground, or at any of the primitive campsites on the trails. But for a warm, dry bed after a day of skiing, try staying at the Wabenaki and Andrew lodges on Lac-à-la-Pêche. Dating from the late 1800s, these beautiful log buildings were once exclusive resorts for private fish and game clubs. Open year round, the lodges are a short, 2-mile (3.5-kilometer) ski-in from the parking lot.

When you go

Parks Canada
La Mauricie District
Place Cascade
C.P 758, 794 5th Street
Shawinigan, QC G9N 6V9
Tel: 1-800-463-6769
Tel: (819) 538-3232

Mont-Sainte-Anne and La Mercier

Just east of Québec City, with a view of the salty St. Lawrence River from its steep slopes, is one of eastern Canada's premier ski destinations, Mont-Sainte-Anne. One of more than a hundred ski areas in the Laurentian Highlands, the name "Mont-Sainte-Anne" conjures up images of its 2,300-foot (700-meter) vertical runs and consistently good snow for most people. For others, visions of the 150-inch (400-centimeter) annual snowfall blanketing a 220-mile (350-kilometer) network of cross-country ski trails come to mind.

In fact, Mont-Sainte-Anne Cross-Country Centre is the largest in Canada. Whether you're a beginner or expert, on classic or skate skis, out for an hour of family fun or for five days of backcountry travel, you'll find plenty to keep you happy here.

All that snow is kept tamed and skiable by a fleet of Bombardier grooming machines, on duty from mid-December to about the end of March. You can wax up in the lodge, pick a trail and head out, knowing there's a friendly ski patrol looking out for your safety and a warm-up shelter (eight in total) where you can stop for a break along the way. One of these, the Ruisseau Rouge, offers overnight accommodation for up to eight skiers. It's located along the easier trail section, so you don't

have to be an expert skier on a marathon tour to enjoy a winter's night in the forest.

Another option is to ski just over a mile (2 kilometers) to L'Auberge du fondeur. There's enough room for 26 people in shared quarters, with a full kitchen, living room, fireplace, bar, sauna and waxing room. Every morning, the innkeeper provides a hearty breakfast to get you on your way. Truly a pampered hut experience!

From Mont-Sainte-Anne, you can hook up with another great cross-country ski area, Camp Mercier. A 40-mile (63-kilometer) backcountry trail links the two centers, with two overnight shelters en route.

Located northwest of Mont-Sainte-Anne in the Réserve faunique des Laurentides, Camp Mercier is

Cross-country skiing at Camp Mercier.

World-Class Mountain Biking

From June to October, Mont-Sainte-Anne becomes a mountain biking Mecca. About 125 miles (200 kilometers) of trails offer excitement and technical challenge to even the most experienced riders. After all, from 1990 to 1996 the resort hosted seven World Cup events in both downhill and cross-country mountain biking. Regional races as well as provincial, national and international-class events are held throughout the summer every year.

Telemark skiing at Mont-Sainte-Anne ski resort.

equally famous for its quality and amount of snow and has an exceptionally long season, from the middle of November to the end of April, depending on conditions. Nearly 125 miles (200 kilometers) of trails are groomed for classic skiers and an additional 16 miles (26 kilometers) for skate skiers, with six warming huts along the network.

There are two long-distance trails at Camp Mercier. A *randonnée* of two

When you go

Mont-Sainte-Anne
CP 400, 2000 boul. Beau Pré
Beaupré, QC G0A 1E0
Tel: 1-800-463-1568
Tel: (418) 827-4561
Tel: (418) 827-5281 (reservations)

Camp Mercier
801 chemin Saint-Louis, Suite 125
Québec, QC G1S 1C1
Tel: (418) 686-1717 (information)
Tel: (418) 890-6527 (reservations)
Tel: (418) 848-2422 (winter)

or more days over 3 to 32 miles (5 to 52 kilometers) can be made through the Vallée de la Jacques-Cartier. There are six yurts along this route, all with capacity for six people. The second long-distance trail, Quatre Jumeaux, is 42 miles (68 kilometers) long and takes four or five days to complete. There are four shelters on this route, accommodating up to eight skiers.

Near the main center, Camp Mercier rents nine winter chalets that can accommodate up to 12 people. These are very comfortable, with hot water, bathrooms and kitchenettes. For the budget-conscious, a dormitory at the center sleeps 20 skiers.

These two great cross-country ski centers are within an hour's drive of the beautiful, historic city of Québec. When you've had your fill of skiing, make sure you visit the city for a taste of its culture, cuisine and old-world charm.

Mountain biking the summer trails at Mont-Sainte-Anne.

Mingan Archipelago National Park Reserve

It takes a special effort to reach a very special place. A long day's drive from Québec City, nearly two from Montréal, the Mingan Archipelago is as off-the-beaten-path as you can get. Still, if you're willing to make the effort, the islands' mysterious landscapes and natural diversity will captivate you.

The Mingan Archipelago consists of more than 40 islands and islets that stretch approximately 56 miles (90 kilometers) along the north shore of the Gulf of St. Lawrence. Created in 1984, the park has exceptional beauty, with spectacular rock formations and the largest concentration of shoreline arches and grottoes in Canada. Frigid ocean currents and chilly prevailing winds produce an unusual tundra-like environment more typical of the Arctic. Moors, wetlands and boreal forest support more than 200 species of birds, and an impressive variety of whales, dolphins, seals and other marine creatures provide intriguing subjects for scientists, whale watchers and photographers alike.

At an average distance of 2 miles (3.5 kilometers) from the mainland, the protected channels and bays of the archipelago make an ideal destination for sea kayaking. Before heading out to the islands, stop at the visitor reception center in Longue-Pointe-de-Mingan or Havre-Saint-Pierre. You'll need to pick up maps and a camping permit (there are 42 primitive sites on six of the islands), and talk to the staff about your intended route.

Although the park is open from June to September, August is the best time for sea kayaking, when there is less wind and rain. Fog and inclement weather, however, are always a possibility, so be prepared. Take plenty of warm clothing and extra food to last at least two days longer than your planned itinerary.

If self-propelled transport is not to your liking, there are plenty of commercial tour boats and water taxis that will ferry you to the islands (these must be arranged in advance). Once you have arrived there, park staff are on hand to lead interpretive hikes.

The limestone monoliths are the most striking topographic feature in the Mingan Archipelago. Their weird shapes are a result of thousands of years of erosion by the harsh winds, the varying sea level and the freeze–thaw cycle that occurs every winter. Up to 20 feet (6 meters) high, these sedimentary giants formed the bottom of a tropical sea 500 million years ago. Over the millennia, the sea dried up, the earth cooled, and an ice sheet 1.5 miles (2.5 kilometers) thick buried the northern region of the continent. When the glaciers receded, the land started to rebound, exposing the limestone ocean floor above the present-day Gulf of St. Lawrence. The Mingan Islands are still rising, uncovering new shorelines and more limestone cliffs to the elements. Île du Fantôme, Île Niapiskau, Île Quarry, Grosse Île au Marteau and Grande Île all have splendid monoliths easily reached on a coastal walk or explored from the seaside vantage of a kayak.

Nearly 15 miles (24 kilometers) of hiking trails lead not only along the island shores, but also into

There are more than 200 species of birds on Mingan Islands.

boreal forests and bogs, moors with short grasses and mosses, and even a tundra-like environment on Île Nue de Mingan (*nue* means naked or bare). The islands support a variety of delicate arctic-alpine plants not usually found at this latitude, and nearly 850 different species of flowers, mosses and lichen.

The islands' rich habitat supports thousands of sea birds. The park is a busy summer breeding ground and stopover for migrating birds, as well as a wintering area for some species. Arctic terns, kittiwakes, gulls, double-crested cormorants, razorbills, black guillemot and common eider ducks are just some of the birds that feed off mussels, sea urchins, capelin and other marine delicacies. Colorful Atlantic puffins nest on three of the islands, arriving in mid-April to lay and hatch one egg, then departing at the end of August. Locally known as sea parrots, puffins mate for life, reuniting in the Mingan Archipelago each

year. Strong and graceful underwater, puffins are quite comical – and clumsy – in the air, sometimes cartwheeling from the sky when they're overstuffed with fish.

The same marine menu that lures sea birds to the Mingan Islands also draws a wide range of marine

When you go

Mingan Archipelago National Park Reserve
PO Box 1180, 1303 Digue Street
Havre-St-Pierre, QC G0G 1P0
Tel: 1-800-463-6769
Tel: (410) 538 3285 (summer)
Tel: (418) 500 3321 (winter)

mammals. But it is the whales that will steal the stage, and no fewer than nine species come to this part of the Gulf of St. Lawrence to feed. Minke whales arrive in June, the best time to see them, and are most often seen close inshore feeding on capelin. Blue whales are encountered farther offshore; though they are not within reach of sea kayakers,

you can take a boat tour to get a glimpse of the largest creature that has ever lived.

As you dip your paddle in the Gulf's frigid waters, let your mind wander to the days of the Montagnais, the native people who plied the sea in their birchbark canoes for 2,000 years and still harvest fish in the Mingan Archipelago today. By the early 1500s, Basque whalers had arrived to hunt the great whales, extracting the precious blubber oil and sending it back to lucrative European markets. Evidence of their ovens still remains on Île Nue de Mingan and Île du Havre. Since the mid-1800s, Acadians have also made their living here by fishing for herring and cod, and hunting gray seals.

Now, the whales, sea birds and other wildlife are protected in the park reserve and are a source of endless fascination for anyone with a keen mind and a sharp eye.

Sea kayaking past the monoliths, Mingan Archipelago National Park Reserve.

Parc de la Gaspésie

The views are spectacular from the summit of Mont Albert and Mont Jacques-Cartier. Across a rolling sea of flat-topped mountains, covered in stark tundra vegetation, herds of woodland caribou roam. And in the forests, deep-cut glaciated valleys, marshlands and lakes, moose and white-tailed deer live in abundance. This is the only place in Québec where these three species live in close proximity.

How can that be? Parc de la Gaspésie is situated in the heart of the Gaspé Peninsula, a thumb of eastern Québec that pokes into the Atlantic Ocean, with the Gulf of St. Lawrence to the north and the Baie des Chaleurs to the south. The Chic-Chocs and McGerrigle mountains, part of the Appalachian Range, form a series of rounded peaks that stretch through the peninsula. Steep-sided plateaus seem to rise right out of the water.

This combination of elevated plateau surrounded by large bodies of water has produced a unique vegetative environment in Parc de la Gaspésie. From valley bottom to high plateau you can wander through lush yellow and white birch groves, boreal forest dominated by fir and black spruce, and alpine tundra with its mosses, lichens and delicate arctic plants. On the summits, the vegetation is almost identical to that found at the 55th parallel – and one of the reasons why woodland caribou can be found here.

Parc de la Gaspésie was declared a provincial conservation park in 1981, though it had been part of a vast forest reserve set aside in 1905. Recreation forms a large part of its services, but it's the caribou that command first consideration. Two small herds totaling approximately 200 animals are split about equally between habitats on the Mont Albert and Mont Jacques-Cartier plateaus. These herds represent the last remaining woodland caribou in eastern North America. Parc de la Gaspésie is their last refuge, and the park is anxious to preserve it. The summit regions of Mont Albert (3,786 feet/1,154 meters) and Mont Jacques-Cartier (4,160 feet/ 1,268 meters) are high protection zones. Here, the caribou are protected from human interference, although their existence is still threatened by their predators –

Le Huard cabin, Parc de la Gaspésie.

coyotes and black bears. The summit areas are closed during the rut (October 1 to 30) and during the calving period (May 1 to June 23).

The park offers interpretive hikes to the summits, or you can simply strike out on your own. The trail to Mont Jacques-Cartier is a jumble of rocks and boulders, which can be treacherous when wet. As you gain elevation, the vegetation becomes progressively more stunted and gnarled, an indication of how fierce the elements can be. On the plateau, stone cairns, closely spaced, mark the trail to an observation tower. In clear weather, you might see the caribou scratching out a living on the tundra, or the fishing boats in the Gulf of St. Lawrence.

Other day hikes will lead you to the lofty summits of Mont Albert,

Hiking on Mont Albert, Parc de la Gaspésie.

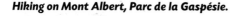

Mont Joseph-Fortin, Mont Xalibu, Pic du Brûlé and Mont Ells. Never trust the weather at the base of the mountains to be the same on the summits. Always carry rain gear and warm clothing, and be prepared for the very strong winds that can whip across the flats. Hold on to your hat!

Mountain bikers will find some amusement on a 27-mile (44-kilometer) trail that leads from Lac Cascapédia to Mont Logan. About 9 miles (15 kilometers) from the lake is a moose observation station on Lac Paul, an area well known for its concentration of *les orignaux*. The bike trail stops short of the summit of Mont Logan, but you can hike the final leg for grand views of the Chic-Chocs, bumping and rolling along as far as the eye can see.

Canoeing is limited to Lac Cascapédia and Rivière Sainte-Anne. The lake is suitable for families, while the river is reserved for experts, and only during spring run-off from the end of May to June 14. Anglers will be delighted with 14 lakes, many small streams and creeks, and Rivière Sainte-Anne,

providing excellent fishing for Atlantic salmon, arctic char, lake trout and brook trout.

In 1993, the park completed La Grande Traversée – a 60-mile (100-kilometer) hiking trail that crosses the park in three sections. The first section, 15.5 miles (25 kilometers) long, traverses the high, barren mountains of the McGerrigle range from La Galène on the far eastern edge of the park to the Gîte du Mont-Albert in the main service sector.

The second section continues to Lac Cascapédia, another 15.5 miles (25 kilometers) over

Mont-Albert and through mature forests. The final 30 miles (50 kilometers) traverse the northern part of the Chic-Chocs from Lac Cascapédia to Mont Logan. The entire traverse takes nine days. From La Galène to Mont Logan, 17 mountain huts and three campsites provide a welcome spot to rest up for the next day's journey.

Winter offers cross-country skiing, telemarking and hut-to-hut touring in the Chic-Chocs, where an average of 16 to 20 feet (5 to 6 meters) of snow, over a season that extends well into April, guarantees great skiing. There are 17 cabins scattered throughout the park, equipped with lanterns, mattresses and wood stoves for heat. Skiers bring their own cooking stove, sleeping bag, food and cooking and eating utensils. Snowmobile transport of gear is available, a luxury you won't want to forgo.

Parc Ami Chic Chocs, the park's "friends" society, offers guided interpretive hikes during the summer (French and English). Club Grand Yétis is an independent outfitter licensed to guide ski trips in the park.

When you go

Parc de la Gaspésie
CP 550, 124–1 avenue Ouest
Ste-Anne-des-Monts, QC G0E 2G0
Tel: 1-800-665-6527
Tel: (418) 763-3301
Fax: (418) 763-7810

Parc Ami Chic Chocs
Tel: (418) 763-9020

Club Grand Yétis
Tel: (418) 763-7782

Woodland caribou on Mont Jacques-Cartier, Parc de la Gaspésie.

Fundy National Park

Canada's national parks are created to preserve environments. Fundy National Park, however, is somewhat of an exception. The small, 80-square-mile (206-square-kilometer) park was established to rescue an environment from nearly 150 years of human misuse.

People had been living in the region long before Fundy became a national park in 1948. Prior to European settlement, the Mi'kmaq people hunted and fished there, living off the land in a way that did not

Fundy National Park.

degrade it. The Acadians, who arrived in the 1600s, were intent on farming, even though the land wasn't arable. In the early 1800s, sawmills were built on the Upper

Salmon and Point Wolfe rivers as part of a thriving logging and ship-building industry. Once-healthy fishing rivers were polluted or dammed, preventing the salmon from reaching their spawning grounds.

Creation of the park put an end to resource extraction, and the wilderness is slowly recovering. Beavers, porcupines, raccoons, hare and coyote dwell in the forests. The endangered peregrine falcon has been reintroduced in the park, as has the American marten. The 200-foot-high (60-meter-high) cliffs along the coast offer the same spectacular views of the bay as they did when the first Acadians arrived, the great tides of Fundy are just as fascinating, and the rivers, waterfalls and forests offer peace and solitude to all those who seek it.

Fundy National Park is located on an arm of the Bay of Fundy called Chignecto Bay, 50 miles (80 kilometers) southwest of Moncton. The park can be accessed from the north-west corner at Wolf Lake, or from the southeast at Alma, both on Highway 114. The major administration center, just inside the park gate west of Alma, offers all sorts of diversions including golf, tennis and lawn bowling, but the natural attractions are by far the most rewarding.

Since Fundy is best known for its coastal features, why not start with some exploration of the tides? The Headquarters Campground on the eastern edge of the park is well situated if you simply want to watch the tides come and go (and this can be a fascinating pastime!). Nearby is the village of Alma, where you can walk far out into the bay at low tide. Within the park, Herring Cove and Point Wolfe are good places to explore the ocean floor and learn about intertidal life. Interpretive dis-

Squaws Cap, Fundy National Park.

plays and guided walks are perfect for the whole family.

There's a magnificent view of the Point Wolfe estuary from the Shiphaven Trail, and superb vistas of the bay from the cliff tops along the Squaws Cap Loop, Matthews Head, Coastal and Coppermine trails. The Devil's Half Acre Trail is short and easy, but remarkable nonetheless. It leads through a red spruce forest that clings to the steep cliffs sloping to the bay, then an area of fractured rock, deep holes and mossy gullies, apparently the work of the devil.

All along the Bay of Fundy, the giant tidal fluctuations affect the climate and vegetation. Moist Atlantic air cools the coastal area, bringing frequent fogs. The interior of the park is a plateau, rising to a height of 1,200 feet (366 meters) above the sea. The dense Acadian forest of red spruce and balsam fir found along the coast gives way to red maple and white birch, with lush ferns and mosses covering the forest floor and lichens draping the trees. The forest is dotted with ponds, lakes and bogs, and three main rivers – the Upper Salmon, Goose and Point Wolfe – drain the highlands.

Many of the park's hiking trails wind through this heavy forest to sparkling waterfalls. The short Dickson Falls self-guiding trail leads through the coastal forest along a boardwalk to the falls. Third Vault Trail, a difficult 4.5-mile (7.4-kilometer) return hike, follows a deep

When you go

Fundy National Park
PO Box 40
Alma, NB E0A 1B0
Tel: (506) 887-6000
Fax. (506) 887 6008
E-mail: Fundy_info@pch.gc.ca

valley to the park's tallest waterfall (52.5 feet/16 meters), and a pool at the base where you can swim or dabble your toes.

The Caribou Plain Trail is an easy, 2-mile-long (3.4-kilometer-long) route through three different environments. From a coniferous forest where pink lady slipper orchids bloom in June, a boardwalk skirts a beaver pond alive with frogs, insects, and wetland birds, then passes a bog of sphagnum moss. Finally, you loop back through a stand of hardwood trees along a ridge.

Of the longer routes, the

30-mile (50-kilometer) Fundy Circuit offers the most variety. It's made up of seven linked hiking trails, and you can complete the entire trail in three to five days, or combine portions of the circuit depending on your time and energy. On this circuit along the coast and through the forests, you'll sample every type of habitat the park has to offer.

In all, about 70 miles (110 kilometers) of trails crisscross the park. Many are reserved for hikers, but nearly 45 miles (70 kilometers) on several of the wider paths are available for mountain biking. The rivers are too shallow for canoeing, but serene Bennett Lake is great for family paddling.

In the winter, Fundy offers 30 miles (50 kilometers) of groomed cross-country ski trails, and two trails flagged for snowshoeing. Camping is available on the Goose River Trail, or at Chambers and Marvin lakes.

During the summer, three fully equipped campgrounds with over 600 campsites are open, and there are a number of backcountry sites. More comfortable accommodation is available in the form of about 60 chalets in or near the park, as well as friendly B&Bs and motels in and around the village of Alma.

Hopewell Rocks

If you arrive at Hopewell Rocks Ocean Tidal Exploration Site at high tide, you'll wonder what all the fuss is about. All that can be seen of the "flowerpots" for which the area is famous are tiny islets crowned with dwarf red spruce and balsam fir. Only as the tide recedes does the fascination become obvious. When the tide is fully out, the immense sandstone pillars are completely exposed, and the power of the Fundy tides is evident.

The Bay of Fundy is justly famous for its extreme tides. An arm of the Atlantic Ocean with only one outlet, the basin acts much like a bathtub, with seawater sloshing up and down in rhythm with the Atlantic's tides. Every outgoing tide

Flowerpot rocks, Hopewell Cape.

drains about 60 cubic miles (100 cubic kilometers) out of the bay – almost as much water as the daily discharge of all the rivers in the world combined!

At the entrance to the bay, the tides reach from 19 to 22 feet (5.8 to 6.7 meters), fluctuating with the lunar phases. The range increases as you approach the head of the bay. Along Nova Scotia's Minas Basin,

the tides are the highest recorded in the world – up to 52.5 feet (16 meters).

At Hopewell Cape, the tides reach 46 feet (14 meters), equal to the height of a four-story building. All that turbulence and millennia of tireless erosion have resulted in the massive sculptures at Hopewell Rocks.

Hopewell Rocks is located 20 miles (32 kilometers) south of Moncton on Route 114. Stop in at the Information Centre and pick up a copy of the tide tables, then descend the stairways to the beach (at low tide only!). You can walk for hours at the edge of land and sea, exploring the ocean floor and the rocky flowerpots. The rocks are a conglomerate of pebbles, boulders and sand

Typical "flowerpot" formation at Hopewell Cape.

covered in barnacles that glue themselves for life to the boulders. The rocky shoreline and base of the "pots" are covered in slippery, brilliant green rockweed, bladderwrack and knotwrack. At your feet, periwinkle snails, clams, crabs and marine worms live in the sand, under the rocks or in tidal pools. Swirling above you are hundreds of noisy gulls and other shore birds that come to feast on the creatures that have been exposed by the outgoing tides, especially the tiny mud shrimp,

corophium volutator. In midsummer, this is a critical feeding stop for 1 to 3 million shore birds on their annual migration to South America.

The Hopewell Rocks site is open for day use only, with several fascinating interpretive activities and facilities

that operate from May to October. Guided beach walks are also offered. To get the most out of your visit, wear waterproof boots with good-gripping soles – most of the beach is wet and sandy, but there are also boulders to clamber over that are covered with slippery algae. When the tide comes in, it's time to hurry off the beach. The flood returns rapidly, rising about 12 inches (30 centimeters) in less than seven minutes. Remember that old adage: time and tide wait for no one!

When you go

The Rocks Provincial Park
Box 29A
Hopewell Cape, NB E0A 1Y0
Tel: (506) 734-3530/3531

Grand Manan

One of the most intriguing destinations in Atlantic Canada is the Fundy Isles, a collection of three large islands and numerous smaller ones situated at the mouth of the Bay of Fundy. The largest of these, Grand Manan (about 77 square miles/200 square kilometers), is also the most isolated, separated from mainland New Brunswick by a 90-minute ferry crossing from Blacks Harbour to the bustling fishing community of North Head.

Outdoor enthusiasts have only recently discovered Grand Manan, but it's long been a retreat for writers, artists, photographers and naturalists. Bird watchers have been flocking to Grand Manan ever since John James Audubon, the great naturalist and painter, visited in 1833. Another great naturalist, Allan Moses, spent a lifetime gathering and mounting several hundred specimens of island birds, now on display at the Grand Manan Museum in Grand Harbour.

More than 363 species of birds have been recorded in the Grand Manan Archipelago, of which an average of 250 are seen on an annual basis, while half that number regularly breed there. During peak migration, a visitor might expect to see a hundred different species. The giant Fundy tides can take much of the credit for attracting such a variety of birds. The Bay of Fundy's rich waters nurture an abundance of marine life that draws birds to feed and nest there.

Red Point, just east of Seal Cove on the southeast coast of the island, is a prime area for viewing birds. You can drive to the point, but a better alternative is to walk the Boardwalk Trail that begins at the Anchorage Provincial Park campground. The trail is suitable for all ages and fitness levels, with boardwalks over the wet spots, and the opportunity to see nesting merlins on the way, plus hundreds of ducks, loons and grebes at the point. The boardwalk leads to the beach access, with great views looking southwest down Seal Cove Sound toward Wood Island and beyond.

East of the Boardwalk Trail, bird-watching blinds have been set up overlooking The Lagoon, Long Point and Great Pond. Not only can you watch cranes, herons, cormorants and other birds at close range without disturbing them, you'll be sheltered from winds and rain. Another good bird-watching area is Castalia Marsh, just a ten-minute drive north up the coast. And the viewing opportunities continue: in the vicinity of North Head at the Whistle and Swallow Tail, you're likely to see both shore birds and sea birds, and possibly finback, humpback and minke whales.

Several offshore islands make great day outings to look for birds and other wildlife. A hiking or cycling trip to White Head Island involves a 20-minute ferry crossing from Ingalls Head (bikes are permitted on the ferry). Along the way, keep an eye

Seal Cove, Grand Manan.

Delicious Dulse

Dark Harbour, on the rugged west coast of Grand Manan, is known for its dulse. This deep red seaweed is harvested by hand at low water, sun dried, rolled into large bales, then ground or packaged in strips. Dulse is a culinary oddity to many people. Found mostly in health food stores, it can be eaten fresh, dried, or ground as seasoning for fish, soups and salads.

House and garden, Grand Manan.

out for harbor seals, bald eagles, common eiders and black guillemots. Following the roads and shorelines, you can hike to Point Prangle to watch the shore birds during migration, or to Langmaid Cove for a possible glimpse of the brown-capped boreal chickadee. The hike to Sandy Cove and the Long Point Lighthouse is especially worthwhile between mid-July and September, when whales can be spotted off the south shore.

At low tide, you can cross "The Thoroughfare" on foot to Ross Island from Grand Manan. A 4.5-mile (7.5-kilometer) trail loops around four ponds on the island, past discarded fishing boats and an abandoned lighthouse. Bald eagles nest on Ross Island, and several species of wildfowl nest and raise their broods on the four

ponds. Islanders come to Ross Island to harvest dulse, dig clams and collect periwinkle snails.

The highlight for any birder is a visit to the Machias Seal Island Bird Sanctuary, 12 miles (19 kilometers) from Seal Cove on Grand Manan.

When you go

Grand Manan Tourism Association
PO Box 193
North Head, Grand Manan, NB E0G 2M0
Tel: (506) 662-3442

Tour boats take a restricted number of visitors to the island for a chance to see the breeding colony of Atlantic puffins, razorbill auks and arctic terns.

Whale-watching tours are very popular in the deeper waters of the Bay of Fundy. En route you might see wilson and storm petrels, greater

and sooty shearwaters, and gannets, among many other bird species – as well as porpoises and basking sharks. Most notable of the whales, which include finbacks and humpbacks, is the rare and endangered North Atlantic right whale. Up to two-thirds of the total world population of 300 right whales migrate to the Grand Manan Basin each year, to feed and mate in its bounteous waters.

Accommodation is available on Grand Manan in charming cottages, B&Bs and campgrounds. Villages line the east coast, the harbors are full of small fishing boats, and the people are friendly and welcoming. Hiking trails crisscross the island, cyclists can pedal along the roads, and commercial operators offer guided sea kayaking trips.

The Dobson Trail

New Brunswick may be best known for its mighty Bay of Fundy tides, quaint fishing villages and other coastal attractions, but the landlocked side has its appeal as well. The northern arm of the Appalachian Mountains in Albert County between Moncton and Fundy National Park offers a rugged woodland retreat suitable for day outings or overnight adventures.

The 36-mile (58-kilometer) Dobson Trail traverses this part of the Appalachians, through soft and hardwood forests, across mead- ows and along brooks, ascending steep slopes to reach expansive lookouts. The brainchild of Dr. Art Dobson in 1959, the Dobson Trail was conceived, built and maintained by volunteers – the first of its kind in the Maritimes.

With three sections of about a mile (2 kilometers) each and six varying from 3.5 to 9 miles (5.8 to 14.8 kilometers) long, hikers, cross-country skiers and snowshoers can bite off a chunk for a day outing or tackle the entire trail in a few days. Numerous secondary roads cross the trail, allowing easy access for day trippers. The trails are well marked, and blazes are placed high enough on trees so as not to be obscured by snow in the winter.

White-tailed deer.

Backpackers intent on completing the whole trail will need about three days to hike its length from Riverview to the Old Shepody Road Boundary of Fundy National Park. Hikers should allow another day to hike the 7.5 miles (12 kilometers) of national park trails to the park headquarters where pickup can be arranged.

There are no designated campgrounds along this wilderness trail, and no amenities. A crude shelter at Beaverbrook Campsite may be used for overnighters, but there are no mattresses or cooking facilities – take your own!

Another first for the Dobson Trail is its one-third-mile (half-kilometer) section designated for the blind. A "feel cable" guides hikers along the level trail; 70 bird feeders have been erected in this section, allowing hikers to revel in the birdsong as they walk along.

The variety of terrain and ecological environments is remarkable on the Dobson Trail. Besides the forests, hikers pass through low-lying wetlands, with beaver ponds, brooks, a lake and marshes. There are several abandoned homesteads to investigate and grown-over fields edged with raspberry and blackberry bushes for late-summer snacking.

Lots of up-and-down travel takes you from the lush lowlands to the higher ground. One highlight is the short, steep side trail leading to Hayward Pinnacle, the highest point in Albert County at about 1,000 feet (300 meters). It's a fine spot to relax and admire the 360-degree views across the countryside all the way to

When you go

Information and a guidebook are available from:
Edwin Melanson, Trailmaster
71 Derby St.
Moncton, NB E1C 6Y8
Tel: (506) 855-5089

Tourism New Brunswick
Dept. 339, Box 12345
Fredericton, NB E3B 5C3
Tel: 1-800-561-0123

Moncton. Another high point is the hike to Prosser Ridge, starting at Berryton. The trail follows the Berryton Brook gorge, then works its way up onto a ridge, where

there's a great view down the other side to Prosser Brook and across to Stewart Mountain.

Although the Dobson Trail is popular year round, fall is perhaps the best season, when the mosquitoes and black flies have disappeared and the landscape is ablaze with the changing colors of the trees. After the leaves have fallen, or in the spring before the leaves are out, the open views permit unimpeded bird watching. At any time of the year, keep an eye out for bear, deer, moose and other small animals that inhabit the Albert County wilderness.

Sugar maples along the Dobson Trail.

Mount Carleton Park

New Brunswick is well known to outsiders for its national parks, Fundy and Kouchibouguac, and its coastal features are admired the world over. But there's an out-of-the-way wilderness area in the north central region of the province, treasured by New Brunswickers, that's only recently come to the attention of out-of-province visitors.

Established in 1969, Mount Carleton is the largest park in the Maritimes. Once a center for logging, hunting and fishing, it's now a haven for hikers, canoeists and cross-country skiers, as well as a host of wildlife. Seven lakes sit in the valleys of a mountainous

plateau; refreshing springs pour off steep cliffs, forming the headwaters of the Tobique and Nepisiguit river systems. Soft and hardwood forests, ablaze with color in autumn, are home to black bears, moose, white-tailed deer and beavers.

Three major peaks are the focal point of the park and the goal for

keen hikers. The most popular trail takes you to the summit of Mount Carleton, at 2,690 feet (820 meters) the highest point in the Maritimes. The 6-mile (9.6-kilometer) loop follows an old road to the ranger cabin and a fire tower. It's a gentle climb all the way, ending in a short, steep scramble to the summit. From here you can see the Nepisiguit Lakes spread below you to the east, and Mount Head and Mount Sagamook to the north. In September, you can scrounge for blueberries and mountain cranberries, or simply enjoy the fresh breeze and changing colors.

From the summit of Mount Carleton there are several options. You can complete the loop and

Hiking on Mount Carleton (the highest point in the Maritimes).

Black bear in a meadow.

return to your starting point, stopping for the night if you wish at a backcountry campground. Or if you have two cars or can arrange a pickup, hike the easy 2.5-mile (4.3-kilometer) connector trail to Mount Head (2,598 feet/ 792 meters) and Mount Sagamook (2,549 feet/ 777 meters), ending at the Lakeshore Road. Alternatively, you can hike the 3.8-mile (6.2-kilometer) loop trail to Mount Sagamook. The approach is quite demanding, zigzagging steeply through a softwood forest. Near the crest, the trail emerges from the forest onto a rock outcrop with a spectacular view of the Nictau Lakes.

Another mountain trail takes you 3.7 miles (6 kilometers) to the summit of 1,847-foot (563-meter) Mount Bailey. It's a steady climb to the peak, but well worth the effort for the inspiring views of Nictau

When you go

Mount Carleton Discovery Site
11 Gagnon Street
Saint-Quentin, NB E8A 1N4
Tel: (506) 235-0793
Fax: (506) 235-0795

Tourism New Brunswick
PO Box 12345
Fredericton, NB E3B 5C3
Tel: 1-800-561-0123

Lake, Mount Sagamook, Mount Carleton, and Bald Mountain Brook Valley, where deer and moose are often seen.

There are several easy trails at lower elevations. The 3.7-mile (6-kilometer) Dry Brook Trail leads past active beaver ponds and numerous waterfalls up to 33 feet (10 meters) high. Big Brook Trail follows 5.5 miles (9 kilometers) of shoreline along Bathurst Lake, with excellent views of the Nepisiguit Lakes. The two can be combined

to make a long 11.5-mile (18.6-kilometer) loop.

Nictau and Nepisiguit lakes, clear and cool, are ideal for swimming, canoeing and fishing. There are two short, easy trails on these lakes. One is a tenth of a mile (0.3 kilometers) to picturesque Williams Falls near Nictau Lake. The other passes through a stand of pure red pine on First Nepisiguit Lake.

In the winter, Mount Carleton draws cross-country skiers and snowshoers to explore its rolling terrain and elevated plateau. Three groomed loop trails of 1, 3 and 4.5 miles (1.5, 5 and 7.5 kilometers) start out from a heated cabin near the park headquarters. Backcountry skiers are free to explore as much as they like, or head to Mount Carleton and Mount Sagamook for long runs of telemark skiing. The best ski conditions are often in March, and the snow lasts well into April.

Kouchibouguac National Park

It reaches a grand elevation of 100 feet (30 meters) above sea level. The greatest height you'll climb is the circular wooden staircase of a 33-foot-high (10-meter-high) observation tower. From here, you can look out over a spectacular expanse of – bog. Exciting you say? Indeed! Kouchibouguac National Park encompasses some of the most intriguing habitats in Canada's national parks system, making it the perfect destination for naturalists and birders.

The name of the park, pronounced *koosh e boo gwack*, is derived from a Mi'kmaq word meaning "river of the long tides." The Mi'kmaq occupied the region centuries before the Europeans "discovered" it, harvesting the bounty of the sea and hunting deer, moose and black bear in the forests. The major cultural influence now is Acadian, and French names, cuisine and music are an integral part of any visit to the region.

Located about 60 miles (100 kilometers) north of Moncton, Kouchibouguac (Koosh for short) was established in 1969 among ill feeling between government and landowners. Acadians had been making a living off the land for nearly 400 years, fishing, clearing its forests for crops, and cutting marsh hay for cattle. Eventually, 92 square miles (238 square kilometers) of parkland were created, and the human inhabitants relocated.

Much of the park has been shaped by the effects of the Northumberland Strait and onshore winds. Along the coast, a chain of barrier islands stretches 15.5 miles (25 kilometers), taking the brunt of the Strait's moods on the seaward side and protecting lagoons on the leeward side. Dunes are constantly being reworked by the shifting wind and waves, and underwater sandbars create an ever-changing navigational puzzle for fishing boats. In the warm, calm lagoons, soft-shelled clams, blue mussels, oysters, fish, and eel grass and other salt-tolerant plants thrive.

Facing the Strait are long white sand beaches where sun worshippers come to soak up rays and swim in the warm seawater. The most popular of these is Kellys Beach, the major activity center. Many visitors come here simply for the beach, and they get to experience at least some of the park's natural attractions just by walking there.

From the parking lot, a boardwalk leads through the forest, over the lagoons, and across the dune ridge to the Strait. In the marsh, in the lagoons and along the beach, you may see greater scaup, red-breasted merganser, osprey and horned larks, along with many other species of waterfowl and

When you go

Kouchibouguac National Park
Kent County, NB E0A 2A0
Tel: (506) 876-2443
Fax: (506) 876-4802
E-mail: atlantic_parksinfo@pch.gc.ca

Boardwalk over dunes and marshes, Kouchibouguac National Park.

shore birds. The endangered piping plover also nests on the barrier beaches.

Away from the beaches are a number of fascinating low-lying habitats that will impress you with their diversity. North of the Kouchibouguac River, the 1.8-mile (3-kilometer) Claire Fontaine Trail loops around a wooded point that juts out into Kouchibouguac Lagoon. Birch, white pine and conifers typical of the Acadian forest provide a shady canopy for trilliums, trout lilies and bunchberries. Keep an eye out for warblers, thrushes, flycatchers, woodpeckers and butterflies throughout the forest. Over the past 200 years, the original Acadian forest either fell to the ax or was destroyed naturally by fire. On the Claire Fontaine Trail and Ruisseau Major Trail, several huge white pines remain, spared the ax because of their slight disfigurement.

South of the Kouchibouguac River, the 1-mile (1.8-kilometer) Bog Trail winds through a forest to a three-story observation tower for that fabulous view of the bog. Raised bogs such as this make up 21 percent of the park area; only this one is accessible to visitors. Layers of multicolored sphagnum moss compact into peat to reach a depth of up to 20 feet (6 meters) in the center. The organic material is ideal for moisture-loving plants such as pitcher plants and some specially adapted orchids. Twenty-five species of orchid may be identified throughout the park.

Cycling is a good way to get around the park. 15.5 miles (25 kilometers) of wide gravel bike paths link up with most of the park's interpretive walking trails and provide access to two of the three primitive campgrounds at Petit-Large and Sîpu. Point-à-

Maxime is accessible by water. That means, while car-campers battle it out at the South Kouchibouguac Campground, which is often full, you can enjoy a quiet evening away from the crowds. In addition, Côte-à-Fabien Campground, also removed from the busier part of the park, has both drive-in and walk-in sites.

Tern Island, Kouchibouguac National Park.

The sheltered estuaries and tidal lagoons of Kouchibouguac are ideal for canoeing and kayaking. Paddling along the outer barrier islands on Northumberland Strait can also be rewarding, if a little more demanding. Check with park staff about tide schedules and currents before setting out, and keep an eye on the unpredictable weather. The view from just above water level allows a close-up look at birds, seals and other wildlife, without having to get too close. For example, at Tern Island, named for these aggressive birds, over 4,000 terns come to nest, so you'll want to keep a respectful distance. The island is off-limits to visitors during nesting season, from mid-June to the end of August. Canoes, kayaks and rowboats may be rented at Ryan's Landing, adjacent to the South Kouchibouguac Campground.

The park is not known for its fishing, although it is permitted with a license. The Visitor Reception Centre is a good place to stop for information on all the activities and natural features.

Kouchibouguac's gentle terrain is ideal for cross-country skiing and snowshoeing in the winter. Trails and warming shelters are outlined in a brochure, and winter camping is available.

Kouchibouguac National Park.

Upper Saint John River Valley

The long, serene Saint John River has always been an important corridor for settlement and transportation. Five hundred years ago, the Maliseet people depended on it for travel to and from summer hunting grounds and winter homes; the Mohawk tribes used it for their raiding parties on the Maliseet. French settlers – the Acadians – settled the lower river, only to be rudely evicted by the British. Loyalists from the United States moved into the region in 1783, settling at what became Fredericton, now the capital city of New Brunswick.

Furs, mail and ancient pine trees have been transported down this river. Now, small pleasure boats and ferries most often use the waterway,

and the Trans-Canada Highway has become the primary transporter of people and products. Along the river, however, are numerous secondary and country roads that are perfect for cycling. Velo New Brunswick, in conjunction with the provincial tourism agency, has mapped out five scenic cycling routes in the upper valley. Quiet and accessible, the circle tours range

in length from 19 to 34 miles (31 to 55 kilometers) – reasonable distances to cover in a day and still allow time for sightseeing.

The tours follow the Upper Saint John River, or head off on country roads to the east or west, through towns like Grand Falls, Bath, Hartland and Plaster Rock, with their colonial-style buildings. Along the way, you'll enjoy exceptional views of the Saint John, called *Woolastook* ("the goodly river") by the Maliseet – an apt name for a river that supports some of the province's most successful farming operations. The longest river in Atlantic Canada, the Saint John begins its serene journey in Maine and ends 415 miles (670 kilometers) later at the Bay of Fundy. The valley

The longest river in Atlantic Canada, the Upper St. John River.

A pastoral village reflected in the St. John River.

is dotted with little towns and villages, forests, and lush green fields of potato plants, the economic mainstay of the area.

Summer and fall are the best times for cycling the Saint John Valley. Summer is a very active time, with plenty of farmers' markets, festivals and special events. Autumn is best for scenic splendor, although many tourist attractions are closed or operating on reduced hours. Two features you won't want to miss in either season are in Grand Falls and Hartland.

At Grand Falls, you'll see the largest waterfall in New Brunswick, spilling 75 feet (23 meters) into a gorge a mile (1.5 kilometers) long and lined with cliffs 230 feet (70 meters) high. It's a spectacular sight, and one worth taking some time to enjoy. You can lock your bike at the Information Centre and visit the observation deck for a thrilling view of the river and thundering falls, then cross the bridge and

When you go

Tourism New Brunswick
PO Box 6000
Fredericton, NB E3B 5H1
Tel: 1-800-561-0123

Recommended Reading

Sienko, Walter. *Nova Scotia & The Maritimes by Bike*. Seattle: The Mountaineers, 1995.

walk along trails overlooking the gorge. Some 250 steps lead down to the "wells," smooth hollows carved out of the rugged cliffs by boulders swirling endlessly in the water.

In the village of Hartland, cross the 1,280-foot-long (390-meter-long) Hartland Covered Bridge, the world's longest. Built in 1921, its roof and sides protect the wooden driving surface from the weather, and, in the early years, "the kissing bridge" sheltered courting couples from prying eyes!

Although not a circle tour, the section from Grand Falls to Hartland on Highways 105 and 103 is ideal for bicycle touring. The route is easy to follow, and there are no busy city streets to negotiate. On all the tours, the roads are generally flat and well paved, and for the most part traffic is light. Occasionally, you'll need to shift into your "granny gears" to make it up steep hills. If you have to venture onto the Trans-Canada Highway, you'll find the traffic much heavier, but the shoulders are wide and you can make good speed.

Rough it or go for comfort – there are plenty of campgrounds and friendly B&Bs en route.

Hartland Covered Bridge, the world's longest.

The Cabot Trail

More than a scenic ride, a cycle tour of the Cabot Trail is a history lesson and cultural experience. Named after John Cabot, the first European to set foot in Nova Scotia, in 1497, the trail climbs through hilly terrain, along rugged coastlines, rolling meadows, sandy beaches and winding river gorges – a visual treat enhanced by the stays at Acadian fishing villages, eating fresh seafood, and meeting some of the friendliest people in Canada.

The 186-mile (300-kilometer) highway circumnavigates the northern part of Cape Breton Island and is one of the most popular coastal tours in North America. For cyclists it is ideal in fall, when the scenery includes the warm hues of maple and birch, traffic volume is less, and the weather is conducive to cycling. This is a maritime climate: anticipate fog, wind and rain any time between May and September. If cycling in July or August, be prepared to share the road (no paved shoulders) with thousands of tourists who may pay more attention to the scenery than to you. An early start will avoid the daytime traffic.

Accommodation is easy to find at numerous roadside inns, B&Bs or campgrounds; reservations are advisable during July and August. For a more pampering experience, let a cycle tour company handle the logistics and just go along for the ride!

Most cyclists start at Baddeck, on the shores of Bras d'Or Lake close to Highway 105. Baddeck was the summer home of Alexander Graham Bell, who wrote, "I have travelled the globe. I have seen the Canadian and American Rockies, the Andes and the Alps and the Highlands of Scotland; but for simple beauty, Cape Breton outrivals them all." Mount your bike and head out of town!

The first 58-mile (93-kilometer) leg of the four-day tour makes a beeline for the Gulf coast along Highway 30 via the Margaree River Valley, then follows the coastline to Chéticamp. The Margaree is famous for Atlantic salmon, and the valley exudes its Scottish heritage; in certain areas Gaelic is still spoken and taught. Approaching the coastal plain near Margaree Harbour, you're in a different world physically and culturally.

Chéticamp is a center of Acadian culture, where you can see traditional activities such as rug hooking and sample fresh seafood and *poutine*, the traditional French fries, gravy and cheese curds. Try to visit the Chéticamp Acadian Museum, or attend a ceilidh for a unique cultural experience.

Leaving Chéticamp, you soon enter Cape Breton Highlands National Park – the first real hill riding on the tour, offering some of the best vistas. For the next 70 miles (113 kilometers) the trail winds along the park's perimeter. Beyond Chéticamp the road clings to the steep, forested hillsides, dipping and climbing like a roller coaster. It then turns inland and climbs to the crest of 1,506-foot (459-meter) French Mountain. After the long uphill haul, the next 7.5 miles (12 kilometers) or so across a rolling plateau will be a welcome respite. From various overlooks, you can gaze down at steep slopes plunging into the shimmering waters of the Gulf of St. Lawrence. The road then dives down to the village of Pleasant Bay, until recently an isolated community of Scottish ancestry.

Again, the road turns inland, following the park's northern boundary,

Margaree River Valley, Cabot Trail.

climbing back into the highlands. Take time to visit the replica of the crofter's cottage at Lone Sheiling, with a 300-year-old sugar-maple-forest backdrop. The Scots, many driven from their homeland by grinding poverty, and attracted by the offer of 40 acres of free land, found a home away from home in this part of Nova Scotia. The similarity between the Cape Breton highlands and the Scottish highlands is striking.

After the height of land at 1,493-foot (455-meter) North Mountain, another exhilarating descent to Sunrise Valley brings the welcome sight of the village of Cape North. Though only 40 miles (65 kilometers), this is a tough leg of the journey, and the point where the trail heads south, back to Baddeck.

The Atlantic coast is less scenic and lush than the Gulf coast; the coastline is craggier and wilder, with bigger surf.

A worthwhile, short detour from the trail starts at South Harbour and hugs the shoreline of Aspy Bay (great for spotting whales) – before turning inland to Neil's Harbour. Shortly after Neil's Harbour you'll rejoin the trail, which now follows the park's eastern boundary. The road follows the shore for

When you go

Tourism Nova Scotia
PO Box 130
Halifax, NS B3J 2M7
Tel: 1-800-565-0000
Tel: (902) 425-5781 outside North America
E-mail: nsvisit@fox.nstn.ns.ca
Website: www.explore.gov.ns.ca/virtualns

15.5 miles (25 kilometers) to Ingonish – first settled by the Portuguese in 1521, but later abandoned. This popular resort area with its sandy beaches is a good choice for an overnight stay.

Beyond Ingonish, the road enters the park one last time, crosses a prominent headland, then exits the park near Ingonish Beach. The route follows the coastline at Ingonish Harbour, then the final 1,180-foot (360-meter) hill climb up Cape Smokey begins. At the top, most of the hilly terrain is behind you; enjoy the ocean view from the Cape Smokey Provincial Park viewpoint.

Though the descent from Cape Smokey is a white-knuckle event – steep, with an abrupt turn at the bottom – the remainder of the trail back to Baddeck is tame and passes through numerous tiny communities (some offer seafood lunches). Of note is the Gaelic College of Celtic Arts near St. Anns, North America's only Gaelic educational institution. In August, the Gaelic Mod features highland dancing, Gaelic singing, bagpipes playing and other cultural events.

The final 12.5-mile (20-kilometer) stretch between St. Anns and Baddeck is along the Trans-Canada Highway, a somewhat anti-climactic finish to a great ride.

Cycling the Cabot Trail on Cape Breton Island.

Mabou Highlands

After crossing the Canso Causeway that links Cape Breton with the mainland, most people follow the Trans-Canada Highway to the Cabot Trail and the justifiably popular and scenic route around the north end of the island. Just to be different, just for the adventure, turn left instead, and follow the Ceilidh Trail into the heart of the Mabou Highlands.

Overlooking Northumberland Strait on the southwest coast of Cape Breton Island, the rugged highlands, made up of hard sedimentary and volcanic rock, reach heights of up to 1,115 feet (340 meters). Clear streams plunge through long, deep gorges that cut through hills cloaked in maple and spruce. Covering an area approximately 58 square miles (150 square kilometers) in size, the hills are crisscrossed by a maze of old logging roads and cart tracks that linked early settlements. Only a few cottages are left now, relics of the Highland Scots who came to Cape Breton to farm and raise sheep. Faced with too short a growing season, most farmers left their fields to look for work elsewhere, and cows have replaced sheep in the pastures that slope down from the highlands.

Situated at the head of a narrow harbor, the village of Mabou is the starting point for hiking excursions. From the town center, drive across the bridge and turn left to Mabou Harbour, continue to Mabou Coal Mines and park your car. This is the start of a network of hiking trails through the highlands, maintained by the Cape Mabou Trail Club. Twelve trails from 1 to 4 miles (1.5 to 6.4 kilometers) long have been cleared and signed, providing access to some of the most beautiful countryside in Cape Breton. You can spend an hour or a day on the trails, hiking to a lookout or combining several short sections to make a long loop.

The "must-do" route begins at Mabou Coal Mines on the Fair Alistaire Mountain Trail, which links up with MacKinnon's Brook Trail, Oak Ridge Trail and *Beinn Bhiorach*, or Steep Mountain Trail. This is a superb coastal

Sugar maple forest, Mabou Highlands.

Tree-lined paths.

walk along the original wagon track used by Scottish settlers in the 1800s. The trail hugs the coast on a rolling, tree-lined path, with fabulous views of Northumberland Strait. You might see pilot whales cruising the coastal waters and majestic bald eagles dive-bombing for a meal of fish. The total distance is about 13 miles (21 kilometers), so pack a lunch and stop frequently to take in the views. Most of the trail is easily hiked, with the exception of the *Beinn Bhiorach* Trail, which involves a scramble along a narrow, exposed edge – don't attempt this section if you have a fear of heights!

After your hike, you can cool off at West Mabou Beach, then head back to town for a bite to eat at the Shining Waters

The majestic bald eagle.

When you go

Cape Mabou Trail Club
PO Box 528
Mabou, NS B0E 2W0

Inverness County Tourism Dept.
PO Box 170
Port Hood, NS B0E 1N0
Tel: (902) 787-2274

Bakery or the Mull Restaurant. Mabou is a lively town, with Gaelic signs in the shop windows, and friendly people who might regale you with some local folklore. You can stay in B&Bs, cottages, inns, a hostel or the campground, and take in some of the traditional summer events. A Gaelic celebration called a ceilidh (pronounced *kay'-lee*) and other festivals are held every week throughout the summer, featuring infectious toe-tapping fiddle music, bagpipes, step dancing and highland dancing. Joining the fun at one of these Celtic gatherings may well be the highlight of your visit. You'll leave Cape Breton with a tune in your head as well as a vision of Mabou Highlands' scenic beauty.

Minas Basin

This is where it *really* happens: the highest tides in the world. Everywhere you travel along the Bay of Fundy, you hear about its record-breaking tides, and now you're here!

The Minas Basin is an arm of the Bay of Fundy, reaching inland at the southeast tip of the bay. Twice a day, every 12 hours and 26 minutes, the tide comes pulsing down the 175-mile-length (280-kilometer-length) of the Bay of Fundy, rapidly covering the vast red sandflats it abandoned at low water. The bay acts as a funnel, amplifying the tides that rise progressively higher as they reach the head of the bay. The surge boils and churns around capes and jagged points, and reverses the outflow of water at the mouths of rivers, creating foaming tidal bores. Over millennia, the powerful tides have scoured the sandstone cliffs that line the basin into intricate sculptures; they'll continue to reshape their works of art in millennia to come.

You could easily spend a week along the Minas Basin, stopping at numerous attractions on the highway routes dubbed the Glooscap

Minas Basin.

Trail and the Evangeline Trail. Basalt cliffs, sandstone stacks, rolling hills and lowlands diked by early settlers provide a rich variety of landscapes to explore. Two provincial parks are of particular note.

Five Islands park, on the north shore of the Minas Basin, and Blomidon park on the south are connected in legend by the demigod Glooscap, creator and protector of the Mi'kmaq people. From his home on Cape Blomidon, Glooscap hurled five giant rocks at his rival, Beaver, who'd destroyed the great chief's medicine garden. Thus Glooscap created the five islands – called Moose, Diamond, Long, Egg and Pinnacle – for which the park is named.

In less colorful terms, the islands are a result of volcanic action, massive erosion and glacial scouring. These are the Basalt Headlands, which stretch along the north shore of the basin and reappear on the south side at Cape Blomidon and Cape Split. The coastal cliffs are capped by the more erosion-resistant basalt, but the underlying red sandstone is easily eaten away. Every spring, after the winter's freeze–thaw cycle, agate, amethyst, jasper and other semiprecious minerals are exposed in the crumbling basalt, making the coastline a paradise for rock hounds.

As for other precious discoveries: *fossils!* In and around Five Islands park, dinosaur tracks and bones have been found – some of the oldest discovered on the planet. As well, fossils of fish and reptiles have been uncovered on the immense tidal flats that extend a mile (1.6 kilometers) from the shore. At low tide, park visitors can search for fossils, collect rocks or try their hands at clam digging.

The park offers 8 miles (13 kilometers) of scenic hiking trails through three different habitats. The 3-mile (5-kilometer) Red Head Trail skirts the 295-foot (90-meter) sea cliffs that overlook the Minas Basin, with views of formations such as The Old Wife and Red Head. Keep well back from the crumbling cliff edges here and on the Economy Mountain Trail, which follows an old logging road 3 miles (5 kilometers) up the mountain to its 698-foot (213-meter) summit. The Estuary Trail is an easy 2.5-mile (4-kilometer) walk along the mouth of the East River.

On the other side of Minas Basin, Blomidon Provincial Park occupies the spectacular wind-blown promontory of Cape Blomidon. Like Five Islands Provincial Park, Blomidon is situated in the Basalt Headland Natural Landscape, one of 80 ecological regions identified by the

province. An 8.5-mile (14-kilometer) network of interconnecting trails traverses a range of ecosystems in the park. Short trails of just over a mile (2 kilometers) lead to waterfalls and through deciduous forests of sugar maple, yellow birch and beech. The longest, the 3.7-mile (6-kilometer) Jodrey Trail, skirts 600-foot (183-meter) cliffs overlooking the Minas Basin. Both provincial parks and their campgrounds are open from June to October.

Just west of Cape Blomidon, Cape Split digs into the Minas Channel like a fish hook, separating the Bay of Fundy from the Minas Basin. The 10-mile (16-kilometer) trail to the cape is primarily forested, but emerges onto the open point in the final half-mile (kilometer), offering breathtaking views from 300 feet (90 meters) above the water. The Fundy tides converge at this point, exhibiting their power in the churning waters below. Beyond the tip of the cape,

A view of Cape Blomidon.

a barren sea stack towers 330 feet (100 meters) over the water, its isolation providing nesting grounds for great black-backed gulls and double-crested cormorants.

Everywhere in the Minas Basin,

tidal flats are home to a variety of marine life – clams, crustaceans, worms, slipper limpets, mussels and barnacles. They're important feeding grounds for hundreds of thousands of shore birds, especially during fall migration when they come to fatten up for the long journey south. Semi-palmated sandpipers, greater yellowlegs, black-bellied plovers and

When you go

Tourism Nova Scotia
Tel: 1-800-565-0000

Blomidon Provincial Park
Tel: (902) 582-7319 (June to October)

Five Islands Provincial Park
Tel: (902) 254-2980 (June to October)

others come in huge numbers – watch to your heart's content!

Exploring the tidal flats is a must for every visitor, but be careful. Never venture onto the ocean floor without first consulting the tide charts, and do not attempt to reach offshore islands. The tides can rise as much as three feet (one meter) in 20 minutes, possibly cutting you off from your return route to the mainland. If in doubt, ask park staff or the local tourist information center for advice.

The many towns and villages along the Glooscap and Evangeline trails offer friendly, comfortable accommodation at inns, B&Bs, cottages, hotels, private campgrounds and even lighthouses. Restaurants serve local fare of fresh steamed lobster, wild blueberry pie and creamy seafood chowders. Stop at one of the provincial information centers en route and pick up a copy of the *Fundy Shore Eco-Guide* for an excellent overview of the region's heritage.

South Shore

High on any coastal kayaker's wish list is the type of coastline that offers interesting coves and islets to explore, sandy beaches to relax on, plenty of safe landing spots, and abundant marine life. The South Shore of Nova Scotia fits this description to a tee. There are nearly 200 miles (320 kilometers) of indented coastline; countless islands, seals, whales; and over 140 species of sea birds and shore birds in the region. Throw in some picturesque villages and convenient road access to the shore and you have an ideal spot for a kayaking vacation.

Highway 103 hugs the coast between Halifax and Yarmouth, giving access to numerous put-ins, so a paddling trip along the South Shore can be as long or as short as you like. With enough time you could paddle the entire coastline, or you can dip

your paddle for just half a day. Likewise, you can choose a trip of any level of difficulty, from island hopping in sheltered bays to trips around exposed headlands. Ocean kayaking has become a popular activity in Nova Scotia, and you will have no difficulty finding a tour company if you prefer to travel with a group.

Hundreds of offshore islands and shoals make this section of coastline tricky to navigate. In fact, the 1866 sinking of the *SS Atlantic* with the loss of over 600 lives occurred along this coast. To make navigation easier, a string of light-

Boer Head lighthouse on Nova Scotia's South Shore.

Atlantic coastal beach on the South Shore.

houses, most of them now automated, was built on prominent points and islands, hence the name "The Lighthouse Route" for this section of coast. Headlands and hidden shoals are generally not a problem for ocean kayakers, but the lighthouses make good reference points.

The limiting factor for paddlers is the weather, in particular fog, for which the coast is famous. A marine map and compass, and the ability to use them, are essential for anything but the shortest trips. It's also wise to carry a good supply of fresh water.

The northern section of the Lighthouse Route, including Lower Prospect, Mahone Bay and the Tancook and La Have Islands, offers good paddling. This sparsely vegetated area is typically rocky with extensive sandy beaches. The salt-laden winds and acidic soils along much of the coast do not support lush vegetation: stunted spruce, tundra-like heath, sphagnum

bogs and salt marshes are typical. Of interest in this area is Oak Island, supposedly the site of vast amounts of buried treasure, and The Ovens, a series of sea caves that were the site of a mini gold rush.

Further south is the 8-square-mile (22-square-kilometer) Seaside Adjunct to Kejimkujik National Park. The adjunct straddles the tip of the Port Mouton Peninsula (named for a drowned sheep!), an area of pristine white sand beaches, rugged headlands and intertidal lagoons. From the north side of the

peninsula, you can take a relatively short jaunt over to the impressive sand dunes on Port Mouton Island, or you can paddle to St. Catherines River on the opposite side of the peninsula if conditions permit. This exposed route passes two headlands and some spectacular, usually deserted beaches. Carry drinking water with you and don't land on closed beaches where the endangered piping plovers nest during spring and summer.

No trip to the South Shore can be complete without a visit to that icon of Nova Scotia tourism – Peggy's Cove. The view from the harbor of the picturesque village set atop a granite promontory is exquisite, but the hordes of tourists might not be to your liking. The area is good for day trips, but not overnighters because of the scarcity of good campsites. If you haven't had enough of the ocean by this time, take one of the whale-watching tours that set out daily from the harbor.

When you go

Nova Scotia Economic Development & Tourism
World Trade and Convention Centre
PO Box 519, 1800 Argyle Street
Halifax, NS B3J 2R7
Tel: 1-800-565-0000

Recommended Reading

Cunningham, Scott. *Sea Kayaking in Nova Scotia.* Halifax: Nimbus Publishing, 1996.

Kejimkujik National Park

In a province renowned for its seaside beaches, it might seem odd to learn that the only stretch of sand you'll find in Kejimkujik National Park is on a freshwater lake. Situated midway between the Bay of Fundy and the Atlantic Ocean, "Keji" is the only landlocked national park in the Maritime provinces.

Established in 1967, the 147-square-mile (381-square-kilometer) park was the ancestral home of the Mi'kmaq, who used its waterways as a canoe highway linking their interior hunting region and coastal fishing grounds. Their history here goes back 5,000 years before the Europeans "invaded" their territory. What followed was two centuries of exploitation – logging, gold mining, sport hunting and fishing – before the area was preserved as a national park.

Canoeing on the Mersey River, Kejimkujik National Park.

Keji's serene landscape is dominated by lakes and rivers, bogs, meadows and young forests that add up to a gentle and accessible wilderness experience for outdoor enthusiasts. The park's calm, warm waters are an invitation to families or novice paddlers to safely strike out on their first flatwater trip. And the easy hiking trails are ideally suited to that first overnight excursion.

Following the Mi'kmaq tradition, canoeing is perhaps the best way to discover the park. The Mersey River, with barely a riffle after the spring flood has waned, meanders slowly from the eastern boundary of the park near the Visitor Centre into Kejimkujik Lake. Along the river's sheltered banks, you can watch for turtles sunning themselves on rocks or logs, or frogs plopping into the water. Keji's moist, warm summers and mild winters are ideal conditions for a healthy population of reptiles and amphibians that make their home in the park. Among these is the endangered Blanding's turtle. Fewer than 250 of this yellow-throated turtle are found in Nova Scotia, most of them within Kejimkujik park.

Kejimkujik Lake is the largest in the park, and a popular spot for canoeing. When the weather is fine, you can paddle to Indian Point at the north end of the lake and have a picnic. There are five backcountry campsites on islands in Kejimkujik Lake, just a short distance from the put-in at Jakes Landing. These make an exciting overnight destination for families with young children.

Energetic paddlers looking for more of a challenge will find it on an extended trip into Keji's wilderness. From Kejimkujik Lake, streams and portages link a number of smaller lakes and rivers, and there are 46 primitive backcountry campsites

Horned puffin, one of many varieties of birds found in Kejimkujik Seaside Adjunct.

els. A minor boom occurred in the late 1800s, and the remains of abandoned mine shafts, ditches and tools can be seen along the way.

The 1.8-mile (3-kilometer) Peter Point Trail leads through several different habitats, making it especially good for bird watching. Watch also for turtles – Blanding's, painted and snapping turtles all breed in the area. The 3.7-mile (6-kilometer) Hemlocks and Hardwoods Trail is a must for any visitor to the park. The trail leads to a grove of 300-year-old hemlock trees, spared the ax because of their inaccessibility. The tall, stately trees completely shade the forest floor and you'll feel like you're in a cool, dark room.

One major backpacking trail, Liberty Lake Trail, makes a circuit of approximately 37 miles (60 kilometers) roughly around the perimeter of the park. Well-spaced campsites provide seclusion and isolation in Keji's wilderness.

Passing by lakes, streams, bogs and meadows, you're sure to spot white-tailed deer, porcupine and beaver, and perhaps see signs of the secretive bobcat.

The best time to visit Keji is during the autumn, when the forests turn a dozen shades of crimson, gold and yellow. Yet winter has its charms as well – the park is well used by cross-country skiers and snowshoers. Over 60 miles (100 kilometers) of cross-country ski trails are available, as well as warm-up shelters and facilities for winter camping.

The small community of Maitland Bridge, just north of the park entrance on Highway 8, offers canoe guides and outfitting services, as well as accommodation, restaurants and groceries. On Kejimkujik Lake, there's a canteen at Merrymakedge Beach, and bicycles, canoes, boats and lifejackets can be rented at Jakes Landing. A large campground at Jeremys Bay is set in natural woodlands along the lakeshore.

where you can pitch your tent and enjoy the park's subtle beauty and tranquility. You'll be lulled to sleep at night to the sound of loons calling across the lake, or the hoot of a barred owl in the woods, or a chorus of coyotes yipping their lonesome songs.

If you prefer keeping your feet on the ground, Keji offers 14 trails of varying lengths, suitable for families and the novice hiker. Most of the hiking trails traverse woodlands and fairly level terrain. Some of the trails are self-guiding, with pamphlets and cassette tapes of recorded interpretations. Park staff members lead interpretive walks to some very special sites to view some of the features that are preserved under national park status. These are the petroglyphs – intricate, curved designs carved into the soft slate along the eastern shoreline of Kejimkujik Lake.

Of the short trails, Mill Falls and Mersey River are two of the most scenic, both following the river through forests of red maple, balsam fir and hemlock, lush ferns and long grasses. The 1.8-mile

(3-kilometer) Gold Mines Trail relates the history of the gold "rush" by way of interpretive pan-

When you go

Kejimkujik National Park
PO Box 236
Maitland Bridge, NS B0T 1B0
Tel: (902) 682-2772
Fax: (902) 682-3367

Recommended Reading

Haynes, Michael. *Hiking Trails of Nova Scotia.* Fredericton: Goose Lane Editions, 1995.

Seaside Adjunct

In 1988, Parks Canada established the Kejimkujik Seaside Adjunct, an 8.5-square-mile (22-square-kilometer) parcel of land on the Atlantic coast, 60 miles (100 kilometers) from Kejumkujik National Park. Coves, salt marshes and a variety of terrain host a diversity of wildlife and birdlife in the adjunct.

Confederation Trail

The building of railways seemed urgent business in Canada in the late 1800s. Indeed it was also important to the tiny colony of Prince Edward Island. In 1871 the government began construction of a railway and two years later reluctantly joined the Dominion of Canada, whose politicians promised to bail out the now financially distraught island.

For a century, the railway linked towns and villages and carried people, mail and freight across the tiny province. But in 1971 passenger service ceased on the Canadian National Railway, and in 1989 the last boxcar load was hauled along its tracks. The provincial government bought the rail corridor in 1994 and is proceeding to convert it into a multi-purpose trail.

With the help of community organizations and provincial parks, the Confederation Trail is being developed and maintained for hikers, walkers, joggers, cyclists and wheelchair users in summer, and snowmobilers in winter. It's part of the larger Trans Canada Trail network of recreational trails that, when complete, will link the entire country.

Like the railway before it, the Confederation Trail links dozens of rural communities. You're never far from civilization; the largest city the trail passes through is Charlottetown, the provincial capital and the birthplace of Confederation. With a population of 15,000, Charlottetown still preserves a small-town atmosphere.

To date, 144 miles (232 kilometers) of the route have been "developed," that is, surfaced with crushed stone on a 10-foot-wide (3-meter-wide) trail, signed and equipped with picnic shelters approximately every 3 miles (5 kilometers). The undeveloped sections are easily accessible; the surface is still covered with grass and stone

Cycling along the Confederation Trail.

Confederation Trail, Charlottetown, P.E.I.

Confederation Trail, Charlottetown, P.E.I.

ballast from the old rail bed, so sturdy hiking boots are recommended.

The eastern section of completed trail begins in Scotchfort near Mount Stewart at the headwaters of the Hillsborough River and ends 45 miles (73 kilometers) later in Elmira. From Mount Stewart to Morell, the rail bed follows the salt marshes along the Hillsborough River, through fields and trees to Morell and the historic swing bridge. From here, the trail winds along St. Peters Bay, dotted with mussel boats and offering views of the Greenwich sand dunes across the bay. As you cross the Midgell and Marie rivers, look for great blue herons and kingfishers in the broad estuaries below.

The trail leaves the coast now and passes through wetlands and maple forests that form a delightful canopy over the trail when the trees are in full leaf. The trail divides at Harmony Junction, and you can follow the spur south to Souris, or east to the terminus at the Railway Museum in Elmira.

The trail's western segment starts at the restored stone railway station in Kensington and continues for 77 miles (124 kilometers)

to Tignish, just short of the North Cape. From Kensington, the trail crosses the narrowest part of the island, a 3.7-mile-wide (6-kilometer-wide) finger of land between Malpeque and Bedeque bays, a major flyway for waterfowl. This is an important agricultural area, with tidy fields of potato plants stretching across the landscape and Acadian flags proclaiming the French influence around Wellington. The trail then turns north toward the Tyne Valley, through wetlands and farming areas to the end of the line at Tignish.

More than a tourist attraction, the abandoned rail corridor is used by islanders who are enjoying it once again as a link between their communities. For those from "away," however, accommodations, food and services are just off the trail. With so many villages en route, you'll have your choice of B&Bs, motels or camping (some private, some in provincial parks), and access to beaches and other attractions. In small communities, farmhouses or towns, you'll always find a friendly hand to help you.

When you go

Island Trails
PO Box 265
Charlottetown, PEI C1A 7K4
Tel: (902) 894-7535
Fax: (902) 628-6331

Tourism PEI
Visitor Services
PO Box 940
Charlottetown, PEI C1A 7M5
1-800-463-4PEI (4734)

Website: www.gov.pe.ca/vg/explore/trail.asp
Trail maps are available at all visitor centers.

Macphail Woods

Just east of Charlottetown is a unique conservation area that offers a retreat for naturalists and bird watchers at any time of the year. The 140-acre Macphail Woods Ecological Forestry Project, started in 1991, is a research and educational site for the restoration of native forests in Prince Edward Island.

Nature trails, guided walks on bird identification and forest ecology, and workshops on natural and cultural history are just some of the activities open to the public. The main center is the Sir Andrew Macphail Homestead, a 19th-century farm built and operated by the Macphail family. The center is named for a McGill University professor, doctor, writer and conservationist who was born and lived at the homestead over the turn of the 20th century. But it was Sir Andrew's mother, Catherine, who lovingly nurtured the exotic shrubs, trees and vines that she planted on the property. Among those that flourish today are linden trees, English oak, apple, Norway maple, English hawthorn, lilac, silver maple and clammy locust. These and other non-native species provide seasonal habitat for downy and hairy woodpeckers, chipping sparrows, red-eyed vireos and cedar waxwings, among many others.

Three short nature trails focus on different aspects of natural history. The Wildflower Trail leads through woodlands that have gradually taken over the abandoned farmland. Dandelions, goldenrod, creeping buttercup and fireweed still grow along its edges and are signs that the land once was cultivated. And on the flat forest floor, blue-bead lily, stemless lady's slipper, sarsaparilla, wood sorrel and bunchberry grow amid white spruce.

On the Streamside Trail, the forest was less altered and looks much as it did prior to European settlement. A dam across a clear stream once provided power for a sawmill and a swimming hole for the young Macphail boy. In the

When you go

Macphail Woods
c/o Gary Schneider
RR 1
Cardigan, PEI C0A 1G0
Tel: (902) 651-2575
Website: www3.pei.sympatico.ca/garyschneider

Macphail Woods.

brook, speckled trout and other fish and amphibians benefit from the cool, tree-shaded water. Along the banks, you might see signs of mink, which feed on fish, small mammals, frogs and insects. In the woods, look for brown creepers spiraling up tree trunks in their search for insect larvae. Snags provide food and shelter for all sorts of critters; birds, bats, frogs, squirrels, raccoons and mice nest, perch and feed in the cavities of these dead or dying trees. The valley is rich in mosses, ferns and lichens, and during the guided mushroom walks in the fall, you may find dozens of varieties of fungi. On the pond,

two viewing platforms over the water allow you to watch for great blue herons, osprey, kingfishers, olive-sided flycatchers, black ducks, juncos and goldfinches. Yellow-rumped and magnolia warblers nest there, as well as robins and cedar waxwings.

From the pond, head up the hill to join the Woodland Trail, which takes you through different forest types, rich in woodland wildlife. The forest floor is covered in twin-flower, stemless lady's slipper, wood sorrel, gold thread and bluebead lily, and lichens droop from the branches. Every season brings something new to look for: toads

and spring peepers in the spring; wood frogs and salamanders in the summer; ruffed grouse and snow-shoe hare in the winter. Black-capped and boreal chickadees, red-breasted nut-hatches, downy and hairy woodpeckers, and barred owls are year-round residents.

A welcome addition to the demonstration project will be the Macphail Woods Nature Centre, housed in the homestead's large barn. When conversion is complete, the center will feature displays of native plants, small mammals, birds, amphibians, insects and a history of what the island would have looked like prior to European settlement.

Boardwalks protect the delicate mosses, ferns and lichens in Macphail Woods.

North Shore

Much of Prince Edward Island's pleasures are related to the sea. Sun worshippers are enticed to lounge on its long, soft sand beaches and swim in its warm waters. Naturalists are drawn to the coastline's unique sandstone formations and intricate dune systems. Bird watchers thrill to the sight of myriad shore birds and sea birds that flock to the island by the millions. Sea kayakers can enjoy all these pleasures – and more – and the North Shore of P.E.I. provides some of the best paddling in the Maritimes.

It's no wonder the native Indians called it *abegweit* – "the land cradled on the waves." Wherever you are in Prince Edward Island, you're never more than a 15-minute drive from the coast, and access to its shores is readily available at public wharves and provincial parks. The warm Gulf of

St. Lawrence bordering the North Shore of the island is perfect for sea kayaking, and its clear waters are an invitation to bring a snorkel and mask.

Prince Edward Island National Park is an ideal starting place for sea

kayaking the North Shore, particularly for novices. Its protected bays and marshy estuaries are easy to explore – accessible and sheltered – and the gently sloping beach provides an easy landing spot except at the gustiest of times. You can spend any amount of time cruising the coast, but allow about three days to paddle the entire 25-mile (40-kilometer) stretch of shoreline within the national park boundaries. Camp only at the designated sites, and be sure to respect all beach closures – some are off-limits to protect the fragile dune systems and the endangered piping plover nesting areas.

If you're a little more adventurous and comfortable with your paddling skills, you can venture farther afield. From New London Bay on the national park's western extremity to the town of Alberton, approximately 37 miles (60 kilometers) of pristine beaches,

When you go

For general information and a list of outfitters, contact:
P.E.I. Visitor Services
PO Box 940
Charlottetown, PEI C1A 7M5
Tel: 1-800-265-6161

Red cliffs along the North Shore.

barrier dune islands and sandstone cliffs will keep you occupied for a week. Just west of New London Bay is Prince Edward Island's largest cormorant colony at Cape Tryon. Huge nests, whitewashed with guano, decorate the 115-foot (35-meter) cliffs below the Cape Tryon Lighthouse.

Malpeque Bay, well known for its oyster culture, lies farther west along the coast. A deserted barrier island chain, 22 miles (35 kilometers) long, separates the bay from the Gulf. Sea kayaking doesn't get much better in the protected bay. The area is a par-adise for migratory shore birds and anyone with a fascination for observing them. Cormorants, terns, gulls and guillemots, sandpipers, ruddy turnstones and 300 other species congregate by the thousands, and the salt marshes attract enormous numbers of waterfowl that nest and feed in the thick grasses.

Between Malpeque Bay and Alberton is Cascumpec Bay, another major oyster-growing area on the island. Oulton Island, just offshore, was once known for the silver fox that were raised in captivity for their fur. With the collapse of that industry, the island has been taken over by a colony of great blue herons and nesting osprey.

Sea kayaking is an exciting way to explore Prince Edward Island, either on your own or with a guide. Several outfitters offer trips on the North Shore as well as other destinations on the island. Trips start at half-day excursions, but why not take an overnight trip? You'll be treated to one of those stunning island sunsets, as well as a lobster feast on the beach.

Kayaking past sea caves on the North Shore, Prince Edward Island.

Blow Me Down Mountains

You shouldn't have to rack your brains too hard to figure out why the Blow Me Down Mountains were so named. Local lore has it that one Captain Mesurvey, a vertically challenged schooner captain, was anchored off Newfoundland's west coast and prayed that the winds wouldn't "blow me down." The name stuck.

The Blow Me Down Mountains are part of the Long Range Mountains that extend along the entire west coast of Newfoundland. They occupy a compact area of about 9 square miles (24 square kilometers) between the Lewis Hills to the south and the Bay of Islands to the north. Their attraction is ease of access from Corner Brook, the island's second-largest city, the spectacular ocean views from the more

than 2,300-foot-high (700-meter-high) summits, and the excellent hiking, biking and skiing.

One of Corner Brook's claims to fame is that it receives an average of 150 inches (380 centimeters) of snow each year, the largest snowfall of any city in Canada. This is good news for skiers, who can enjoy a visit to Marble Mountain Ski Resort, or to the 22 miles (36 kilometers) of groomed trails at the Blow Me

Down X-C Ski Club. At higher elevations the snow stays well into May and offers some of the best spring skiing in eastern Canada.

Backcountry skiers can climb to the treeless slopes that characterize the upper part of the mountains and enjoy spring telemark skiing with a stunning ocean view. An additional treat might be the sighting of white arctic hares or ptarmigan, or even the woodland caribou that roam these mountains.

By July, the snow has mostly disappeared and hikers can enjoy the breezy ridges and summits. In summer, the unique nature of the mountains becomes apparent. Despite their relatively low elevation, the tops of the mountains are almost bare of vegetation. This is due to the toxic chemical makeup of

Blow Me Down Mountains, from Blomidon Bottle Cove, Newfoundland.

Catching sight of a caribou.

the soil produced by weathering of peridotite, the local bedrock. Only certain species can survive both the harsh climate and soil. Hardy alpine wildflowers such as moss campion, and Newfoundland's insect-eating provincial flower, the pitcher plant, are able to survive. The result is an area of bedrock, boulders and sparse vegetation that sustains faint trails but no established hiking paths. You need good navigation skills if the weather socks in while you're above the treeline.

The 2,132-foot (650-meter) summit of Blow Me Down Mountain itself can be reached in a day from the Blow Me Down Nature Trail on Highway 450, 29 miles (47 kilometers) west of Corner Brook. The trail ascends

through dense boreal forest that gradually thins until the "barrens" are reached. From there it's a two-

When you go

Newfoundland and Labrador Tourism
PO Box 8730
St. John's, NF A1B 4K2
Tel: 1-800-563-6353
E-mail: info@tourism.gov.nf.ca
Website: www.public.gov.nf.ca/tourism

Corner Brook Chamber of Commerce
10 Main Street
Corner Brook, NF A2H 1B8
Tel: (709) 634-5831

hour scramble to the summit, where you'll be entranced by the panoramic views.

If the weather gods are not smiling, there are rewarding hikes that are shorter and closer to sea

level. The Blow Me Down Nature Trail, a well maintained kilometer-long boardwalk, leads to two scenic swimming pools on Blow Me Down Brook. And at the western end of Highway 450, near Bottle Cove, cliff top hiking trails in Blow Me Down Provincial Park take you to spectacular ocean viewpoints. The park is a beautiful place to camp and explore the western extremities of the Blow Me Down Mountains.

Closer to Corner Brook, several of the cross-country ski trails are used for interpretive hikes and for mountain biking in summer. Marble Mountain opens certain areas to mountain bikers, so if you enjoy an adrenaline rush try some of the resort's challenging rides.

Gros Morne National Park

Newfoundland is variously described as desolate, bleak, harsh and untamed, but its largest park, Gros Morne, is nevertheless a place of great beauty. In 1973, Canadians set aside 697 square miles (1,805 square kilometers) of this wild and majestic landscape in a national park. Little more than a decade later, in 1987, the rest of the world acknowledged Gros Morne as a UNESCO World Heritage Site.

A mineral called "peridotite" can take much of the credit. In Gros Morne, peridotite was pushed from the earth's upper mantle to the surface about 480 million years ago, a result of plate tectonics, or continental drift. The peridotite in the park forms part of an exposed cross-section of an oceanic plate that is one of the best examples in the world.

This ancient rock is most evident in the southern portion of the park, in an area called the Tablelands. On Highway 431, heading south

Western Brook Pond, Gros Morne National Park.

toward Trout River, the flat-topped Tablelands appear before you – stark, orangey-brown rock rising sharply over 1,950 feet (600 meters). From a small, secluded campground near road's end, you can explore those awesome heights in a number of different ways.

The two-hour, one-and-a-quarter-mile (2-kilometer) guided hike to the base of the Tablelands massif is perhaps the best way to learn about the geological history of the park – the continental collisions, the effects of the Ice Age, and how plants and animals survive in a seemingly barren landscape. High in iron and magnesium, peridotite,

combined with the unforgiving winds, supports very little vegetation. As in a desert, though, a variety of plants do survive – two are harebell and moss campion, which cling to tiny pockets of soil. Stunted tamarack, dwarf birch and juniper, some hundreds of years old, hug the ground for protection.

To get a feel for the grandeur of the Tablelands, it's well worth taking the interpretive boat tour down the 9-mile (15-kilometer) length of Trout River Pond. For a different perspective, the 4-mile (7-kilometer) Trout River Pond trail takes you to the narrows that divide the landlocked fjord into Big Pond and Small Pond. It's a moderate hike that takes about four or five hours, and the views overlooking the pond are magnificent. Back at Trout River, notice the terraces that step up from the sea. These were former coastlines that rebounded in stages after the glaciers retreated, severing Trout River Pond's link to the ocean.

The Green Gardens trail leads out to the battered coast, past lush meadows where sheep graze in the summer. Volcanic action has been at work here, forming convoluted patterns of pillow lava and dramatic sea stacks that stand isolated from the cliffs. There are two choices on the Green Gardens trail, both fairly strenuous and not suitable for children. The full trail is a 10-mile (16-kilometer) loop, while the shorter version is 5.5 miles (9 kilometers) there and back.

When you've explored the southern portion of the park, head to the north side of Bonne Bay. The park's visitor center is just outside the town of Rocky Harbour, as is the main campground at Berry Hill. From here, two short, easy hikes take you up the hill to a lookout or around a pond. The 6-mile

(10-kilometer) trail to Baker's Brook Falls travels through bog and forest and a colorful display of wildflowers in spring and summer.

Also in the vicinity, a couple of short trails allow exploration of the shoreline near Lobster Cove Head Lighthouse. The long, windswept cobble beaches are littered with bleached logs and battered lobster pots and are lined with fishing sheds and cabins. In June and early July, you may see pilot whales, minke whales, and sometimes humpbacks and fin whales plying the waters for capelin.

East of Rocky Harbour is the trailhead for one of the most popular and difficult hikes in the park, the 10-mile-long (16-kilometer-long) James Callaghan Trail to the summit of Gros Morne. The highest in the park at 2,644 feet (806 meters), Gros Morne is part of the Long Range Mountains, which stretch from Port aux Basques to the tip of the

Northern Peninsula. The landscape is dotted with ponds and exposed rock covered by subarctic heaths, grassy fens and those stunted, twisted bands of dense spruce and fir called "tuckamore." In summer, woodland caribou seek out snow patches that linger long into July,

When you go

Gros Morne National Park
PO Box 130
Rocky Harbour, NF A0K 4N0
Tel: (709) 458-2417
Fax: (709) 458-2162
Website: www.grosmorne.pch.gc.ca

standing in the cool air to escape the insects.

No trip to Gros Morne would be complete without a visit to its most photographed feature, Western Brook Pond. As it is set amidst the towering Long Range Mountains, you must first walk

inland to reach the landlocked fjord. An easy, 45-minute walk lands you at the wharf, where you can board a tour boat that will take you down the lake's 10-mile (16-kilometer) length. Alternatively, you can hike through forests and coastal lowland to Stag Brook on the west side of the pond, or to Snug Harbour on the north side. Both are moderately easy trails that allow glimpses of the gorge and the high plateaus. A difficult trail continues on from Snug Harbour, leading to an exhilarating view of the fjord from above.

Although August and September are the best times for hiking, every day can bring unpredictable weather. Whether you're strolling or setting out on a long day hike, always be prepared with extra clothing, food and water. Clear skies in the morning could turn to fog and drizzle by afternoon. It's all part of the experience in Gros Morne.

Lookout Hills overlooking Bonne Bay, Gros Morne National Park.

East Coast Trail

Everyone has heard of the West Coast Trail on Vancouver Island, and everyone, it seems, is clamoring to hike it. Now, however, there is an east coast counterpart – Newfoundland is proud to present the East Coast Trail. Just as the West Coast Trail is set on the extreme western edge of the country, the East Coast Trail is perched at the opposite end of Canada, on the easternmost shore of the Avalon Peninsula.

The similarities stop there, for, unlike the West Coast Trail, virtually *nobody* has heard of Newfoundland's version. Not to boast too much, but visitors don't have to line up for the East Coast Trail, or make reservations, or pay hefty fees to hike it, or race to campsites to be assured a spot, or …

In fact, you may not see another soul on the portion you choose to hike. Currently about 150 miles (250 kilometers) long, the East Coast Trail will be 210 miles (340 kilometers) when it's complete in 2000. Ready access all along the trail means you can hike as much or as little as you like, skip sections altogether, do a series of loops or a linear route, take a day, or take a week. You can pack a tent and camp along the way, or just your toothbrush and stay at B&Bs.

The trail follows traditional paths that have been used for centuries by fish-

When you go

East Coast Trail Association
General Delivery
Bay Bulls, NF A0A 1C0
Tel: (709) 334-2976/2977
Fax: (709) 334-2994
E-mail: ecta@thezone.net
Website: www.ecta.nf.ca

East Coast Trail from The Spout to Bay Bulls.

ermen and hunters, as links between communities, and even by European sailors who escaped from their ships to settle in the "newe founde launde." Thirty-eight fishing communities between Cape Race in the south and Topsail in the north are connected by the trail. Some of the villagers who once made their living off the sea are now turning to the land by providing meals to hikers and accommodations that range from modern B&Bs to converted convents, fishermen's cottages and stageheads.

The East Coast Trail is divided into six sections called "paths," each with a cultural and geographical personality all its own. The shortest is the Cape Spear Path, which, at 14.5 miles (23.5 kilometers) long, can be hiked in two days. At the other end of the spectrum, the Colony of Avalon Path is 84.5 miles (136 kilometers) long and takes seven to nine days to hike. The paths are further divided into walks and community links, where accommodation and other services are available.

Whatever path you choose to follow, you'll be rewarded with the peninsula's striking landscape and numerous natural and cultural attractions. The route follows along rugged cliffs, over coastal meadows and through boreal forest. There's even a section of barren tundra, the most southerly in Canada, where large herds of caribou roam among the tuckamore. One path, the Spout Hike, leads to a natural geyser. Powered by the sea to a height of 165 feet (50 meters), the Spout has been used as a

navigational aid by mariners for generations.

Abandoned villages, graveyards, old lighthouses and shipwrecks are onshore attractions, while above you soar eagles and myriad sea birds. Offshore islands are home to puffins, murrelets and other colorful birds, and from May to early July you may see a procession of icebergs marching by. In July and August, at any point along the trail, you can watch 30-ton humpback whales breach and lobtail in the ocean below you.

An extra attraction: in the winter, you can go snowshoeing and ice fishing along the East Coast Trail, something you can't do on that *other* trail!

Whaleback Rock on the East Coast Trail, between Beamer Rock and Tappers Cove.

Witless Bay Islands

A 20-minute drive from St. John's, the oldest city in North America, is the fishing community of Bay Bulls. Boat tours from here take you to the Witless Bay Islands, home to 2.5 million sea birds and the largest puffin colony in the northwest Atlantic. A spectacular site!

Sea stacks seen from the East Coast Trail.

Bay of Islands

The sea kayak is an unobtrusive boat, which makes it ideal for observing wildlife and, in particular, whales. In summer, the Bay of Islands on Newfoundland's southwest coast is the temporary home of hundreds of pilot and minke whales, so what better way to see them than from a kayak? The sheltered waters of sections of the bay make whale watching an exciting and relatively safe experience.

The 135-square-mile (355-square-kilometer) Bay of Islands, named by Captain Cook when he charted this part of the coast in 1767, consists of a large open bay and three fjord-like arms, Humber Arm, Middle Arm and North Arm. The bay is dotted with islands and bordered to the south by the rugged Blow Me Down Mountains and to the north by the North Arm Mountains. It's a place of exceptional beauty that offers accessible wilderness.

The town of Corner Brook at the mouth of the Humber River is a good place to start your explorations. Kayak outfitters are located here, and you can rent a boat if you prefer self-guided trips. Corner Brook can be used as a base for day trips, or there is a choice of inns and B&Bs along Highway 450. A scenic oceanfront campground is located near Lark Harbour, on a peninsula that juts out into the bay, about 28 miles (45 kilometers) west of Corner Brook.

The best time to see the whales is in August when they move closer to shore to feed on squid, mackerel and herring. The 2.5- to 3.7-yard-long (4- to 6-meter-long) pilot whales supposedly earned their name because of their ability to locate schools of fish. By observing their movements, fishermen were piloted toward a good catch. Large pods of whales, sometimes as many as 20 or 30, ply the waters of Humber Arm and may pass within meters of your kayak. The best time of day to spot the whales is early in the morning when the sea is calm. The prevailing northwest wind often kicks up a chop by early afternoon, making whales difficult to spot and paddling more challenging.

It should be noted that whale watching is a bit of a crapshoot. Some years they are numerous, other years they are scarce, for reasons not yet understood. However, there are sufficient areas of interest that you're guaranteed an enjoyable visit even if you don't see whales.

Highway 450 snakes along both the south and north shore of Humber Arm, and offers many put-in locations. York Harbour, in a sheltered cove on the south shore, is a good spot for a half-day excursion to Seal Island, where you can stretch your legs and explore the grass-covered island. In June, many sea birds, including terns, guillemots, cor-

Bay of Islands.

morants and eider ducks, nest on Seal and other islands in the bay. The sight of bald eagles and diving osprey will also thrill bird lovers.

Wood's Island, at the mouth of the Humber Arm, is a historic site that can be reached from either Frenchman's Cove on the south shore or from McIver's on the north shore. Once home to a bustling fishing and canning community, the population was resettled by the government in the 1960s and the island is now almost deserted. The sandy beaches make a great lunch spot.

For experienced paddlers, the Middle and North arms make interesting and exciting destinations. Paddling trips start from Cox's Cove on the south shore of Middle Arm, which further splits into Goose Arm and Penguin Arm. Numerous multi-day trips using primitive campsites can be planned. There is more exposure to wind and waves, particularly in the North Arm, so experience and skill are required to paddle safely in these areas.

When you go

For a list of kayak outfitters contact:
Newfoundland and Labrador Tourism
PO Box 8730
St. John's, NF A1B 4K2
Tel: 1-800-563-6353
E-mail: info@tourism.gov.nf.ca
Website: www.public.gov.nf.ca/tourism

Ospreys may be seen flying above the Bay of Islands.

Terra Nova National Park

Driving through Terra Nova National Park can be a bit misleading. The Trans-Canada Highway is buffered on both sides and as far as the eye can see with boreal forest bumping over low hills. Yet, if you stray from the artery that might otherwise whisk you through the park with nary a thought to what you might be missing, you will find that water is an equally important feature here.

The sea: long fingers of the Atlantic creeping inland from Bonavista Bay, glacier-carved fjords lined with shallow coves, rocky cliffs and sand and pebble beaches. But, in addition to the sea, and true to its boreal nature, the park is pocked with fens, bogs, freshwater ponds and streams. Cool, moist ferns, mosses and fungi are abundant in the forest, and spring mists roll in from the ocean, following the valley contours.

For 5,000 years, people have been lured here by the land and the sea. First the native peoples, dating back to 3000 BC; then pirates, who found the indented coastline to their

Sundew.

liking; and European settlers who came for the fish and lumber. Logging and shipbuilding were important industries for over 200 years, but the forests were depleted of their best trees by the time the park was established in 1957. Protecting 155 square miles (400 square kilometers) of land on the northeast coast of the province, Terra Nova is a superb park for people of all ages to explore.

With over 100 miles (160 kilometers) of coastline, perhaps the best place to start is with the sea. The Marine Interpretation Centre at Saltons day-use area, overlooking Newman Sound, gives a good introduction to marine life, with exhibits, aquariums and a touch tank. You could easily spend a few hours here, then venture out to look for periwinkles, whelks, mussels, rock crabs and clams on the mudflats of the Sound. You can also get out to open water with an interpretive boat tour, where you might see dolphins, whales or icebergs, and bald eagles nesting along the exposed coast.

Paddling is a wonderful way to get close-up views of coastal life. The secluded waters of the southwest arm of Alexander Bay and the sheltered coves near Lion's Den are excellent sea kayaking areas. Newman Sound and Clode Sound are more open and therefore require greater caution. The major inland canoe route begins at Sandy Pond, where canoes and kayaks can be

rented. A short portage links Sandy Pond to Dunphy's Pond, where there are several secluded campsites. Another portage takes you outside the park to Pitts Pond; experienced canoeists can continue along the Terra Nova River to the sea at Alexander Bay, a long and difficult journey that takes several days.

Sandy Pond is a great spot for families. For an introduction to the plants and animals of the boreal landscape, take the 1.8-mile (3-kilometer), self-guided trail around this freshwater pond. Newfoundland's provincial flower, the insect-eating pitcher plant, can be seen along the boggy edges of the trail.

There are more than a dozen other trails in the park, most less than 3 miles (5 kilometers) long, that take just a few hours to walk. Many of the trails are wet in spots, so be prepared with rubber boots or waterproof hiking boots. There's good bird watching on Dunphy's Pond Trail – red and white-winged crossbills nest in the area, and you might hear or see finches, great horned owls and boreal owls. Woodpeckers, warblers, grouse and gray jays also make their homes in the forest. Nearer the shores, you'll see sandpipers, greater yellowlegs, red-breasted mergansers, terns and gulls feasting on everything from

Iceberg Alley

Icebergs that drift past the east coast of Newfoundland originate from glaciers on Baffin Island and Greenland, and take 3 to 5 years to travel, driven by the Labrador current. The ice is thousands of years old. Only the summit may be seen above the surface.

aquatic plants to marine mammals. Look for bald eagles and ospreys along the Coastal Trail. The Buckley Cove Trail leads to Saltons barachois where salt and fresh water meet, creating a good habitat for shore birds.

On forest trails, you may see signs of moose, black bear, lynx and snowshoe hare. On the Blue Hill West Trail, you may see signs of the pine marten. This primarily nocturnal creature, once well established in Newfoundland, is now on the endangered species list.

The Louil Hills Trail and Malady Head Trail offer spectacular views of the park, as do the barren, boulder-strewn slopes of Blue Hill and Ochre Hill. The lower Ochre Hill Trail leads through sphagnum bogs and fens punctuated by scraggy tamarack and

Terra Nova National Park.

When you go

Terra Nova National Park
Glovertown, NF A0G 2L0
Tel: (709) 533-2801
Fax: (709) 533-2706

Recommended Reading

Burzynski, Michael. *Fingers of the Sea: A Guide to Terra Nova National Park.* Glovertown: Heritage Foundation of Terra Nova National Park, 1994.

Maryniak, Barbara. *A Hiking Guide to the National Parks & Historic Sites of Newfoundland.* Fredericton: Goose Lane Editions, 1994.

spruce. Pitcher plants are very prominent along this trail.

For avid hikers, the park offers one long backcountry route, the 30-mile (50-kilometer) Outport Trail. This trek begins and ends at Newman Sound Campground, forming a loop that follows the coast southeast to Park Harbour then turns inland via Ochre Hill. The 1-mile (1.5-kilometer)

side trip to the top of Mount Stamford provides a spectacular view across Bonavista Bay. In late spring and early summer, icebergs driven by the Labrador Current appear on the horizon, and during the summer, pilot, humpback and minke whales ply the waters of Newman Sound. The trail continues over the rocky shores of Hefferns Cove to the former settlements at Minchin Cove and South Broad Cove, and from there to Lion's Den. From here on, hikers traverse the least traveled area of the park, and arguably the most scenic.

In the winter, the park is open for cross-country skiing, snowshoeing, ice fishing and winter camping. There are four trails ranging from 1.2 to 6 miles (2 to10 kilometers) long and rated easy to difficult. Skiers are welcome to ski ungroomed trails in the park, provided they register before heading out.

Baccalieu Trail

You'll want your camera within arm's reach on this superb three-day cycling tour on the historic Baccalieu Trail. Rugged cliffs, rocky beaches and countless small coves and inlets describe a coastline where tiny villages once thrived on the bounty of the sea. Now, with the closing of the fisheries, life on the harsh Avalon Peninsula is even more of a struggle. Even so, the people are warm-hearted and friendly, always willing to stop and chat.

Anyone attempting this trip should be in good shape *before* starting out, and willing to brave a few steep hills! The cycle tour begins at Gushue's Pond Park, just west of the provincial capital of St. John's. The first day covers 57 miles (92 kilometers) to the next campground at Northern

Bay Sands Park, so plan an early start to allow for sightseeing.

Head out on the Trans-Canada Highway, then turn north on Route 70. The road dips and climbs, with a couple of grueling hills that afford magnificent views of Conception Bay and some thrilling descents. Several short detours will take you into picture-postcard fishing villages, or you can make a bee-line for Harbour Grace. First settled by the French in 1550 as "Havre de Grace," this was a quiet

fishing port until 1610 when the infamous British naval admiral-turned-pirate Peter Easton built a fort and terrorized the western North Atlantic. Easton's fort is now the site of a museum, with three floors of exhibits on the town's colorful past, including its role in the history of aviation. Many attempts to fly across the Atlantic began in Harbour Grace, of particular note, Amelia Earhart's successful 1932 solo flight.

From Harbour Grace, continue on to Northern Bay Sands Park. The road roller-coasters through a wild and rugged landscape, hugging the coastal cliffs overlooking the bay. Get a good night's rest – the second day is as long as the first.

The terrain now becomes less hilly, but a strong headwind is not unusual. You start out along a

Cycling on the Baccalieu Trail.

Avalon Peninsula.

beautiful coastal stretch, then veer inland to Old Perlican. From here you can take the 3-mile (5-kilometer) detour to Bay de Verde, the jumping-off point for boat tours to Baccalieu Island Ecological Reserve. Eleven species of sea birds nest here in the summer, including 3.3 *million* pairs of Leach's storm petrels, and thousands of puffins and black-legged kittiwakes.

You can continue past Bay de Verde a few miles to Grates Cove – the legendary spot where John Cabot landed and carved an inscription in a rock. Stretch your legs with a walk to that boulder, which still stands. (The inscription was stolen in the 1960s – chiseled out of the rock!)

Back to Old Perlican, continue cycling over rolling hills on the peninsula's northern edge and

When you go

Newfoundland and Labrador Tourism
PO Box 8730
St. John's, NF A1B 4K2
Tel: 1-800-563-6353
Tel: (709) 729-2830

Recommended Reading

Sienko, Walter *Nova Scotia & The Maritimes by Bike.* Seattle: The Mountaineers, 1995.

south along Trinity Bay. At the village of Heart's Content (followed by Heart's Desire and Heart's Delight), stop at the old Cable Station, a fascination to anyone interested in communications technology. The first successful trans-atlantic Morse code signals were sent from here in the late 1800s. The road becomes flatter from here and follows Trinity Bay shore to the Backside Pond Park campground.

The final day sees you pedaling 30 miles (50 kilometers) back to your starting point at Gushue's Pond Park. At South Dildo, visit a remarkable sealing and whaling museum with exhibits on the great whalers and artifacts discovered at local Maritime Archaic Indian archaeological sites. The road climbs gently out of Trinity Bay and joins with the Trans-Canada Highway. From here, it's a deserted 13-mile (21-kilometer) stretch back to Gushue's Pond Park. Situated so close to St. John's, the area is fairly populated, but traffic is only moderate. There are plenty of stores and restaurants along the Baccalieu Trail, as well as B&Bs, inns, cottages and motels if camping is not your style. Be sure to reserve well in advance.

The Torngat Mountains

While sitting out an Atlantic storm, which you almost invariably will do if you visit the Torngat Mountains for a week or more, you might wonder at the fortitude of the people who have occupied these coastal mountains on and off for over 6,500 years. The Torngats, named after the Inuit god of wind and storm, are notorious for their harsh weather and terrain – but there's no finer place for anyone seeking unspoiled wilderness and the opportunity to see exotic wildlife.

Like the tip of a spear, northern Labrador juts out into the Atlantic Ocean, separating Ungava Bay from the Labrador Sea. The Torngat Mountains stretch along the eastern edge of this tip, their rugged sides pierced by long fjords, their treeless slopes home to caribou, wolves, black bear, golden and bald eagles, peregrine falcons and the endangered harlequin duck.

There is no road access to the Torngats. Visitors arrive by boat from Nain, nearly 250 miles (400 kilometers) to the south or by Twin Otter or floatplane, and usually head for Saglek or Nachvak fjords. Because of the logistical problems and expense, most people join an outfitted trip rather than arrange their own.

The spectacular nature of the Torngats is best appreciated from the air. Soaring cliffs rise straight from the ocean, fjords punch their

The Steeker River Valley, Torngat Mountains.

way through the mountains, creating a deeply indented coastline, and rivers in broad U-shaped glacial valleys snake their way down to the fjords. The subarctic landscape is treeless, covered in moss, lichens, grasses and dwarf shrubs.

Caribou thrive in this type of terrain – the Torngats are home to part of the 500,000-strong George River herd, one of the largest in Canada. Sharing the land are black bear, uncommon north of the treeline, wolves and, in the coastal regions, polar bears.

A flight into the Torngats is also a great opportunity to spot icebergs. The cold Labrador Current sweeps along the coast, bringing with it icebergs that probably started their journey at some tidewater glacier in western Greenland. These behemoths can be seen in bays and offshore as they slowly drift south. Some reach the shipping lanes south of the 48th parallel, others drift around for years before disintegrating. Iceberg watching can be a fascinating pastime: the blue-and-green-tinged ice comes in all shapes and sizes, from freshly chiseled to smooth and worn. Some are four or five stories high and may be many thousands of years old.

The fjords are a good location for spotting whales that come to feed in the nutrient-rich waters during the summer. It was the abundance of sea mammals that sustained the Thule Inuit and their ancestors through the harsh Labrador winters. Remains of their winter dwellings, partly subterranean and with whalebone rafters covered with caribou skins, can be found at the end of Nachvak Fjord.

There are no established trails in the Torngats. Like the caribou, you travel through a corridor, picking your way through rock-strewn valleys, crossing bridgeless streams, coping with the black flies as best you can. Experienced hikers escape the worst of the insect hordes by traveling at a steady, constant pace on breezy, open ridges or slopes and avoiding, where possible, low-lying

When you go

For a list of outfitters contact:
Newfoundland and Labrador Tourism
PO Box 8730
St. John's, NF A1B 4K2
Tel: 1-800-563-6353
E-mail: info@tourism.gov.nf.ca
Website: www.public.gov.nf.ca/tourism

boggy areas. It's crucial to have a tent with strong, reliable zippers and netting so you can be guaranteed at least one bug-free space.

Most groups tackle an overland route between fjords, scrambling to the top of some of the 4,900-feet-plus (1,500-meter-plus) peaks when the opportunity arises. Probably the most frequently traveled route is between Saglek Bay and Nachvak

Fjord. En route there's the opportunity to climb Cirque Mountain, or Newfoundland's highest peak, 5,420-foot-high (1,652-meter-high) Mount Caubvick, which straddles the border between Newfoundland and Québec (where the mountain is called Mont d'Iberville).

With luck, the Torngats may soon be declared a national park, Labrador's first. The region was first considered for national park status in 1969, but disputes over land claims delayed the process. These were recently resolved and the way has now been cleared to create the new park. The unique landscapes, cultural history and wildlife habitats will be preserved for future generations of hardy visitors.

Looking out over the Torngat Mountains.

Whitehorse

Many travelers to Yukon pass through Whitehorse on their way to other northern attractions, stopping for a day or two to enjoy what the city has to offer. What they don't realize is that the recreational opportunities from this historic city can fill several more days or even weeks.

Whitehorse, the territory's capital of about 23,000 people, sits on the west bank of the Yukon River, which cuts through rounded mountains reaching some 985 feet (300 meters) in elevation. During the brief summer, the boreal forest, lakes and wetlands come alive with birds and wildlife that feast on plants and shrubs bursting with colorful flowers and berries.

Easily accessible from Whitehorse is an impressive network of hiking and mountain biking trails that has been mapped out by the Yukon Conservation Society. Thirteen of these, ranging from 1 to 11 miles (2 to 18 kilometers) long, are within the immediate vicinity.

The Miles Canyon and Yukon River trails are the most popular, and a must for visitors to Whitehorse. The 3-mile (5-kilometer) Yukon River interpretive trail follows the east side of the river opposite the city's downtown core. It's an easy trail well used by hikers – mountain bikers check your speed!

Leading through sun-dappled stands of trembling aspen and poplar, the trail follows the route of the old tramway that ran nearly 5 miles (8 kilometers) between Canyon City and Whitehorse. The tramway was built in 1898 to skirt an unnavigable section of the Yukon River, the main highway for thousands of stampeders on their way to the Klondike gold fields. Imagine their disappointment after having lugged a ton of provisions over the Chilkoot Trail to be faced with the formidable White Horse Rapids and Miles Canyon, described by one prospector as "five miles of foaming hell"!

The 11-mile (18-kilometer) Miles Canyon Trail extends south from the Yukon River Trail, beginning at a point overlooking Schwatka Lake and the hydroelectric dam that created it. Built in 1957–58, the dam tamed the wild White Horse Rapids. The trail leads across the top of the escarpment. Below you, steep basaltic cliffs line the canyon, the columnar rocks formed by volcanic activity. Keep an eye out for bald eagles, often seen soaring above the water, looking for a meal of salmon. At the trail's turn-around point, you'll see rusted tin

Alpine flowers in the Boundary Ranges near Whitehorse.

cans, broken glass and old building foundations strewn among the poplars – all that remains of the Gold Rush town of Canyon City.

From anywhere in Whitehorse, Grey Mountain, once called Canyon Mountain, is a prominent feature. During the Klondike, it served as a warning to travelers on the Yukon River that they were approaching the dreaded White Horse Rapids. The 7.5-mile (12-kilometer) trail leads to the gray exposed limestone on its slopes and grand views of the surrounding valleys. Strictly a hiking trail, the alpine ridge walk can be a bit demanding in places, especially where it crosses the bedrock.

The trails at the base of Grey Mountain and all around the outskirts of the city are a mountain biker's Mecca. Single track, double track and some 4-by-4 roads traverse the rolling hills through spruce and pine forests, around lakes and ponds, and across the top of the Yukon River escarpment. The maze of trails offers a variety of terrain, from easy to feverish.

The Yukon Conservation Society has published an excellent guidebook of hiking and mountain biking trails in the Whitehorse area. The book includes maps and route descriptions, information about the First Nations, and wonderful detail about plants and animals.

When you go

For information and a copy of their guidebook, *Whitehorse & Area Hikes & Bikes*, contact:

Yukon Conservation Society
Box 4163, 302 Hawkins Street
Whitehorse, YT Y1A 3T3
Tel: (867) 668-5678
Fax: (867) 668-6637

Cycling in an aspen grove outside Whitehorse.

Kluane National Park and Reserve

The lure of Yukon is as strong today as it was a century ago, when prospectors flocked there in an attempt to make their fortune in the gold fields. Now only the focus of people's attention is different. Instead of material riches, people seek solitude, wilderness and the opportunity to escape from urban life. Unlike gold, these rewards are easy to find in Kluane National Park and Reserve.

The park is tucked into the southwest corner of Yukon and, at 8,500 square miles (22,000 square kilometers) is Canada's second largest. It is bordered on the west by Alaska's Wrangell–St. Elias National Park and Preserve, and on the south by the Tatshenshini–Alsek Wilderness Park and Glacier Bay National Park and Preserve. Together these parks form the largest international protected area in the world. In 1980, Kluane was declared a UNESCO World Heritage Site in recognition of its cultural and natural values.

Kluane is accessed from Whitehorse along the Alaska Highway or from the Alaska ferry terminal at Haines and the scenic

Haines Highway. Both routes converge at Haines Junction on the eastern edge of the park. The Alaska Highway continues north to Burwash Landing and Kluane Lake, Yukon's largest. The Visitor Centre at Haines Junction should be your first stop to obtain current information about the park. An excellent way to become familiar with the geology, fauna and flora is to join one of the interpretive walks, which can last from a couple of hours to a full day.

There is one campground inside the park at Kathleen Lake, 20 miles (32 kilometers) south of Haines Junction, and others outside the park at Dezadeash, Pine or Kluane lakes. If you prefer not to camp, either Haines Junction or Kluane

Lake near Sheep Mountain are good bases for day trips. Both areas have a range of motel accommodation, B&Bs and restaurants.

The hiking season runs from late May to mid-September. May and early June are often periods of stable weather, but the best time to view the short-lived alpine flowers is late July and early August. Expect up to 19 hours of daylight in mid-summer with temperatures ranging from 55°F (12°C) to 70°F (20°C).

Most of the park is still in the grip of an Ice Age, with the western-most two-thirds of the park permanently snow- and ice-covered. In fact, this is the largest continuous icefield outside the polar regions; Canada's highest peak, 19,550-foot (5,959-meter) Mount Logan, is located here. The lower-lying southeastern third of the park is more accessible to hikers. Because the treeline is low, between 3,450 and 3,950 feet (1,050 and 1,200 meters), it is relatively easy to reach open alpine areas with their magnificent displays of arctic poppies, purple saxifrage, moss campion and mountain heather. Wildlife is abundant. The park boasts the highest population of Dall sheep in North America. Large groups of up to 20 or more sheep often can be seen on high, grassy ledges. You might also be fortunate enough to hear the chilling howls of the park's wolves.

Hikers follow routes into the backcountry, not established trails. Depending on the route you choose, you may need considerable map and compass skills. There are no signs and few conveniences such as bridges over creeks and rivers. Be prepared to ford such obstacles –

The Lowell Glacier, Kluane National Park and Reserve.

Hiking in Kluane National Park and Reserve.

a pair of light runners is useful so your regular hiking footwear doesn't get wet. Also bear in mind that most of the rivers are fed by meltwater and increase in volume and difficulty during the day, especially during warm spells. Be prepared for cold winds from the icefields, called katabatic winds, which can become quite ferocious at times. Always expect cool, windy weather.

The most dynamic and scenic areas of the park are where the glaciers, some of the longest in the world, meet the greenbelt and deposit their meltwater and silt into long, braided rivers and lakes. Some glaciers have been known to "surge" more than 40 feet (12 meters) a day! The most accessible glacier for hikers is the Kaskawulsh, 40 miles (65 kilometers) long and 1.8 to 3.7 miles (3 to 6 kilometers) wide. Observation Peak, the best vantage point for viewing the glacier, is an 18.5-mile (30-kilometer), day-and-a-half to two-day trek up the Slims River. The 4,265-foot (1,300-meter) slog to the top of Observation Peak rewards you with one of the most spectacular vistas in the park. Moose can often be seen in the marshy areas of the river valley, as well as black and grizzly bear. The

Parks Service sometimes closes this valley to hikers when problem bear encounters might occur.

If you are not an experienced backcountry traveler, there are outfitters who will guide you to this and other glaciers in the park. An alternative way to view the glaciers is from the air. Several commercial, small-plane operators offer sightseeing flights when the weather permits.

If your objective is not to reach one of over 4,000 glaciers in the park, consider excursions from Kathleen Lake. These can range from day hikes to the four- to five-day, 50-mile (80-kilometer) Cottonwood Trail hike that starts at Kathleen Lake and ends at Dezadeash Lake back on the Haines Highway. This is the park's showpiece trail, which, unlike most routes in the park, is signposted and maintained, though you still have to ford some creeks.

Alternatively, you can stay at the campground and fish for landlocked Kokanee salmon, or try to identify the dozens of birds that live by the shoreline.

Though Kluane is principally a park for hikers and mountaineers, there are opportunities to cycle and paddle. Mountain bikers can tackle the 16-mile (26-kilometer) Mush Lake Trail with its numerous creek crossings and mud puddles, or visit abandoned prospectors' cabins along the 18.3-mile (30-kilometer) Alsek Trail.

Several of the lakes in the park are accessible to canoeists and offer pleasant half-day or day-long trips in combination with a short hike or a couple of hours of fishing. Stay close to shore on the bigger lakes to avoid the almost daily buildup of wind and waves. River trips such as the Dezadeash and the upper Tatshenshini can be tackled by experienced paddlers. Non-paddlers can take a guided day-long rafting trip on the upper Tatshenshini River and enjoy spectacular scenery and the opportunity to see riverside moose, elk and bear.

When you go

Kluane National Park and Reserve
PO Box 5495
Haines Junction, YT Y0B 1L0
Tel: (867) 634-7250
Fax: (867) 634-7208
Website: www.parkscanada.pch.gc.ca/

Recommended Reading

Lougheed, Vivien. *The Kluane National Park Hiking Guide*. Vancouver: New Star Books, 1997.

Nahanni National Park Reserve

It's been called "The Dangerous River." It's also been the site of mysterious deaths involving headless corpses. Hoards of gold have been found, then lost. Shangri-La supposedly exists here. Nahanni: it's a place of myth and legends, but it's also one of the most scenic and exciting areas in Canada, if not the world.

The value of the area was recognized in 1972 with the creation of the Nahanni National Park Reserve, a 1,840-square-mile (4,766-square-kilometer) strip of land bordering a 186-mile (300-kilometer) stretch of the South Nahanni River. In 1978, the park was designated a UNESCO World Heritage Site, the first natural area on earth to receive this designation.

Nahanni is a wilderness park. No roads enter the park, and the only access to the river is by float-

plane from Fort Simpson at the junction of the Nahanni and Liard rivers. A quota system for visitors is imposed to preserve the wilderness experience. Because of the difficulty of organizing a trip to the park, most people use an outfitter to supply guides, equipment and a safe paddling and hiking experience.

Most trips start at one of three places: the headwaters of the river at the Moose Ponds, 132 miles (213 kilometers) north of the park boundary; at Rabbitkettle Lake near

the northern boundary of the park; or just above Virginia Falls, about midway between the northern and southern boundaries. The white-water section between the Moose Ponds and Rabbitkettle Lake is reserved for experienced, skilled paddlers only. An alternative, in order to miss most of the technical rapids, is to put in at Island Lakes, about 60 miles (100 kilometers) north of the park boundary.

Trips starting at Rabbitkettle Lake usually last about 10 to 14 days, whereas trips from Virginia Falls are between 7 and 12 days. Take time to hike, explore side valleys and climb to high lookouts offering great views of the river and surrounding mountains.

If you start at Rabbitkettle Lake, you're rewarded with a trip to the hot springs. Multicolored, tiered tufa mounds up to 88 feet (27 meters) high have been deposited from the mineral-rich spring water. During the summer a resident warden conducts interpretive hikes. From here you take to your boats and begin the 217-mile (350-kilometer) journey downstream to the take-out at Blackstone Territorial Park. Most outfitters offer clients the choice of a canoe or raft. If you prefer to take it easy, soak up the scenery and be a shutterbug, take the raft. Paddling a canoe is more energetic and requires coordination, though it's more thrilling in faster stretches.

The first few paddling days allow you to find your river legs. The river is wide and sluggish as it meanders across a broad glaciated valley. Near Sunblood Mountain is the only portage on the river. Miss

Nahanni National Park Reserve.

Dall ram are often seen grazing around the Nahanni National Park Reserve.

it and you hurtle through the Sluice Box rapids and over Virginia Falls, twice the height of Niagara and twice as deadly. Thanks to adequate warnings and numerous pull-outs, no one has yet been swept over the falls.

Seen from below, or preferably from the summit of Sunblood Mountain, the 384-foot-high (117-meter-high) rapids and falls are magnificent. Split by a huge pinnacle of rock, two waterfalls cascade into a seething cauldron, throwing mist high in the air and creating spectacular rainbows. Most groups stop for a night or two to admire the falls and take day hikes. It is also the most crowded area as float-planes ferry in groups that are starting their trip from the falls.

Below the falls, the pace of the river and the scenic splendor pick up considerably. Hell's Gate, a.k.a. Figure 8 Rapids, is a tricky set of rapids, an exciting run when water levels permit. During high water most paddlers portage around the rapids. Then, for the next 50 miles (80 kilometers), the Nahanni flows through three immense limestone canyons with walls soaring to 4,920 feet (1,500meters) above the river. The canyons are home to Dall

sheep, often seen grazing unconcerned on the high, narrow ledges; you'll also spot cave entrances high up in the limestone walls.

Between the canyons are tributary valleys, such as Lafferty Creek, Prairie Creek and Deadman Valley, that offer superb hiking and the opportunity to climb to lookouts offering views of the river snaking through the canyons far below. Deadman Valley is named for Willie and Frank McLeod, whose supposedly headless skeletons were found in 1908 on a gravel bar. Rumor has it that they had discovered a fabulous gold mine, but their secret died with them.

Beyond First Canyon, the river again flows through a broad glacial valley. The final stop in the park is Kraus Hot Springs, where you can luxuriate in the hot, sulfurous pools. The next day, you'll leave the park and spend a last night out at Nahanni Butte, where the Nahanni and Liard rivers join; some groups fly out to Fort Simpson from here. If you continue, the river is sluggish as it meanders across a broad floodplain. With luck you might spot some shaggy, free-ranging wood bison.

Your journey ends at Blackstone Territorial Park, a half-day paddle down the Liard River, where vehicles wait to take you back to Fort Simpson.

Guided trips on the Nahanni usually run from early June through September. July and August offer the most stable weather, but mid September is often fine and the fall colors along the river are spectacular.

When you go

Nahanni National Park Reserve
PO Box 348
Fort Simpson, NT X0E 0N0
Tel: (867) 695-3151
Fax: (867) 695-2446

Nahanni–Ram Tourism Association
PO Box 177
Fort Simpson, NT X0E 0N0
Tel: 1-800-661-0788

Recommended Reading

Hartling, Neil. *Nahanni, River of Gold ... River of Dreams.* Canadian Recreational Canoeing Association, 1993.

Jowett, Peter. *Nahanni, the River Guide.* Calgary: Rocky Mountain Books, 1993.

Hood River

What inspires people to travel to a land of extreme climate and isolation? Explorers have been drawn to Canada's "frozen" North for centuries, lured by the idea of a route through the Northwest Passage to the riches of the Orient.

The Hood River, draining into Arctic Sound on the north coast of Nunavut, drew one such team of explorers nearly 200 years ago. Sir John Franklin's First Arctic Overland Expedition in 1820–21 turned into a nightmare – like others before and since. The 20-man expedition descended the Coppermine River to the Arctic Ocean in two freighter canoes, intent on meeting ships sailing west from Hudson Bay that would carry them back to England. The ships never made it, their progress halted by thick sea ice, and Franklin and his men were forced to

Polar bears.

return to Fort Enterprise, where they'd spent the previous winter.

Their return route led them up the Hood River, named for expedition member Lieutenant Robert Hood. It proved impossible to ascend, however, and just beyond Wilberforce Falls, Franklin and his men began the 250-mile (400-kilometer) overland trek to Fort Enterprise. En route, 11 men died of starvation, the others barely surviving on shoe leather and lichen. Among the dead was Hood,

murdered by a demented Iroquois guide.

Today's explorers make their way down the Hood River in sleek, lightweight canoes, wearing warm fleece clothing and Gore-Tex waterproof jackets, and carrying several weeks' supply of good food and wine. It's still a remote northern trip, though, best undertaken with a guided group.

Most trips leave by floatplane from Yellowknife, arriving two hours later in a land of unnamed lakes and rivers. The Hood River trip begins on Lake 414, just north of the Arctic Circle on the rocky tundra. The first 60 miles (100 kilometers) is through a series of long, narrow lakes connected by rapid-laced channels and rivers. It takes a few days to get your paddling arms in gear, but you'll soon fall into a rhythm.

At every campsite, take the opportunity to exercise your legs and set off on a tundra walk. Soft, wet and spongy underfoot, the tundra in July is a wild palette of purple, pink, yellow and white with the blossoms of willowherb, arctic lupines, arctic poppies, moss cam-

Canada's New Territory

On April 1, 1999, Nunavut became Canada's third northern territory. The Nunavut Land Claims Agreement of 1993 set the stage for the eastern portion of the Northwest Territories to be governed and managed by the Inuit, who have inhabited this vast, far northern region for thousands of years.

pion, lousewort, arnica, anemones and avens.

Massive eskers mark a change in topography where lake travel ends and the river proper begins. Walking on sand and gravel ridges is much easier than the tundra, and you can see several days of river travel ahead and behind you, giving some perspective of where you've been and where you're headed.

When you're not reading the river, scan the hills for signs of wildlife. Although the diversity of species is not great, the numbers are – hundreds of thousands of caribou migrate every year. You might also see the archaic-looking muskoxen, arctic hare, arctic fox, ptarmigan and possibly gyrfalcon and wolverine.

In all, you'll be about

Rafting the Hood River.

When you go

NWT Canoeing Association
P.O. Box 2763
Yellowknife, NT X1A 2R1
Tel: 1-800-661-0797
Tel: (403) 873-3032
Fax: (403) 920-4047

Nunavut Tourism
PO Box 1450
Iqaluit, NT X0A 0H0
Tel: 1-800-491-7910
Tel: (867) 979-6551
Fax: (867) 979-1261
E-mail: nunatour@nunanet.com
Website: www.nunatour.nt.ca

Recommended Reading

McCreadie, Mary. *Canoeing Canada's Northwest Territories.* Canadian Recreational Canoeing Association, 1995.

Raffan, James (ed.). *Wild Waters: Canoeing North America's Wilderness Rivers.* Toronto: Key Porter, 1997.

two weeks on the river, depending on your take-out. By the time you reach Wilberforce Falls, you'll have scouted and run a good many Class I to III rapids, and portaged or lined around at least eight or nine more. The falls, which Franklin named after British Chief Justice William Wilberforce, are the most spectacular in the Arctic, spilling 160 feet (50 meters) over two ledges into a red quartzite canyon.

Wilberforce Falls is where most parties get picked up. Closer to the coast, fierce winds can prevent planes from landing, which could mean several days of waiting. The Hood is a technical river for confident canoeists – exploring it with the ghosts of Franklin's desperate men will bring history alive.

Burnside River

From the air, the land to the west of Hudson Bay looks like a vast mosaic of interconnected lakes and treeless tundra. Glance out of your plane window a few hours later and there's no perceptible change; the mosaic seems to go on forever. These are the Barren Grounds or Barrens, also referred to as the barrenlands, named by early explorers who imagined that nothing could live in such an inhospitable land. Of course, we now know that the barrenlands are anything but barren. They have

Arctic hare.

supported generations of Inuit and other native groups, and they support a rich variety of fauna and flora.

However, the barrenlands *are* unforgiving, as many ill-prepared explorers have found to their cost. Even with modern equipment, high-tech clothing and communications, a trip on one of the many rivers that cross the barrenlands is a serious undertaking. Unless you are experienced and skilled at northern travel, it is probably best to join an outfitted canoeing or rafting trip and leave the organization and logistics to the experts.

The Burnside is a typical northern river in that it has dramatic scenery, abundant wildlife and long stretches of quiet water interspersed with rapids up to Class III. A typical trip takes between 10 and 14 days, allowing for hiking and exploratory hikes onto the tundra. The Burnside has an added attraction in that Bathurst Inlet Lodge, a naturalist lodge, is located near the mouth of the river.

Most trips start from the outlet of Contwoyto Lake, 266 miles (430 kilometers) by floatplane from Yellowknife. An alternative start, which avoids the fast water and difficult Belanger Rapids, is from Kathawachaga Lake, 14 miles (23 kilometers) downstream. From here, the river flows 146 miles (235 kilometers) to Bathurst Inlet, passing through rolling tundra, caribou migrating grounds and the spectacular Wilberforce Hills.

For much of its distance, the river follows a broad valley with uninterrupted views and the chance to spot caribou and muskoxen. There's even the chance of a rare grizzly bear sighting. The river cuts through glacial till and eskers that can be climbed to provide a 360-degree view of faraway horizons. The tallest vegetation you'll see will be waist-high willows and alders, among carpets of lichen and moss. It's easy to be over-whelmed by the scale of things, so bring everything back into perspective by peering at the wildflower detail.

After about two-thirds of the journey is complete, near the meeting of the Burnside and Mara rivers, you cross the Arctic Circle and the pace of the river picks up. The broad valley becomes more of a classic V-shape as it enters the Wilber-force Hills. Their rugged slopes climb up to 1,600 feet (500 meters) above the river until, 10 miles (16 kilometers) from Bathurst Inlet, it flows into a canyon and over Burnside Falls.

When you go

For a list of outfitters and expediters contact:
Tourism Marketing Division
Government of the Northwest Territories
PO Box 1320
Yellowknife, NT X1A 2L9
Tel: 1-800-661-0788
Website: www.nwttravel.nt.ca/

Bathurst Inlet Lodge
PO Box 820
Yellowknife, NT X1A 2N6
Tel: (867) 873-2595 or 920-4330
Fax: (867) 920-4263
E-mail: bathurst@internorth.com
Website:
www.canadiana.com/vnorth/bathurst

This section is unnavigable and a 2-mile (3.5-kilometer) portage must be made around the falls. From the base of the falls it's a short paddle to Bathurst Inlet and the option of

pickup by floatplane or spending time at the lodge.

The lodge, an old Hudson's Bay Company trading post and Roman Catholic mission that were abandoned in 1964, is now jointly run by Trish and Glenn Warner and their Inuit partners. Knowledge-able guides will ensure that your visit is an exciting, educational experience. The relatively mild but short summer climate makes the Bathurst Inlet area a naturalist's nirvana: over 125 species of wild-flowers, 80 varieties of nesting birds, as well as caribou, muskoxen, grizzly bear, wolves, arctic fox and arctic hare can be found here. Anglers can catch arctic char, lake trout, whitefish and grayling. Barren, indeed!

Rafting the Burnside River.

Auyuittuq National Park

Canadians often puzzle at the outsider's impression of our parks as vast tracts of untamed wilderness. To us, the busy townsites, crowded highways and networks of hiking trails tracking up Canada's parks seem a far cry from the real backcountry of a century ago. Perhaps only a trip to the Far North will recapture our sense of the wild.

Set aside as a park reserve in 1976, Auyuittuq (pronounced *eye-you-ee'-took*) will do just that. The park lies almost completely north of the Arctic Circle on Baffin Island, 1,488 miles (2,400 kilometers) north of Montréal. The Penny Ice Cap, a remnant of the ice sheet that smothered much of Canada during the last Ice Age, covers more than a quarter of its 7,607-square-mile (19,700-square-kilometer) area. Long glaciers pour off the Penny Ice Cap, reaching down through the treeless valleys between immense peaks with names like Odin, Thor and Asgard, taken from Norse mythology. Huge moraines, erratics and other glacial debris litter the landscape.

Auyuittuq truly lives up to its Inuit name, which means "the land that never melts." Even during its brief summer in July and August, when the valleys are free of ice and snow, the land remains frozen just below the surface. Meltwater from the glaciers flows down from the mountains as chortling streams in the morning, turning to torrential outpourings in the heat of the afternoon sun. Barely dipping below the horizon, the northern sun coaxes tiny arctic plants to take root in the thin soil. These stalwart little gems huddle together for warmth and

Auyuittuq National Park.

Thor and Asgard mountains, Auyuittuq National Park.

protection against the fierce winds that whip down the valleys.

One such valley is the broad, glacier-carved Akshayuk Pass (formerly Pangnirtung Pass), which cuts across the Cumberland Peninsula from Pangnirtung Fjord in the south to Broughton Island in the north. In the winter, it's the main travel route, by snowmobile, between local communities. In the summer, wilderness seekers come from all over the world to hike the pass and experience the grandeur of Auyuittuq.

Most visitors come to the park in July and August to make the 41-mile (66-kilometer) trek to Summit Lake. The lake marks the height of land in Akshayuk Pass (1,640 feet/500 meters), and two rivers flow from its basin – the Weasel hurries south to Cumberland Sound, and the Owl drains north into Davis Strait. Some people even hike the full 60-mile (97-kilometer) length of the pass (a 7- to 14-day undertaking), though

they start from the opposite end, at North Pangnirtung Fjord.

The hike to Summit Lake begins with a 15.5-mile (25-kilometer) boat trip from the community of Pangnirtung to the park entrance at Overlord Mountain. This majestic peak rises 4,887 feet (1,490 meters) above the Weasel River, where it enters Pangnirtung Fjord. There's a warden station here as well as the only designated campground in the park; all others are "random" sites.

From the warden station, the route follows the silt-laden Weasel River, with the occasional *inukshuk* – a rock cairn built in the shape of a person – to guide you across moraines and rivers, and through particularly fragile terrain. Some streams are spanned by an ordinary footbridge, suspension bridge or cable crossing, but many more will need to be cautiously forded.

The round trip to Summit Lake takes five to seven days, more if you take the time to hike into the valleys

that radiate from the pass. One such trek would take you to Schwartzenbach Falls, a maelstrom that pours off the ice sheet 2,165 feet (660 meters) down to the Weasel River. Akshayuk Pass is bordered by impressive granite peaks – so impressive that rock climbers from around the world clamor to scale their lofty heights. Flat-topped Mount Asgard (6,611 feet/ 2,015 meters) and its twin cylindrical towers are highly sought-after by international expeditions, as is Thor Peak. This imposing mountain, reaching 5,505 feet (1,678 meters), has the longest uninterrupted cliff face in the world – about half a mile (one kilometer) long.

With time and food to spare, you can hike beyond Summit to Glacier Lake, where the Highway, Turner and Norman glaciers converge. If you're experienced in glacier travel, and have ropes, ice axes, crampons and other specialized equipment, you can hike up onto

Mountain ranges, Auyuittuq National Park.

the glaciers for incredible long-distance views of the valley. The arctic air is so clear, you'll find the distances deceiving, bringing yesterday's hike as close as today's.

The few inches of earth that thaw in the summer cause unsteady footing on the tussocks, gravel and mud along the Weasel and Owl rivers. This thin layer of soil supports a surprising amount of vegetation, given the short growing season, bitter winds and cool summer temperatures. (July is the warmest month, with an average temperature of about 50°F/10°C.) Plenty of moisture and 24 hours of sunlight help to compensate for the climate, and you'll be delighted to see masses of fluffy white cotton grass, startlingly yellow arctic poppies and showy pink

willow herbs along the rivers and streams. Hardy mosses, lichen and arctic heather grow in the gravel outwash from glaciers and on the mountain slopes, and the tundra sports grassy tussocks up to a meter tall.

This sparse vegetation supports a limited number of animal species: lemmings, arctic hares, weasels and arctic fox may make a shy appearance, depending on the year. A "low lemming" year will yield fewer sightings of its predators, the weasel and the arctic fox. Although there are polar bears and a few small herds of caribou in the park, their range does not normally include the Akshayuk Pass.

To avoid treading on the fragile vegetation, stick to the trail if there is one, or hike on sand or rocky terrain. You'll find the going easier than the

ankle-twisting tundra anyway! Along the Owl River, be careful not to step on the nests of snowy owls and eiders, just two of the 32 species of birds that nest in the park between June and August. Circling high above, you might see a peregrine falcon or gyrfalcon – two magnificent and rare birds.

Inuit guides from Broughton Island operate trips to the much less visited northern area of the park to see seals, walrus, beluga whales, narwhals, polar bears and sea bird colonies. The coast is extremely rugged, with deeply incised fjords that radiate from the inland mountains and jagged peninsulas. Remote and difficult to get to, the northern part of the park attracts a host of scientists and researchers studying climate change, geology, botany, history, birds, wildlife and many other subjects.

The park's Visitor Centre in Pangnirtung, where you must register before and after your trip, has a collection of books concerning the park environment and the North, and an art exhibit on Inuit history. The museum and library at the Angmarlik Visitor Centre is also worth a stop, and you can arrange for a guided tour of the community and nearby historic sites.

In the North, everything

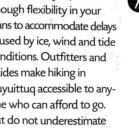
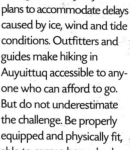

When you go

For general information and a list of licensed operators, contact:

Auyuittuq National Park
PO Box 353
Pangnirtung, NT X0A 0R0
Tel: (867) 473-8828
Fax: (867) 473-8612
E-mail: Nunavut_Info@pch.gc.ca

Nunavut Tourism
Toll free within North America: 1-800-491-7910
Outside North America: 1-800-979-6551
Fax: (819) 979-1261
E-mail: nunatour@nunanet.com

depends on the weather. Take a healthy dose of patience with you, and allow enough flexibility in your plans to accommodate delays caused by ice, wind and tide conditions. Outfitters and guides make hiking in Auyuittuq accessible to anyone who can afford to go. But do not underestimate the challenge. Be properly equipped and physically fit, able to carry a heavy backpack for long distances over sometimes demanding terrain. This *is* the "true north strong and free." To travel its wild reaches is humbling – and inspiring.

Auyuittuq National Park.

Ellesmere Island National Park

Here is the ultimate northern experience – the chance to visit a mountainous High Arctic desert populated by muskoxen, wolves, caribou and herds of arctic hares, all within spitting distance, relatively speaking, of the North Pole. The nearest tree is over 1,200 miles (2,000 kilometers) away, the Pole about a third of that distance. You'll have plenty of time to mull over its remoteness on the five-hour flight north from Resolute, itself a remote northern community.

The rugged nature of this desolate region is best appreciated from the air. In the northern portion known as Grant Land, rocky peaks, called *nunataks*, poke through a vast ice sheet up to 2,900 feet (900 meters) thick. One of these, 8,580-foot (2,616-meter) Mount Barbeau, is the highest mountain in eastern North America. The ice sheet gives birth to valley glaciers up to 50 miles (80 kilometers) in length. Long fjords poke their way inland, creating a deeply indented coastline ringed with thick shelf ice – freshwater ice that is permanently attached to the shore – and broken floes in constant motion. On the north coast, tidewater glaciers calve into the Arctic Ocean. Here, at the top of the world, the last Ice Age never really left.

It's a magnificent, wild area, an appropriate choice for Canada's most northerly park. The 14,586-square-mile (37,775-square-kilometer) park is administered by Parks Canada, and all visitors are required to register their arrival and departure and participate in an orientation. Park wardens stress self-sufficiency, self-reliance and the difficulty of rescue should a mishap occur. Because of the high cost of air travel (a return flight by Twin Otter from Resolute to Hazen Camp runs about $27,000), most visitors use the services of outfitters who are licensed to operate in the park and who can bring together groups of nine or ten to share expenses.

The park sees an average of about 400 visitors a year, of which between 80 and 100 are hikers. Hazen Camp and Tanquary are the main jumping-off points for day hikes or extended trips; experienced, fit hikers can tackle the 80-mile (130-kilometer), ten-day trek between the two camps. This ultimate northern experience starts on the shore of Lake Hazen, one of the largest freshwater lakes north of the Arctic Circle. The 48-mile-long (78-kilometer-long) lake enjoys a reputation as a (relatively) warm desert oasis, though you won't find any swaying palms here. July, the warmest month, ranges between about 44° and 57°F (7° and 14°C). The area is classed as a desert because it receives only about 2.5 inches (6 centimeters) of precipitation a year!

There are no established trails between the two camps, though there are emergency caches. Walking is fairly straightforward: the treeless, open terrain allows you to see where you're going and where you've been. However, getting from A to B can involve crossing swollen glacial streams and picking a route through ankle-twisting hummocks or boggy terrain.

In July, you'll experience the Arctic in glorious bloom – yellow arctic poppies, white mountain

Air Force River Valley, Ellesmere Island National Park.

Navigating among ice floes is one of the hazards for kayakers at Ellesmere Island.

avens and red moss campion poke through a multi-colored carpet of lichen and moss. Ankle-high dwarf willow, the nearest thing to a tree in these parts, offers some protection to the delicate plants and serves as food for thousands of arctic hares. Weighing up to 11 pounds (5 kilograms), hares, in turn, feed a population of arctic wolves and foxes.

Those denizens of the Arctic, the shaggy muskoxen, can also be found in the park, as well as the rare Peary caribou. Polar bears, the most dangerous northern predator, roam the coastal areas.

If a ten-day hike isn't for you, use either Tanquary or Hazen camps as a base and explore the immediate region on day or overnight hikes. The fjord area offers lots to the student of archaeology, including ancient foundations, stone traps and opportunities to discover new sites and artifacts, which should be reported to the resident wardens and left undisturbed. Despite its inhospitable climate, northern Ellesmere Island has been inhabited, on and off, for over 4,000 years. Today, the only permanent settlement is the tiny village of Grise Fjord (pop. 148) on the southern coast.

At Hazen Camp, you can

When you go

Ellesmere Island National Park
PO Box 353
Pangnirtung, NT X0A 0R0
Tel: (819) 473-8828
Fax: (819) 473-8612

Nunavut Tourism
Toll free within North America: 1-800-491-7910
Outside North America: (819) 979-6551
Fax: (819) 979-1261
E-mail: nunatour@nunanet.com

fish for arctic char, or visit Glacier Pass or Blister Creek, two superb hiking destinations. Be aware that distances can be deceptive – a feature appearing to be only 3 miles (5 kilometers) away may, in fact, be three times that distance. Because

Arctic tern.

of its relative warmth and wetness in July and August, this is the best region to view wildlife. About 30 species of birds have been identified here, including long-tailed jaegers, ringed plovers, red knots and well traveled arctic terns, having recently returned from their "winter" in Antarctica.

With plenty of advance planning, you can visit the lonely outpost of Fort Conger southeast of Lake Hazen and see well preserved relics of its era. The outpost was used by generations of Arctic explorers, including Robert Peary on his controversial 1909 attempt to reach the pole.

Though most visitors come to hike on the interior plateau, it is possible to try ski mountaineering in the Grant Land Mountains or sea kayaking on the northeast coast at a latitude nudging, 80°N. The opportunity to see walrus, narwhal and polar bears makes this a unique, exciting and challenging experience. Kayaking in the High Arctic requires special knowledge and skills and is best done with an experienced outfitter.

A trip to the High Arctic may well change your life forever. Chances are, only a return trip will measure up.

Index

Algoma Central Railway, 156
Algonquin Provincial Park, 184, 188
Alpine Rafting, 78
Athabasca Sand Dunes, 126
Auyuittuq National Park, 290

Baccalieu Trail, 270
Banff National Park, 92, 94, 96
Barkley Sound, 28
Bay of Exploits, 272
Bay of Islands, 266
Bird watching
Baccalieu Trail, 270
East Coast Trail, 264
Grand Manan, 228
Grand River, 170
Kouchibouguac National Park, 234
Last Mountain Lake National Wildlife
    Area, 124
Macphail Woods, 256
Mingan Archipelago National Park
    Reserve, 218
Point Pelee National Park, 172
Rouge Park, 176
Saugeen River, 168
Sleeping Giant Provincial Park, 146
Blackcomb, 38
Blow Me Down Mountains, 260
Bon Echo Provincial Park, 190
Bow Valley, 98
Bowron Lake Provincial Park, 50
Bruce Peninsula, 164
Burgess Shale, 74
Burnside River, 288

Cabot Trail, 238
Canmore, 98
Canoeing
    Algonquin Provincial Park, 184
    Athabasca Sand Dunes, 126
    Bon Echo Provincial Park, 190
    Bowron Lake Provincial Park, 50
    Burnside River, 288
    Grand River, 170
    Hood River, 286

Lac La Ronge Provincial Park, 130
La Vérendrye Wildlife Reserve,
    212
Milk River, 116
Quetico Provincial Park, 144
Rideau Corridor, 194
Saugeen River, 168
Seal River, 138
Temagami, 160
Cape Breton Highlands National Park,
    240
Cathedral Provincial Park, 56
Caving
    Crowsnest Pass, 106
    Gold River, 20
    Rats Nest Cave, 100
    Charlevoix Traverse, 208
    Chilkoot Trail, 46
    Clayoquot Sound, 24
    Confederation Trail, 252
Cross-country skiing
    Charlevoix Traverse, 208
    Haliburton Highlands, 182
    Kananaskis Country, 102
    La Mercier, 216
    Mansfield Outdoor Centre, 166
    Mont-Sainte-Anne, 216
    Crowsnest Pass, 106
Cycling
    Baccalieu Trail, 270
    Cabot Trail, 238
    Charlevoix Traverse, 208
    Confederation Trail, 252
    Icefields Parkway, 90
    Kettle Valley Railway, 58
    Prince Edward County, 196
    Silver Triangle, 60
    Upper Saint John River Valley, 236
    West Coast, P.E.I., 250
    Whitehorse, 280
Cypress Hills Interprovincial Park, 120

Dinosaur Provincial Park, 112
Dobson Trail, 230
Dog sledding

Algonquin Provincial Park, 188
Rocky Mountain House, 88

East Coast Trail, 264
Estrie, Les Sentiers de lí, 206
Elk Island National Park, 118
Ellesmere Island National Park, 294

Fathom Five National Marine Park,
    164
Fundy Coastal Trails, 226
Fundy National Park, 222

Ganaraska Trail, 180
Garibaldi Provincial Park, 42
Gaspésie, Parc de la, 220
Gatineau Park, 200
Georgian Bay Islands National Park,
    162
Glacier National Park, 68
Gold River, 20
Grand Manan, 228
Grand River, 170
Grasslands National Park, 122
Gros Morne National Park, 262

Haliburton Highlands, 182
Hiking
    Chilkoot Trail, 46
    Confederation Trail, 252
    Dobson Trail, 230
    East Coast Trail, 264
    Fundy Coastal Trails, 226
    Ganaraska Trail, 180
    Juan de Fuca Marine Trail, 32
    Les Sentiers de líEstrie, 206
    Oak Ridges Trail, 174
    Rideau Corridor, 194
    Rockwall Highline Trail, 80
    Rouge Park, 176
    Torngat Mountains, 274
    Voyageur Trail, 150
    Waterfront Trail, 178
    West Coast Trail, 30